TURNING TO FACE THE EAST

To Sarah

TURNING TO FACE THE EAST

LIAM BYRNE

guardianbooks

First published in 2013
by Guardian Books
Kings Place, 90 York Way
London N1 9GU

Published with Guardian Books
Guardian Books is an imprint of Guardian Newspapers Ltd
www.guardianbooks.co.uk

Typeset by seagulls.net
Printed in England by CPI Group (UK) Ltd, Croydon, CR0 4YY

A CIP record for this book is available from the British Library

ISBN 978-0852653302

FSC
www.fsc.org
MIX
Paper from
responsible sources
FSC® C020471

10 9 8 7 6 5 4 3 2 1

CONTENTS

ACKNOWLEDGEMENTS

First and foremost, this book simply would not have been possible without all the team at the GB–China Centre, and in particular the far-sighted leadership and extraordinary dedication of its former director Katie Lee, its chairman Peter Batey, and vice-chair Hugh Davies. I owe great debts to all three. Our relationship with China would be far weaker without them.

Over the years, I've learned heaps from many of the Foreign Office's brilliant China team: Peter Wilson, Dan Chugg, David Ellis and Richard Pullen; and successive British ambassadors in Beijing: Sir Christopher Hum, William Ehrman and Sebastian Wood. But this book really would not have been possible without the great number of Chinese friends who have taught me so much and worked together with me on projects and conferences over the last six years, in particular Liu Jieyi, Vice-Minister, Communist Party of China (CPC) Central Committee International Department; Vice-Foreign Ministers Zhang Zhijun and Madame Fu Ying; Lu Hao, First Secretary of the Communist Youth League; Wang Xiao, President of the All-China Youth Federation, together with his outstanding vice-presidents Lu Yongzheng and He Junke; and, crucially, the indispensable Ma Hui, Director-General, CPC Central Committee International Department, and Dong Xia, Deputy Secretary-General, All-China Youth Federation; along with China's ambassador in Britain, Liu Xiaoming. A number of

Chinese academics have also helped me piece together my ideas. In China, I was especially grateful to be able to spend time with Prof. Zhou Hong at the the Chinese Academy of Social Sciences, Prof. Wang Changjiang at the Central Party School, Fu Jun, Dean of the School of Government, Peking University, and Tao Ran, Director of China Center for Public Economics.

Here in the UK, we are extremely lucky to have some of the best China specialists in the world. At Oxford University, many were incredibly generous with their time, in particular Prof. Andrew Dilnot, Warden of Nuffield College, Dame Jessica Rawson, Rana Mitter, Jessica Wong, and Patricia Thornton, who was kind enough to share an insightful analysis of the Bo Xilai affair. At Birmingham University, Prof. Edward Peck offered a glimpse into how universities will become key links in the bridge to China. Prof. Peter Nolan at Cambridge University opened completely new horizons for me on the development of Chinese business, as did Prof. Kerry Brown, University of Sydney, on questions of political reform.

Martin Jacques was a great inspiration. Mark Leonard, Co-Founder and Director of the European Council on Foreign Relations, and Charles Grant, Director of the Centre for European Reform, were constant sources of advice.

Iain Ferguson and Adela Gooch and the team at Wilton Park were generous enough to include me in their ground-breaking new partnership with the CPC's Central Party School. A huge number of leaders from the fields of politics, business, economics and cultural relations were good enough to share thoughts and views as I put this book together. In particular, I want to thank Peter Mandelson, Jim O'Neill at Goldman Sachs, Gerard Lyons formerly of Standard Chartered, John Hughes at BP, Martin Davidson at the British Council, Alan Parker, chairman of Brunswick, Mike Wright at Jaguar Land Rover, Paul Walsh at Diageo,

Alex Wilson at Flamingo Research, and Christine Dalby at the European Commission's London office. David Sainsbury's visionary work and advice has been a source of immense inspiration, and a number of colleagues in and out of the Shadow Cabinet helped me develop my ideas, in particular Douglas Alexander, Chuka Umuna, David Miliband and Andrew Adonis. BP, Rolls-Royce, Standard Chartered and Prudential have all been crucial conference partners.

Sir Trevor Chinn and the wonderful team at Labour Friends of Israel, Ben Garrett and Tali Halpin, organised our 'start-up nation' research trip to Israel and the Palestinian Authority in October 2012, where a host of people including HM Ambassador Matthew Gould and his team were good enough to give us their time. I want to praise Sir Trevor in particular for being such a staunch and far-sighted friend. HMA Simon McDonald and Economic Counsellor Simon Gallagher were invaluable in making the right connections in Berlin, and my old friends Matthias Machnig, Minister for the Economy in Thuringia, and Jakob von Weizsäcker, Head of Department, Thuringian Economics Ministry, opened my eyes to some of the extraordinary strengths of German economic development.

A number of people were incredibly generous and offered me detailed comments on my draft manuscript, including Lord Mandelson, David Miliband, Katie Lee, Sir Andrew Cahn, Kerry Brown, Peter Nolan, Jessica Rawson, Rana Mitter, Charles Grant, Edward Peck and David Mills. The errors, however, are all my own.

This book would not have happened without the inspiration and help of my two marvellous special advisers in government, Tony Danker and David Mills, my agent Georgina Capel, who did so much to help me shape concepts for the book, Katie Roden at Guardian Books, a fabulous editor, Virginia Catmur, and backup from an extraordinary team in London and Hodge

Hill: Peter Starkings, Cathy Sprent, Tom Dunn and especially Rachana Shanbhogue; and, in Birmingham, Gill Beddows, Sarish Jabeen and Anne Marie Byrne. Laura Allen provided invaluable research. Finally, my debts to Sarah and Alex, John and Lizzie are boundless. For putting up with the absences and ramblings on China over the dinner table, I owe you everything.

ABBREVIATIONS

3G	third-generation (mobile telecoms networks)
ASEAN	Association of South-East Asian Nations
AVIC	Aviation Industries of China
BBO	billion barrels of oil
BIRD	Binational Industrial R&D programme (Israel–USA)
CIC	China Investment Corporation
CNOOC	China National Offshore Oil Corporation
CNPC	China National Petroleum Corporation
CPC	Communist Party of China
EIC	East India Company
EXIM	Export–Import Bank of China
FCO	Foreign and Commonwealth Office
FDI	foreign direct investment
FIE	foreign-invested enterprise
GDP	gross domestic product
IMF	International Monetary Fund
IPR	intellectual property rights
JLR	Jaguar Land Rover
JVP	Jerusalem Venture Partners
LDV	Leyland DAF Vans
MofCom	Ministry of Commerce (China)
NAFTA	North Atlantic Free Trade Agreement

NPC	National People's Congress (China)
OBR	Office for Budget Responsibility (UK)
OECD	Organisation for Economic Cooperation and Development
PISA	Programme for International Student Assessment
PLA	People's Liberation Army (China)
RMB	*renminbi*: official currency of China, measured in *yuan*
SMEs	small and medium-sized enterprises
SOE	state-owned enterprise
SSE	Shanghai Stock Exchange
TSB	Technology Strategy Board (UK)
UKTI	UK Trade and Investment
USTR	US Trade Representative
VC	venture capital
WTO	World Trade Organisation

CHAPTER 1

Drawing level

I was ten seconds from facing Gavin Esler live on Newsnight. The polls had just closed. Minutes before, my friend James Purnell had dramatically resigned on the 10 o'clock news and demanded a leadership challenge to Gordon Brown. Clamped to my ear was a phone with Peter Mandelson on the other end speaking from the 'war-room' at No 10 Downing Street. 'Its down to you, Liam', Peter said calmly. 'You've got to say no one will forgive us for fighting amongst ourselves when the country's in crisis'.

Eight months later, just after eleven in the morning, I was standing in the stillness of the Chancellor's study in No 11 Downing Street. On Alistair Darling's red-leather topped desk perched Gladstone's famous red box. It was Budget Day and Alistair and his wife were about to lead the Treasury team into Downing Street for the famous photos before the hop to the cock-pit of the Commons to present Labour's last budget.

When I arrived in the Treasury Alistair had his suspicions of me, fearing I was a No 10 spy. But we formed a close partnership and he was now about to present some big plans we'd worked on together to a sceptical world. They were bold plans, but not bold enough to stop our election defeat months later. Battered by the giant storm-waves of a political and financial crisis, politics rarely gets tougher than Labour's final year. And yet, we had nailed down a plan that would have locked in recovery from the greatest crash since the 1930s.

Now, three years on, our country's prospects don't seem better than on that day when I left the Treasury along with Alistair Darling. They seem worse. It seems clearer than ever that our country needs a bold plan to rebuild, to renew, to jump-start for the new world taking shape around us. Just as we had after the second world war.

In the middle of the bear-pit of the House of Commons is a very good memorial of how we did it once before. Whenever a politician gets up to speak from the Opposition front bench, they rest their elbows on a beautiful box of puriri wood, decorated with an ornate filigree. It's a gift of New Zealand. The table it stands on is a gift of Canada. Behind that table sits the Speaker's chair, a gift of the people of Australia. The Bar of the House is from Jamaica. The doors to the Chamber are from India and Pakistan. Friends from all over the world helped us rebuild the Chamber after the fateful nights of 10 and 11 May 1941 when German incendiary bombs hit the Commons Chamber and sent it up in flames. The Chamber was left a smoking shell. A copy of the Bible damaged by fire that night now sits in the dispatch box. That Bible, that box and the Chamber around it are a wonderful symbol of how in those tough, postwar years, our friends helped us rebuild not just the House of Commons but our country.

The second world war destroyed swathes of the British economy. As the battering of war was felt, the economy lost a seventh of its value by 1947.[1]

When my political hero Clement Attlee took his seals of office in the summer of 1945, his cabinet faced an economic situation of the bleakest proportions. Their answer was tough and determined. Britain would export its way back to health. In December

1945, the Cabinet agreed a vast sales push[2] to be pursued 'with the same energy as in time of war, whatever measure of industrial and marketing reorganisation and reconstruction may be necessary'.[3] New assistance was negotiated from the Americans. Our industry and infrastructure were rebuilt. And as our neighbouring markets in America and Europe began to blossom, our exports boomed and our economy with it.

Amid all the difficulties of demobilising hundreds of thousands of troops, creating the welfare state, managing the balance of payments and rebuilding a bombed nation, production picked up so fast that by 1952 the economy was 15% bigger,[4] with an astounding three-quarters of the boost driven by exports mostly sold in America and Europe.

By 1959, exports to the US had quadrupled in the space of a decade.[5] Exports to Europe rose over 50%. By the end of the 1960s, as the European recovery gathered pace, Britain's trade with Europe tripled on its postwar value. For all the disagreements with America and our diffidence towards the new-fangled European Union, it was our neighbours across the Channel and the North Atlantic that became the key to our recovery.

The great global crash of 2009 did not do as much damage as the second world war. But here in Britain, it destroyed one million jobs and £400 billion of wealth. Now, just as in 1945, we have to rebuild by trading our way back to prosperity.

The problem is this: the friends who helped us in 1945 are in as much trouble as we are. America is mired in slow growth and fierce arguments about how to pay its debts; Europe is trapped in disagreements about how to save its currency.

It is said that China's great philosopher, Confucius, teaching around 500 BC, never wrote anything down. But his students did. And the famous Analects of Confucius begin with a simple question: 'Is it not delightful to have friends coming from far away?'[6]

It is the question to which we in Britain must answer 'yes'. The revolution unfolding in China and the East Asian economy around it is quite simply the most important event to shake the world since the Industrial Revolution. China is industrialising today at 10 times the speed of Britain and on 100 times the scale. But today, we trade more with Ireland than we do with Brazil, Russia, India and China put together. We need more friends far away.

This book is just one contribution to what I hope will be a much bigger debate about how we make that happen. I do not pretend to have many of the answers. But for five years, I've been convinced that a revolution in our links with China, and the great East Asian trading zone of which it is the centre, home to one-third of the world's population, is critical to our future wealth and well-being. It is a book born of determination: in the debates I've joined all over Europe since the last election, no one talks much about the opportunity unfolding over the eastern horizon. Historians often try to label different eras with the seas around which the great powers of the time faced each other: the Mediterranean century or the North Atlantic century. Well, we always knew that the 21st century could be the Pacific century. But the global crash means something big: the new order is arriving faster than anyone expected – and we're not ready. So this book is simply a personal story of the travels, the debates and the conversations I've had over the last five years in search of answers to a simple question. How does Britain prosper in the Pacific century?

The crash

Governments and bankers have a love–hate relationship. They always have had. When one has a crisis only the other can sort it out. Sometimes it ends well. And sometimes it doesn't.

Outside the House of Commons stands Carlo Marochetti's great bronze statue of Richard the Lionheart, the king kidnapped on his way back from the Third Crusade and saved only when Italian bankers stumped up a loan to pay the ransom. They were richly rewarded. But Italian bankers were smashed when Edward III defaulted on his huge war loans.[7] The business run from their offices on Lombard Street in the City of London never quite recovered.

Six hundred years later major Western countries do not leave their lenders high and dry any more. The banks, however, have proved perfectly capable of manufacturing problems of their own. And when banks go wrong, only governments – and taxpayers – can bail them out.

Deep beneath the Cabinet Office on Whitehall is the suite of rooms known as COBRA (Cabinet Office Briefing Room A) – perhaps the closest we have to a White House-style situation room. Surrounded by video-screens full of gloomy news, it was here in the bright white light that the National Economic Council met sometimes every day, to plot a way through the crisis. As a minister working in No. 10, helping coordinate our policy and communications across government, I remember sitting through the key meetings as we wrestled with how to explain what was happening to the public. It was actually pretty simple. The economy was having a heart attack. Nothing was pumping the life-blood of credit through the nation's veins and arteries.

When a bank explodes, an awful lot of people get hurt. Banks take in money – like savings – on a short-term basis. But they lend many times over to long-term projects. They keep enough cash on hand to cover what might be needed to pay out, day by day. But if a bank run starts, the cash runs out fast and loans are called in. Rarely can anyone pay back quickly and so they sell off what they can. As the market is flooded by sellers, prices fall and a bank gets back far less than needed. If the bank is lucky, it might stay in business. If it doesn't, it goes bust and takes what's left of everyone's savings with it. And when a bank stops pumping credit, the heart of the economy stops, the nation's commerce goes into reverse; the taxes stop flowing to the Exchequer and the national debt balloons.

I'm afraid to say these 'heart attacks' are rather more common than we would like to think. In fact Britain has had 12 of them since 1800[8] – and the world's major economies have been hit 18 times since the second world war.[9]

But none were on the scale of the shock that hit the world in 2009.

In the years before the crash interest rates were low as China parked its giant export surpluses in American Treasury bills.[10] With low interest rates, house prices boomed. By 2005, Americans were borrowing against the new value of their homes to the tune of *$1 trillion dollars* a year. American banks were reselling the debts to Western banks now so intertwined that some 40–60% of US securities were in portfolios of foreign investors. And so the asset price boom spiralled. You could see it in Dubai, Australia, Ireland, New Zealand, Spain, Ireland, Vietnam, Estonia, Lithuania, Thailand, China, Latvia, South Africa and Singapore. In 2005, The Economist estimated the total value of residential properties had doubled between 2000 and 2005 to $40 trillion: 'it looks like the biggest bubble in history', it reported.[11] As house prices rose, consumers borrowed more and, crucially, so did the banks. By June 2008, leverage ratios (the ratio of debts to assets) at European banks had grown gigantically; at ING it stood at 49 to 1. Deutsche Bank's stood at 53 to 1. Barclays's stood at 61 to 1. In fact, bank balance sheets ballooned in the UK to *five times* the size of the whole economy.

When the bubble burst, problems spread like wildfire. American house prices peaked in 2005. Within a year mortgage lenders

were going bust. Ten failed by the end of 2006. Fifty fell by
the end of March 2007. In April 2007, New Century Financial
collapsed, triggering the collapse of two hedge funds and Bear
Stearns. By the summer, BNP Paribas reported major losses. So
did the German bank, IKB. Then Iceland's entire banking system
collapsed. Ireland's system was totally underwritten and the UK's
banking system effectively nationalised. Finally, on 15 September
2008, Lehman Brothers imploded, followed by America's big five
investment banks, two mortgage lending giants and the world's
largest insurer, AIG.[12]

The 'average' bank crisis is bad enough. In an average bank
crisis, economic growth falls by around a tenth, unemployment
goes up by 7%, house prices fall by a third,[13] and government debt
tends to double as tax receipts fall off a cliff.

But this was no 'average'-sized crash. This was a monster.
Without the work of Gordon Brown and Alistair Darling at the
G20 group of advanced Western nations, the Western world
might have been plunged into a Great Depression. But following
the policies of the last few years the hit to our economic growth
in Britain has been allowed to outweigh the catastrophe of the
1930s. Back in the 1930s, our national output recovered after 50
months. But 50 months after this great crash, we are still 4.3%
worse off than before the crisis started.

Recessions that are allowed to last a long time are very,
very bad news. The scars they cause can last literally for generations. People invest less in their skills.[14] Workers with a history
of unemployment get offered less secure jobs and lose valuable
work experience.[15] Spells of unemployment lead to careers that
are low paid and unstable.[16] Business investment stays low[17] as
firms lack confidence in future demand.[18] Low levels of investment[19] mean the pace of innovation slows. New ideas struggle
to find backing. Economic theory tells us that low investment in

skills, falling investment in the nation's capital stock and falling levels of innovation and enterprise result in a much slower growth rate for years to come. In other words, the 'trend rate of growth' – the rate at which the economy can grow without driving up inflation – gets smaller. It's a terrible circle. And it is precisely what's unfolding in Britain today.

Since I left the Treasury, forecasts for growth have been downgraded and downgraded again (see Table 1.1). We were supposed to be bouncing back in 2012. No more. But worse is what's happening to the *foundations* of our economy. Business investment has fallen off a cliff. It's not moved up for three years and now stands £18 billion below the pre-crisis level. Science spending has been cut 12% while in Germany, one of our main competitors, it has increased by 8%.[20] The President of the Royal Society, Sir Paul Nurse, is warning that we're falling behind. In fact, even the government's own reports say: 'Other countries are outpacing the UK in terms of growth in number of researchers and spending on research. The UK is well positioned, but its ability to sustain its leadership position is far from inevitable.'[21]

In our schools, our exam grades have hit a plateau – and we're now sending fewer young people to train for the future at university. Productivity growth now lags America, Germany and China. Yet our big corporates are awash with cash: £34 billion more than before the crisis (Table 1.2). They simply lack the confidence to invest and the banks aren't stepping in. In fact bank lending is still pretty frozen. Together, this is deeply damaging our country's entrepreneurs – the people we rely on to found the new businesses that will be the success stories of tomorrow.

Nearly 60% of people in Britain are employed by small businesses. They are vital to bringing down unemployment. Yet the business start-up rate is falling fast and because more businesses now are going bust, our country's entrepreneurs are weakening;

32,000 fewer businesses were founded in 2010, compared to 2008 (Table 1.2). And export growth, much boasted about, is actually anaemic. Exports have grown by just 2%.

Together this is terrible for the public finances. The government has already had to increase its forecasts for Public Sector Net Borrowing by £150 billion because tax receipts are falling short, because incomes, profits and asset prices are not growing fast enough. *What this means is that it is going to take longer to pay down our national budget deficit.*

Sounds bleak? There's more.

A little west of the White House is the formidable Eisenhower Old Executive Building. Built in French Second-Empire style in the 1870s, it is home to a raft of the President's closest advisors. It reminded me a bit of the Cabinet Office where I used to work on Whitehall. The most exquisitely beautiful rooms sit off utilitarian corridors painted a drab olive green.

In 2009, I dropped by to listen to a man who had just told me why Labour was about to lose the next election.

Jared Bernstein, then chief economist to Vice-President Joe Biden and the intellectual force behind Barack Obama's Middle Class Taskforce, was explaining the crisis unfolding among middle-income Americans. 'The moment we knew John McCain had lost [the presidential election]', said Bernstein, 'was when he said there was nothing basically wrong with the American economy. In fact most voters knew there was everything wrong!'

I suddenly realised that what had been described in America was almost certainly unfolding in Britain. When I came home, Alistair Darling let me investigate and, sure enough, three months later my civil servants confirmed that Britain's lower middle classes were under huge pressure. Our policies since 1997 meant we had avoided the hit to working people seen in America. But from 2004 onwards, beneath the miraculous arc of rising average incomes, families on 'median incomes' – millions of workers

(some 25–30% of Britain's workforce) grafting as small employers, sales assistants, cashiers, construction and factory workers
– were feeling the strain. Between 1997 and 2004 they had done
well under Labour; their incomes grew faster than average. But
from 2005, the economy changed. 'Real disposable income'[22] had
been growing at just 0.14% a year – barely noticeable – and well
behind the national average. The hours people were working had
not fallen; people were working just as hard as ever – but were
not getting on. With rising fuel, food and housing costs across
the Western world, they felt squeezed. Without the protection
of tax credits, families would have been absolutely hammered.
Productivity was rising – by over 9% between 2001 and 2008 –
but workers' share of national earnings was falling: from 73.5%
to 69.6%. What did that mean? Well in 2009, workers' share of
national earnings was around £768 billion. Yet if workers' share of
the national economic pie had matched the postwar averages, an
extra £23.4 billion would have headed into people's pay-packets.

I presented the findings to Cabinet two months before the
general election – but we had too little time to make a difference.
At the polls, we lost the 'squeezed middle' – and with them the
general election.

Yet back in 1945, the outlook was far tougher than today.
Full employment at home and full engagement abroad pulled us
through. And our neighbours across the Channel and the wide
Atlantic were there to help us. Now, once again we need a plan
for full employment at home and booming sales abroad. We need
a plan to export our way back to growth. If we're to grow at the
rate hoped between now and 2018, at a time when government
spending is falling and growth in consumer demand will be anaemic, exports have to grow by a *massive* 45% above their 2009
level.[23] Today exports[24] make up around 30% of our economy. By
2018 they need to reach 36%. That's a massive change. And I'm
afraid our neighbours aren't going to be quite the help they were.
They are in just as much trouble as we are.

CHAPTER 2

The state of the neighbours

It was all meant to be so different.

Like me, millions of Europeans of my generation watched the spectacle of Berliners smashing down the Berlin Wall in a stunned wonder. As I goggled at the scenes on a dodgy TV in a student common-room in Manchester, I remember those dark fears of teenage years lived in the final stage of the cold war swirling away, vapour-like. I set off the next summer to Berlin, Prague and Budapest, to see at first hand grand and stately but rather empty capitals, run-down, like old country homes.

We didn't know it then but what we were watching, said foreign-policy guru Robert Cooper, 'was far more far-reaching than the events of 1789, 1815 or 1919 ... [It was] a fundamental change in the European state system itself.'[25] The door was suddenly flung open to a new world of mutual security and cooperation in which politicians could come together 'and make deals on everything, from the conditions for battery hens to the size of their budget deficits'.[26]

Before 1989, the cold war balance of terror haunted European life. After 1989, the spectres were gone. The very notion of joining the European Union galvanised reform and democracy across a continent. Until 1989, half of Europe lived under dictatorship. By 2000, more Europeans lived in liberal democracies than ever before. From Spain and Portugal to Croatia and Turkey, the prospect of joining Europe improved life, and in the years after peace descended on the Balkans, the European Union doubled in size. Within just a decade of those scenes on my TV, 12 new nations joined a political union of 450 million citizens that was now a real potential counter-balance to the United States of America: 'a remarkable and unique political order', European President Barroso called it, extending a 'zone of stability from Tipperary to Tallinn'.[27] Around the borders of this new Europe lived an incredible 1.3 billion people in 80 nations of the former Soviet Union, the Balkans, North and sub-Saharan Africa and the Middle East.

Across these border lands – a 'Eurosphere' – it is European ideas and ideals that now influence people, governments and regimes, just as Ancient Rome once did. European trade, foreign investment, aid and diplomacy helped settle the Orange Revolution in the Ukraine, shape human rights in Turkey, keep peace in Sarajevo, negotiate on nuclear weapons in Tehran and train the police in Palestine. Eighty thousand pages of law, a common market and a common defence force unite the continent. European troops served in Sierra Leone, Congo, Ivory Coast, Chad, Lebanon and Afghanistan. Europe dispenses half the world's foreign assistance. Alongside the US, Europe remains the only continent able to project the full spectrum of hard- and soft-power resources. It contributes more to the UN than any other group of nations. New global institutions and treaties, argue writers like Mark Leonard,[28] from the World Trade Organisation (WTO) to the International Criminal Court to the Kyoto Treaty, owe their shape to Europe, its market size and influence.

And then the people spoke. As Europe celebrated its fiftieth birthday in a reunited Berlin, the citizens of France and the

Netherlands rejected a new constitutional treaty. Not because they had studied the text. But because they wanted to send a signal that this new Europe was not working. Literally.

Before the crisis, Europe boasted the world's largest marketplace and a bigger share of world trade than America; seven nations were in the top 10 World Economic Forum Competitiveness Index and there was a $30 billion trade surplus with the rest of the world.

But for years, Europe's economy had lacked dynamism and direction. Twenty million were unemployed, productivity rates were behind those of the US, India produced more science graduates and 'on any relative index of a modern economy – skills, R&D, patents, IT, [Europe] is going down not up'.[29]

When Europe's leaders gathered in Lisbon to welcome in the new millennium they resolved to forge a continent that was different: 'the most competitive place to do business in the world by 2010'. But with honourable exceptions – the Nordics, Austria, and Netherlands – the project was failing by the time the crisis hit.

Progress had been made; more Europeans completed secondary and university education; the age of retirement had generally gone up, relieving pressure on strained and expensive pension systems; female employment rates had surged; there was more competition in energy and telecoms; Europe was 'greener'. But few nations were anywhere close to hitting their targets and the gap between the best and the worst was bigger in 2010 than in 2000.[30] Some countries took the lower borrowing rates that Eurozone membership brought, and simply spent the money. Spain, Portugal, Greece, Italy all held back others' progress in delivering social equity, employment, innovation, R&D and environmental sustainability.

And then the crisis hit. Within four months of the first American sub-prime lender going bust in April 2007, the German bank

Sachsen announced it needed rescue. IKB Industriebank soon followed. Then the UK's Northern Rock. Then the Swiss bank UBS announced $3.4 billion losses. As 2008 unfolded, one European bank after another announced catastrophic results and new efforts to raise money from shareholders. When Lehman Brothers failed, HBOS, Bradford & Bingley, Glitnir, Fortis, Dexia, Hypo Real Estate, Kaupthing, UniCredit, RBS, Landsbanki, Icesave, Heritable, ING, Anglo-Irish, Lloyds TSB, all needed huge government intervention to save them. And as the recovery took hold in 2009, it became clear that the costs of the crisis – the collapse of tax revenues as business dived – had shattered the fortunes of those governments that had gone into the crisis in poor shape.

Greece was a nation that had spent 100 of the last 200 years in default. Even when it joined the euro in 2001, its debt stood at 100% of gross domestic product (GDP). Tax evasion was high. Public administration wasn't efficient. There wasn't much of a grip on public spending and pensions were unaffordable. Yet after joining the euro, the Greek government simply borrowed more because its interest rates fell to within 2% of Germany's. But when the government realised the budget deficit was nearly twice the size it thought in October 2009, Greece's lenders took fright. Its credit rating took a battering. Emergency loans have been needed ever since.

Portugal was in better shape, but it was one of only two EU countries to see its employment rate fall between 2000 and 2009.

Spain suffered an almighty crash in its construction sector, which had ballooned with the property bubble and left Spanish banks holding big losses on property loans, and very, very high unemployment. Italy had huge debts – 120% of GDP, or €2 trillion, and had done almost nothing to reform either its labour markets or its pension system. Its employment rate – at

58% in 2008 – was about the worst in the EU, and an astonishing 20% behind high-performing Denmark. Finally, the Irish economy had done well since the millennium. But the Irish property bubble, when it crashed, wrecked the banking system and as the government in its wisdom stepped in to underwrite all the liabilities of the Irish banking system, it was trying to swallow far more than it could hope to chew.

The response from Europe's leaders was frustrating and slow. Summit after summit 'kicked the can down the road', leaving two basic problems. Eurozone countries with lots of government debt could not make their debts any more attractive to foreign investors by letting their currency depreciate.[31] With a shortage of foreign investors, the money had to come from the International Monetary Fund (IMF) or other Eurozone governments. Eurozone governments invented one bail-out fund after another with tougher and tougher rules to try to bring some order to national budgets. Eventually, the grandly titled Treaty on Stability, Coordination and Governance in the Economic and Monetary Union mandated everyone except Britain and the Czech Republic to bring down their structural deficit to 0.5% of GDP. But the rules were so tough that voters kept sacking their governments.

Worse, Eurozone governments refused to allow the European Central Bank to behave like a normal central banker and act as the lender of last resort to banks which have a problem. In other words, there is 'common money and national banking'. When banks – like Spain's – are full of bad debts, and governments are so overloaded that no one trusts the government to ride to the rescue, then there's a really serious problem of a run on the banks. Yet the ECB does not have any power to step in, and recapitalise banks that are about to fall over.

Now, political historians will tell you that Europe has always been a 'process'. There's always been a crisis to keep us busy. The

French voted 'no' to defence cooperation in 1954. De Gaulle vetoed British membership in the 1960s. Denmark voted 'no' to Maastricht. The Irish rejected the Treaty of Nice in 2001, and the Swedes rejected the euro in 2003. But, like a river hitting rocks, Europe does not 'stop'; it moves ahead in a slightly different direction. That dynamic process is slowly delivering a single market that is half a billion people in size, with a single currency underpinned by a new degree of fiscal harmony, and a more coordinated foreign policy.

But the bottom line for Britain is this.

In December 2011, the Organisation for Economic Cooperation and Development (OECD) forecast that European imports would grow at half the pace of before the crisis. And since then, the Eurozone has gone back into recession. Our European markets are flat on their backs.

American dream?

So, what about America?

Back in the 1940s, despite all the disagreements about the end of Lend-Lease, the British economy would have been sunk without Marshall Aid. Seventy years later, I am afraid it doesn't look like America is there to save us.

It's funny but it doesn't seem so long ago that the world saw in America the world's only 'hyper-power'. Writers were prone to marvel at the country which had become 'the most powerful nation since Imperial Rome ... for the last 20 years that dominance has been unrivalled, a phenomenon unprecedented in human history'.[32]

'Suddenly', wrote British foreign policy expert Robert Cooper,

everyone is talking about America as an imperial power ... Pax
Americana is ... the best way to describe the world system.
Whatever foreign policy question is discussed, sooner or later
the question is asked: where does the US government stand
on this?[33]

The British historian Niall Ferguson even urged the US to go the
whole hog and set up shop as proper empire, for 'empire it is', he
wrote, 'in all but name'[34].

Yet in a decade the burden of war, the explosion of debt and
the heart-attack in the world's financial system has left America
weak. In any election year, you can expect a few expressions of
self-confidence. In his last State of the Union Address before
re-election, President Obama was emphatic: 'The renewal of
American leadership can be felt across the globe ... America
is back.'[35] On one level President Obama was right. But what
worries most American commentators is not the risk of over-
stretch abroad but 'under-reach' at home. After all, 'Rome',
Joseph Nye reminded us, 'rotted from within'.[36] Here was the
key insight of President Obama's election team. They knew that
most American voters have felt for years what Time called 'the
death of the American Dream'. Writers like Paul Krugman,[37]
Robert Reich,[38] Jacob Hacker,[39] and Lane Kenworthy[40] have
now set out how, since the early 1970s, the gigantic growth in
American productivity has barely produced any improvement at
all in the real income of the average American family. American
consumers no longer enjoy ever-cheaper goods; they compete
for fuel and food in a more demanding global marketplace and
wages aren't rising to compensate. Wages are flat and the prizes
are carried off by a richer and richer super-elite. As Paul Krugman put it:

the value of output an average worker produces in an hour has risen almost 50% since 1973. Yet the growing concentration of income in the hands of a small minority has proceeded so rapidly that we're not sure whether the typical American has gained anything from rising productivity.[41]

Nor was this 'inevitable' or 'automatic'. Political choices have widened what Jacob Hacker calls 'pre-distribution': a massive new gap between the way markets reward those at the top and those in the middle.[42]

These powerful long-term shifts are making it harder and harder to take tough decisions in America. But long-term decisions are needed, for the United States has been buoyed up for years by what Valéry Giscard d'Estaing once called an 'exorbitant privilege'.

It does not cost the US Treasury much to print a $100 bill. But to buy one, foreigners have to supply $100 worth of goods or services. In a world where everyone wants dollars (and foreign central banks own around $5 trillion of them), demand is high. That keeps US interest rates low; almost 1% lower than they would be otherwise.[43] That's a giant subsidy to the American consumer and American business. But as economist Barry Eichengreen points out, unless America takes action to deal with its debts:

> We will no longer be able to consume and invest a trillion dollars more than we produce each year just because central banks and other foreign investors have a voracious appetite for dollars that require no real resources to supply.[44]

Just like Europe, America has to find the way to bring its debts under control – and that means painful decisions on taxes and spending. In 2012, America's federal deficit stood at $1.1 trillion.

American national debt is now over $16 trillion – or $53,000 per citizen. Yet tax revenues stand at the lowest share of GDP since 1950 (about half the level of Europe). Health costs are mounting. And from 2015, the baby boomers will start retiring and demanding pensions.

Can Americans find a way of taking decisions big enough to fix the problems they confront? It's not clear. America is simply a far more divided country than before. Occupy Wall Street and the Tea Party movement are opposite but equal expressions of rage in a country when the old certainties have broken down.

I was very privileged to study in America. A few months after I got married, I was lucky enough to win a Fulbright scholarship to go and take my MBA at the home of American capitalism, the Harvard Business School. When I went left Harvard, there was exhilaration in the American economy. The dotcom bubble was ballooning. You only had to ring a venture capitalist and say you had a business plan, and they'd fly you to London. Ten years later when I went back for my tenth year reunion, the mood was very different. Times were very tough. On the Saturday morning, David Gergen, who has worked for American presidents of all stripes, gave a superb talk on just how hard it is for American presidents today. Presidents who served in the second world war, says Gergen, could expect an approval rating from their opponents 35% lower than among their own supporters. Now the gap is some 70%. When two sides are that polarised, it's far, far harder to achieve bi-partisan solutions to big problems.

Today in America there are plenty of policy wonks and politicians now reminding anyone who will listen that 'America isn't done'.

But this is the key point for us.

Before the crash, an amazing 20% of global GDP was powered by the American consumer. As the US savings rate fell from 10%

in the early 1980s to zero in 2007, US consumers spent *$10 trillion* a year – twice the amount of the next largest economy, Japan. Those days are now gone. The locomotive of the American consumer is not going to be pulling the world train in the decade to come. The great crash has destroyed something like $8 trillion of American wealth. Levels of personal debt are astronomical. The recovery in the US, hitherto, has been relatively jobless. It is simply not clear that growth great enough to create lots of jobs is going to return to America soon. If there is a US plan for fiscal consolidation, it is being kept pretty quiet. You should never underestimate the power of an American recovery. But we shouldn't bet on it either. And that's why we need to start looking to some new friends far away.

CHAPTER 3

The world shifts east

It was long predicted that China would be the giant of the 21st century, and the crash has not dimmed its rise. Far from it. 'Beware the sleeping dragon', said Winston Churchill, 'for when she awakes the Earth will shake'. In 1967, searching for a way out of Vietnam, Richard Nixon wrote,

> We simply cannot afford to leave China outside the family of nations, there to nurture its fantasies, cherish its hates and threaten its neighbours. There is no place on this small planet for a billion of its potentially most able people to live in angry isolation.[45]

It was nine years ago that economists at Goldman Sachs forecast that China could become the world's richest nation by 2041.[46] Last year China became the world's number two economy. It will be number one within a decade – perhaps, say OECD economists, by the first year of the next Parliament. It is a decisive shift in the globe's balance of power which could mean that by 2050 China, together with India, Brazil, Egypt, the Philippines, Indonesia, Iran, Mexico and a few others will control 60% of the world's wealth[47] in a revolutionary shift that could push 2 billion people into the global middle class.

It amounts to what Gerard Lyons, former chief economist at Standard Chartered, calls the third great economic 'super-cycle' since the Industrial Revolution 200 years ago. The first, from 1870 to 1913, saw the global growth rise to 2.7% a year and lifted America to world leadership. The second, from 1946 to 1973, saw global growth of 5% and lifted Japan and the Asian tigers to prominence. The super-cycle now under way will be faster than the first but slower than the second and more revolutionary than both. And like all revolutions, it has arrived overnight. It's been a long time coming.

It was fortunate for Richard Nixon that Chairman Mao had come to the conclusion that China's isolation from the world must draw to an end.

In the spring and summer of 1969, skirmishes with Soviet troops on the border around Xinjiang escalated dangerously. One million Soviet troops were massed on the border confronting China. Mao decided to recall four former marshals of the People's Liberation Army (PLA) to reassess US relations. The marshals soon reached an interesting conclusion: in any Sino-Soviet war, they opined, America could not sit 'on top of the mountain to watch a fight between two tigers'. America would have to take sides. And China wanted America in its corner. Suddenly engagement with America was a matter of self-defence – and necessity.

When Zhou Enlai, China's premier for 22 years and Mao's associate for 40, finalised the terms of Nixon's visit to China he told Henry Kissinger: 'Our announcement will shake the world.' In fact, China would prove perfectly capable of shaking the world with an energy of its own.

Four years after his handshake with Nixon, Mao was dead; and for the third time, an extraordinary Chinese statesman returned from internal exile. I am convinced that history will prove Deng Xiaoping to be among the greatest leaders of the

20th century. He had returned to power in 1974 only to be purged again months before Mao's death. But he re-emerged as a subordinate to Mao's successor, Hua Guofeng, and quickly Deng began to articulate a very new direction for China born of a frustration with the state of his nation. 'We are so poor and backward', he said in 1977, 'that, to be frank, we fail to live up to the expectations of our people. Foreigners are questioning how long the Chinese people can endure. We should pay attention to such remarks.'[48]

Deng was not wrong. In 1978, China accounted for 1% of the world's output. Its wealth per head ranked 190th in the world and was on a par with Zaïre. The following year, 'seeking to learn truth from facts', Deng had begun to endorse some consistent themes: decentralisation, modern technology and learning from the West. Deng was careful to present his arguments as an evolution of Mao's thought. In 1978, he told the All-Army Conference on Political Work: 'Isn't it true that seeking truth from facts, proceeding from reality and integrating theory with practice form the fundamental principle of Mao Zedong Thought?'

When the party gathered for the Third Plenum of the Eleventh Central Committee of the CPC in December 1978, Deng gave one of the most important speeches in Chinese history: 'Reform and Opening Up'. 'Economic construction' was put at the heart of the Party's mission and facts, not ideology, should guide the way, argued Deng: 'It doesn't matter if it is a black or a white cat. As long as it can catch mice, it is a good cat.'

In China you will often hear senior leaders describe their journey as like 'feeling for the stones to cross the river'.[49] But China's leaders were remarkably sure-footed. By the beginning of the new millennium, Deng's reforms had created such a high and consistent rate of growth that a revolutionary new balance of power was in sight.

Deng was happy for some areas to take a lead 'to prosper before others'. Economic powers were devolved to regions, and competition was encouraged between them. From 1979, four special economic zones were established in South China where foreign investment was allowed in. Fourteen coastal cities followed in 1984, then huge economic and technical development zones, helping create three vast economic belts along the Pearl river delta, the Yangtze delta and a 'Silicon Valley' around Beijing.

From 1980, 'individually owned business licences' were issued to the first privately owned businesses in Wenzhou, Zhejiang province, and soon this corner of the economy mushroomed so fast it began to power some 70–80% of China's economic growth.

'Township enterprises' were encouraged to diversify – by the mid-1990s they accounted for a third of industrial output. Pay was linked to output in the vast rural economy.

To push the business of learning from abroad, Deng encouraged students to begin study overseas: 20,000 started abroad in 1978. National plans were adopted to drive technology research: the Spark programme for rural economic development; the Torch plan for hi-tech industries and the 863 programme for hi-tech research began to drive innovation from ChangZheng carrier rockets to high-yield rice. In September 1986, China opened its first securities market and, in November 1986, Deng presented John Phelan, President of the New York Stock Exchange, with share certificate 05743, in Shanghai Feilo Acoustics, the first stock listed in China (it is today in a display cabinet in the NYSE).

Finally, Deng pushed through painful reform of state-owned enterprises (SOEs). He had described 'township enterprises' as 'a new force that had just come into being spontaneously'. Reform of China's massive SOEs was to prove harder work. Competition and 'opening up' left over 6,500 operating at a loss by 1997.

Reform of bankruptcy law, however, left many to simply go to the wall.

When Margaret Thatcher came to visit China in 1991 she gave President Jiang Zemin a lecture on how socialism was completely incompatible with a market economy. Deng had a very different view: 'A market economy is not capitalism', he told leaders in South China a few months later in January 1992, 'while a planned economy is not identical with socialism. Planning and market forces are both means of controlling economic activity.'

Here was the advent of what Jiang Zemin was later, in 1992, to call 'the socialist market economy'. It was, on any measure, a spectacular success.

A year before Hu Jintao took the stage as General Secretary of the Communist Party of China in 2002, Jim O'Neill, head of economics at Goldman Sachs, finished a paper which began to look at the relationship between the world's leading economies and the big new emerging economies, the BRICs – Brazil, Russia, India and China. The BRICs, argued Jim O'Neill, would over the course of the next 10 years overtake most members of the G7 group of richest industrialised nations: 'The world would have to pay attention', he concluded.[50]

Two years later, Goldman Sachs's team extended the work and concluded to most people's surprise that China might in fact become the world's largest economy by 2035.

At the time, interviews with Chinese leaders in the West were still relatively rare. When they spoke, they were careful to underline China's status as merely a 'developing nation' with immense challenges to confront. But from 2009, China's leaders took equal care to seed another thought: a belief that the course of history was now bending towards 'the larger trend', a multi-polar world in which America was no longer the undisputed leader. And by now batteries of facts were pouring forth in the Western media to reinforce the point.

Since 2001, China's economy has grown at an average of 10% a year, quadrupling in size. The economy has doubled in size every eight years. By 2005, China had 28 billion sq ft (2,600 sq km) of space under construction. For the 2008 Olympics, China built in Beijing six subway lines, 43km of light railway, 25 sq km of new property, a 125km ' green belt' and a 12 sq km Olympic Park. China has become the largest mobile phone market. It manufactures two-thirds of the world's photocopiers, microwaves, DVD players and shoes. According to the OECD, China's investment in innovation nearly doubled from €34 billion ($44.56 billion) in 2006 to €65.7 billion in 2009. In 2010, China completed 15 space launches, including its second lunar probe and five Beidou navigation satellites – the first stage in a network of 35 navigation satellites by 2020; completed its 7,531km of high-speed rail, more than in any other country; it became the fifth country to develop deep-diving technology capable of going beyond the 3,500m mark, and overtook the United States in developing the fastest supercomputer (the Tianhe-1A can perform 2,507 trillion calculations a second).

Between 2001 and 2010, China's domestic spending grew $1.5 trillion – the size of the entire UK economy. China now buys nearly 2 million more cars than America. Four hundred million people have been lifted out of poverty and the average Chinese person's income has grown seven-fold. Around 5% of China's population – 65 million people – have incomes of $35,000 a year; one in every 1,400 people is a dollar millionaire – and 200,000 millionaires live in Beijing alone. In 2011, Forbes listed 115 billionaires living in China; and many believe there are now more billionaires in China than America.

China's economy has in fact performed far better than Goldman's team believed possible: by 2008, it was an astonishing $1.7 trillion bigger than initial forecasts.

But it's the future forecasts, not the history, that should really grab our attention.

China might be a low-middle income country where hundreds of millions still live on less than $2 a day. It may be unique as a large country with barely any globally known firms and burdened with high pollution and carbon emissions. It might be ageing almost faster than it is getting wealthy. But the OECD now believe that China will become the world's largest economy in 2016.[51] Standard Chartered forecast that between now and 2030, 50% of the world's growth will arrive from east Asia – more than a fifth of it from China; the European Union may provide 15%; America may account for around the same. If these scenarios are correct, says Jim O'Neill, 'the BRIC markets will dominate certain industries, notably cars, luxury goods, travel and tourism'.[52] Indeed over one-third of all cars bought in the world will be bought in China: 25 million of them.

Comparing the wealth of countries is, as you might expect, a tricky business. Often economists do their sums using what's called PPP, or purchasing power parity. On a PPP basis, China's national output is much larger than its nominal output computed at market exchange rates because PPP sums take into account the lower level of prices in China. So forecasters expect China to overtake the US in PPP terms before it overtakes the US in market exchange rate terms; when China overtook Japan to become the second largest economy, it did so in PPP terms in the early 2000s, but in market exchange rates only in 2011.

As you would expect this is not an uncontroversial topic. Arvind Subramanian, from the Peterson Institute, argues that China has in fact already overtaken the US in PPP terms. The IMF expects this to happen in 2017. On market exchange rate terms, US GDP will still be nearly 50% bigger – but even on this basis China is expected to overtake the US some time between 2020 and 2027 (see Table 3.1).

But I think the message is fairly clear: if we want to trade our way back to prosperity, we had better start looking east.

A lesson from our history:
how the world order can change

A change in the world order does not happen overnight. Geopolitical power only passes decades after the economic fundamentals have shifted. But the power does pass and this is the shift that is under way in the world order today. My argument is that in Britain we should see this and decide to act ahead of the game, strengthening our links with China now, not later.

In America, there is a level of political paranoia about what is coming. That is understandable. Since the revolution in East Germany on 9 November 1989, America's writ has, by and large, run supreme. Weeks after George Bush Sr and Mikhail Gorbachev declared the cold war over on 2 December 1989, America invaded Panama. Two years later the Allies took back Kuwait. By the time George W. Bush landed his plane on the USS *Abraham Lincoln* to declare 'mission accomplished' in Iraq, America had led coalitions delivering victory in two Gulf wars and against the Taliban in Afghanistan, and had expanded NATO right up to the Russian border.

Today, America spends some $600 billion on defence, more than the rest of the other great powers combined.[53] Its generals, like Anthony Zinni, have been known to compare themselves to Roman pro-consuls. At the peak of conflict in 2003, 200,000 troops were stationed in Iraq and Afghanistan and a further 160,000 in Europe and East Asia; 752 bases are dispersed around 130 countries; at sea sail nine 'super-carrier' battle-groups; the US Air Force boasts three different stealth aircraft. Yet all this costs America less than 4% of GDP. America is not 'over-stretched' and its projection of power stands on the foundations of a remarkable economy.

America has been generating between 20 and 30% of world output for 125 years. Its economy's roots are nourished by the world's most advanced, best-financed, and most successful eco-system of innovation. American productivity growth remains way ahead of Europe; at 2.5% p.a. before the crash, it was a full 1% p.a. higher than Europe, underpinned by a global lead in R&D spending.[54] The sinews of that productivity are in rude health. Seven of the world's 10 best universities are American and the US spends twice as much on higher education as France, Germany, Britain or Japan. American firms dominate R&D spending in IT hardware, software, aerospace and defence and pharmaceuticals. 'The rise of the rest' has actually helped America's bottom line; between 1980 and 2007, as the world economy boomed, America's share of global exports fell just 1%, from 10% to 9%. As the 21st century began, wrote Joseph Nye, 'the US accounted for about a quarter of the world's product, nearly half of global military expenditures and the world's most extensive cultural and educational soft power resources'.[55]

But in Britain we should remember our own history. Good things, as they say, don't last forever. We've learned the hard way how world orders can change. We should know. It happened to us.

On 27 July 1866, the SS Great Eastern reached the Canadian coast to complete an extraordinary task: connecting the United Kingdom and North America by submarine telegraph cable. It was the latest link in the metal chains that connected together the greatest empire on earth; by the late 1870s, the telegraph linked Britain, Canada, India, Australia and Africa in a network 97,568 miles long, part of a global network of rail lines and steam-ship routes that had collapsed distance.

The Great Eastern was among the finest symbols of Victorian engineering excellence. It dominated the last six years of the life of Britain's greatest engineer, Isambard Brunel. Brunel was fascinated by the idea, conceived in 1851, of creating a ship big enough to carry its own fuel all the way to the Far East and back. By 1853, he had designed a ship nearly 700ft (200m) long and carrying 4,000 passengers, driven by both paddles and propellers. James Watt of Birmingham supplied the engines. Robert Stephenson advised on the launch. Its design would redefine modern shipbuilding; no ship was bigger for another 49 years. But it was a commercial disaster. Cursed by accidents the ship eventually found its niche laying submarine cable across the world's ocean floors.

Within a year or two of the Great Eastern touching shore in North America, Britain deployed the new technology of the telegraph to mobilise imperial forces from the two continents to crush a disagreeable dictator holed up in a third. The Emperor Theodore of Abyssinia, frustrated at Britain's failure to recognise his regime, had imprisoned a collection of Europeans in his mountain fortress in Magdala in the Ethiopian highlands. When Queen Victoria's appeal for their release went unanswered, the Prime Minister, Lord Derby, dispatched a telegraph message across 10,000 miles to the Governor of the Bombay Presidency with orders for Lord Napier: 'Break thou the chains.' Napier mobilised 13,000 British and Indian soldiers, 26,000 camp-followers, vast amounts of livestock, a prefabricated harbour replete with lighthouses and a railway system, and 44 elephants. Napier landed, marched over 400 miles of desert and, in a 'butcher and bolt' assault lasting just two hours, stormed the fortress, killing 700 people and releasing the hostages. The Emperor committed suicide. It was an extraordinary demonstration of Britain's global power.

Three decades later, on 22 June 1897, one quarter of the world's population got a day off. The occasion: Queen Victoria's jubilee. In Portsmouth the largest fleet ever assembled lay at anchor: 165 ships carrying 40,000 seamen and 3,000 guns. Through London marched 50,000 soldiers from every corner of an empire which now encompassed a quarter of the world's land mass, connected together by 170,000 nautical miles of ocean cable and 662,000 of aerial and buried cable strung between the 'five keys' to the world's sea-lanes; Singapore, the Cape of Africa, Alexandria, Gibraltar and Dover.[56]

Watching the soldiers march was a young Arnold Toynbee: 'I remember the atmosphere', he wrote in later life. 'It was: "Well, here we are on top of the world, and we have arrived at this peak to stay there forever."'[57]

On the eve of the first world war, Britain still invested twice as much as anyone else abroad. Between 1865 and 1914, Britain exported some £4 billion to the rest of the world. London was the centre of the world's finance. The pound was the global reserve currency.

Yet, just as the SS Great Eastern reached North America in 1866, the United States surpassed the United Kingdom as the largest economy in the West. Within six years of Victoria's Diamond Jubilee, the average American had become wealthier than the average Briton.[58]

While Britain had been building a global empire, America had built an economic powerhouse that in time would comprehensively overhaul us.

As late as 1842, Charles Dickens on his first visit to America had labelled Washington DC a 'City of Magnificent Intentions'; the grand ambitions of its architect Pierre L'Enfant were in some contrast to the reality of Washington's muddy environs. Within living memory, the President's wife Dolley Madison had actually had to evacuate the White House before the British troops arrived to burn it down.

Three years after Dickens sailed home, America elected the president that would transform the country into a continent. James Knox Polk isn't famous in Britain. Yet he has a reasonable claim to be one of the most successful American presidents. The son of a successful land speculator, he grew up in Tennessee, graduated first in his class, became a lawyer and, on a rainy 4 March 1845, he took office aged just 49, as the eleventh – and youngest – president in American history. Not known for his elegance, he was very clear-eyed about his agenda, which he confided to just one man, his Secretary of the Navy, George Bancroft:

> There are to be four great measures of my administration: the settlement of the Oregon question with Great Britain. The acquisition of California and a large district on the coast. The reduction of the tariff to a revenue basis. The complete and permanent establishment of the constitutional Treasury.[59]

Within just four years, Polk had achieved everything he had set out to accomplish.

Polk did not name his political philosophy; it was named for him. In the summer after he took office, an anonymous journalist writing about Texas for the Democratic Review argued: 'it is now time for opposition to the annexation of Texas to cease. [Texas's annexation represents] the fulfilment of our *manifest destiny* to overspread the continent allotted by Providence for the free development of our yearly multiplying millions.'[60]

Manifest destiny was precisely what drove a generation of Americans towards the new frontiers of their country. While war raged in Mexico in 1846, the writer Francis Parkman described the scene in St Louis at the confluence of the great Mississippi and Missouri rivers and the great jumping-off point for the pioneers heading west. Here, the great polyglot mass of pioneers busily prepared to venture west to Oregon and California:

> The hotels were crowded, and the gunsmiths and saddlers were kept constantly at work in providing arms and equipments for the different parties of travellers. Steamboats were leaving the levee and passing up the Missouri, crowded with passengers on their way to the frontier.[61]

By the 1890s, those pioneers had settled the west and created a distinctive American character. The frontier which had once moved so quickly became, in the words of the historian Frederick Turner, 'the line of the most rapid and effective Americanisation', a crucible in which 'immigrants were Americanised, liberated and fused into a mixed race, English in neither nationality nor characteristics'.

By the time of Queen Victoria's diamond jubilee, that pioneering spirit had produced some of the greatest capitalists on earth. In the decade after James Polk left office, 21,000 miles of railroad was laid. Alongside it ran the telegraph spanning the continent from the Atlantic to the Pacific. To manage these new businesses, Americans invented the modern corporation to coordinate finances, accounts, engineering, timetables, cash-handling, pricing and staffing for huge inter-continental networks. By 1900 several employed over 100,000 people.

To finance them, new banking businesses were born. By 1859, $1.1 billion had been invested in railroad securities[62] and New York had become the centre for raising the funds. In 1830, just 31 stocks were traded on the New York Stock Exchange. By 1850, hundreds of thousands of shares were traded every week; in one four-week period, a million shares changed hands.[63] New trading techniques were invented; puts and calls were perfected. Margin trading was born. Call loans appeared. Manipulators like Jay Gould became nationally infamous.

The giant new market fostered huge new companies. Before 1880 few US businesses were worth more than $1 million. By 1901, the billion-dollar corporation was born when J. Pierpont Morgan created the $1.4 billion US Steel Corporation. In a huge wave of consolidation between 1897 and 1904, 4,227 companies were merged to form 257 combinations, like Standard Oil and American Tobacco. By 1904, 318 large firms controlled 40% of the nation's manufacturing assets. At the end of the 20th century half of the largest companies could trace their roots to this extraordinary era, 1880–1930.

It did not take America long to elect the president who epitomised the new nation: Theodore Roosevelt. The son of a wealthy and influential partner in the old New York importing partnership, Roosevelt and Son, his character was forged not in genteel New York but in the west, where he became a rancher at the age of 25, after the death of his wife. Roosevelt went to blaze a trial as an ebullient, forceful, Republican reformer, as a civil service administrator, president of the Board of Police in New York, Assistant Secretary of the Navy and then Governor of New York and war hero of the 1898 conflict with Cuba. In 1900, he was unable to resist his party's nomination for Vice President, and when McKinley was shot dead in Chicago in 1901, Roosevelt became the country's youngest ever President and, in a new demonstration of American power, he sailed the country's 'Great White Fleet' around the world. 'Manifest destiny' ran through Roosevelt like words through a stick of rock.

There is a simple lesson from this story. A nation's geopolitical presence can hide for a very long time a change in the economic order.

Right now, America is the world's geopolitical leader. But the world economic order is now changing as radically as it did between President Polk's election and the SS Great Eastern reaching the coast of North America.

Between 1990 and 2007, the size of the global economy more than doubled – from $22.8 trillion to $53.3 trillion; half of this growth was from 'emerging markets'.

Writers like Fareed Zakaria condemn the 'arrogance and unilateralism which [have] handicapped America abroad [in which] American politicians constantly and promiscuously demand, label, sanction and condemn whole countries for myriad failings'.[64] Even the Republican Robert Kagan admits that America's responses to 9/11 have alienated allies: 'the detainment facilities at Guantánamo, the use of torture against suspected terrorists, and the widely condemned invasion of Iraq in 2003 have all tarnished the American brand and put a dent in America's soft power.'[65]

Former presidential foreign-policy advisors like Zbigniew Brzezinski now write articles called 'After America' and quote high-ranking Chinese officials saying to American counterparts: 'please, let America not decline too quickly'. Analysts point to the risk of new, assertive regional powers threatening America's allies and new difficulties in managing the 'global commons': sea-lanes, space, cyber-space and the environment. When America's National Intelligence Council surveyed the country's prospects for 2025, it concluded; 'the US will remain the preeminent power, but ... American dominance will be much diminished.'[66]

I want our relationship with Europe and America to be strong. As someone who has had the privilege of living, studying, travelling, and doing business all over America, I can happily say I love the country.

But, let's remember our history. If Britain had seen the coming shift in the world order in 1897, I think we would have done a few things differently. We would have worked much harder to build business connections. Today we have £184 billion invested in America – that's nearly 20% of everything we own abroad. But a century ago, British entrepreneurs didn't – or couldn't – join forces with the new giants of Roosevelt's America. We would have worked harder to forge links with the American universities then taking shape. And I think we would have worked much harder to understand American politicians who played such a crucial role in the decisions which shaped our fortunes throughout the 20th century, from joining us in world wars, to cancelling Lend-Lease in 1945, to standing against us in Suez.

So, this book is the story of one quest to pin down some of the ways we might build exactly those links. And here's a simple back-of-the-envelope calculation to focus the mind. If we managed to double the annual growth rate in exports to China, from 15% to 30%, we would increase GDP by £5 billion, or 0.3% of GDP. If we tripled the growth rate, we'd add £7 billion, or 0.5% of GDP (see Table 3.2).

Just to illustrate the point: say we trebled the pace of our exports and then kept at that pace for the next five years. Five years later our economy would be 5.8% larger. In real money? That's £87.6 billion larger. So: turning east could mean some great prizes. If this century is to be the Asian century we need to ask: are we ready?

CHAPTER 4

Turning east

Is the UK ready for the arrival of the Asian century? I don't think so.

Our history as a post-Imperial global trading power means that we have relationships, investments, trade and a dialogue with China that, despite the ups and downs of the last year following the Prime Minister's meeting with the Dalai Lama, are fundamentally in excellent shape. In the race to prosper in the Asian century, we are definitely on the starting grid. But I think we are a long way from the front.

Americans might not like the idea, but their relationship with China is deep, good for America and fast blossoming into something even more intricate and complicated for the years ahead. In the last 30 years the American consumer has forged an extraordinary interdependence with the Chinese factory worker. Closer to home, Chinese politicians have forged an extraordinary rapport with their Pacific neighbours, even if it remains a community fraught with the suspicions and jealousies of any old neighbourhood. In a decade, the five major East Asian economies – China, Japan, Taiwan and the two Koreas – have achieved a degree of economic interdependence that it took the nations of Europe 50 years to master.[67]

Here in Europe, there are three nations that dominate China relations: Germany, France and us. We're 'ahead' of France. But I'm afraid Germany is now many, many miles ahead of us. The past we bear, the products we make, the political priorities we've struck are all very different to Germany's; and the result is now plain to see.

That's the bad news. But the good news is this: our position is eminently fixable. And fixing the problem requires we know a little about the history of Sino-British relations.

East and West

There isn't a Western nation that can boast a long and great history of intimacy with China; China's long history, its progress, its pride all meant that the Celestial Empire could stand aloof from the world behind its Great Wall to the north and its sea wall to the east.

Take a stroll through Room 33 of the British Museum, where there is a rather nice illustration of just why. There sits the magnificent bronze bell featured in the BBC series, A History of the World in 100 Objects,[68] the size of an elliptical beer barrel intricately etched with flying geese and topped with a magnificent pair of dragons. Originally part of a set, it was played by an orchestra in a musical tradition that epitomised a Confucian ideal of harmony and order. It was cast some 2,500 years ago – 1,500 years earlier than anything in Europe, an instrument of music but also representing a philosophy 500 years older than Christianity.

For almost Europe's entire history, China was not only a nation far away. It was a civilisation far ahead, and its lead over us was early. Man probably spread to Asia anywhere between 1 and 1.8 million years ago – possibly half a million years earlier than the colonisation of Europe.[69] Seven and a half thousand years ago, China became one of the first five centres of civilisation to domesticate plants and animals, including water buffalo, ducks, geese – and silk worms. Bronze metallurgy was under way by the 3rd millennium BC in fortified towns where the bronze bells and vessels of exquisite beauty like those in the British Museum were cast. In Britain, by contrast, our ancestors were humping around large rocks at Stonehenge.

In the centuries that followed, China's precocious inventors created canal lock gates, cast iron, drilling, animal harnesses, porcelain, stern-post rudders and wheelbarrows[70] and the 'big four': paper-making; moveable type printing; the magnetic compass and gunpowder.[71]

But for a politician like me, the extraordinary achievement of ancient China was political. By 221BC, as the Romans fought the Second Punic war and united merely the Italian peninsula south of Florence, the Qin dynasty had united the Warring States into an empire greater than Rome ever reached at its height, into a civilisation that is still recognisable today. Its two great rivers – the Yellow river in the north and Yangtze in the south – connected the coast to the deep interior and in turn were connected to each other by the Grand Canal, one of the miracles of early engineering that was complete by AD610: around the time King Arthur was resisting the Anglo-Saxon conquest of England.

Chinese thinkers could perhaps be forgiven for acquiring something of a superiority complex. One writing system pervaded throughout the land (unlike the dozens of modified languages and forty-odd languages of Europe),[72] and a thousand years before Tacitus[73] a Zhou dynasty writer was using it to describe the 'barbarians' of the neighbouring tribes – people who tattooed their foreheads and ate their food raw.

For sixteen hundred years, this new Celestial Empire was unknown to the West. Alexander the Great came close. If you head south-east out of Islamabad, in Pakistan, on the N5 – the Grand Old Trunk road – for an hour you get to Jhelum on the Jhelum river, where Alexander defeated King Porus in the battle of Hydaspes in 326BC.[74] For centuries, this marked the eastern extent of Western exploration. But not interest. For the Romans not only knew but adored Chinese goods. The Emperor Elagabalus, AD218–22, shocked Rome not just with the capricious murder of children but by powdering his face, removing all body hair and flaunting a wardrobe made entirely of Chinese silk.[75] A century after Christ, the Roman poet Juvenal complained of luxury-loving and women's fondness for the mysterious fabric the Romans believed grew on mulberry trees.

By the time Chinese silk reached Rome, it was literally worth its weight in gold and the prize of Eastern trade was so great it would fuel generations of European commercial violence. For the bazaar at the end of the Silk Road was an enormously profitable place to be. In the years after Rome's fall, that marketplace was Constantinople, the capital of Byzantium, the city which, wrote Edward Gibbon, 'attracted the commerce of the ancient world'.[76] Byzantium's last Latin emperor, Justinian, knew exactly the value of eastern routes. He fought the Persians to forge a road through the Crimea, Lazica (present-day Georgia) and the Caucasus,[77] and if you wander through Istanbul today you can still see the prize of the wealth he won in what is for my money the most beautiful building in the world: Justinian's Hagia Sophia, the church which prompted him to murmur on 27 December 537, 'Solomon, I have surpassed thee.'[78]

Wealth that great was worth a fight, and when the fight came it was led by a blind eighty-something Italian politician: Doge Dandolo of Venice. Amid the chaos of the Fourth Crusade, it was Dandalo who persuaded Europe's princes to join an attack on Constantinople, which he personally led against the city's great sea walls. After an orgy of violence across the city – 'the booty gained was so great', wrote one solider, 'that none could tell you the end of it'[79] – Venice imposed a commercial treaty which at a stroke moved the market at the end of the Silk Road from the Golden Horn of Constantinople to Venice.[80] So Venice became the 'masters of the gold of Christendom'[81] and, in the streets around the small church of San Giacometta[82] by the Rialto Bridge, its merchants haggled for control of Europe's trade in pepper; spices; Syrian cotton; grain; wine; salt – and silk.

Yet still, medieval Europe knew little about the *source* of spices and silks that arrived through trade with the East. The Silk Road, as it was known, ran east over land opened by Han Chinese emissaries in the decades before Elagabalus: a network of roads that shifted with politics and the weather, through Samarkand, Isfahan, Herat – and Europe. Cheaper and more popular was the sea route along which Chinese traders sailed around the Malay peninsula to the Bay of Bengal and Sri Lanka. There they traded with Indian merchants who shipped to the south-west coast of the sub-continent to meet the Greeks and Arabs who would sail on to Socotra (or Diocordia) and through the Red Sea to Berenice in Egypt, before they met the camel trains to the Nile, the only north-flowing river in Africa, and from there across the Mediterranean to the old Roman ports of Puteoli and Ostia.[83]

First-hand accounts of what actually lay at the end of the road didn't arrive until Marco Polo's journals in 1298, and they were widely dismissed as fantasy.[84] But 140 years later, another Venetian, Niccolò de' Conti, relayed to Pope Eugenius IV a rather more enticing image: of Sri Lanka's cinnamon trees, Sumatra's fields of pepper and camphor, the island of 'Sanday' where nutmeg and mace grew, and Bandan, thick with cloves.[85] This sounded more like money, and it wasn't long before adventurers and their patrons were pushing forward into the seas in search of the sea route east. Three years after the monarchs of Portugal and Spain met in the sleepy town of Tordesillas to divide the world – along an east–west line – between themselves,[86] Vasco da Gama finally set sail on the most momentous maritime journey in history.

Heading south to the equator, passing Sierra Leone, da Gama turned west into the Atlantic tacking against the wind and then swinging east on to the winds that would take him beyond the Cape of Good Hope. Rounding the Cape, he drew into Malindi, 60 miles from Mombasa, resupplied and re-equipped with a pilot furnished by the Sultan, and set sail north on 24 April 1498. He crossed the equator five days later, took bearings from the North Star, and on 18 May 1498 he spied the south-west coast of India. In just 23 days, da Gama had crossed 2,800 miles of ocean, missed his destination of Calicut in India by just seven miles and opened the sea route from Europe to the east.

The Portuguese captain was a better navigator than trader. When he arrived in Calicut he had but 'four *capotas* or cloaks of scarlet cloth, six hats, four branches of coral, 12 *almasares* [pieces of cloth], a box containing seven brass vessels, a chest of sugar, two barrels of oil, and a cask of honey'.[87] It wasn't much. But when he left Calicut, da Gama packed up enough cinnamon and cloves to pay for this expedition *60* times over.

And so the dam was breached. Europeans now poured east to fight it out for profit. The first Portuguese ships were unloading cargos of peppers, cinnamon and saffron on the quaysides of Antwerp within four years of da Gama arriving home, and within a century, the mighty Dutch VOC (East India Company) had built an extraordinary trading zone across which were shipped Spanish silver, Chinese gold and silk; Japanese copper; Bengal cottons; East Asian mace, nutmeg, cloves, cinnamon and pepper;

coral, pewter, deer pelts, saltpetre, rice, lacquer, precious stones, cowry shells, slaves, tea, porcelain – and elephants. By 1650, the company had become the world's biggest transnational corporation and boasted 200 ships in ports in Jakarta. Throughout the Indies, 30,000 men sailed under the company's colours.

But outside the borders of their emporium lay China. For in China, the Europeans confronted the largest, most sophisticated and most united realm on earth, home to 120 million people,[88] governed by a massive bureaucracy of ministries, military, tax officials, scholars imbued in a philosophy a millennium old, organised around a vast palace complex of court women, eunuchs, bodyguards and imperial staff, at the centre of which sat the Son of Heaven, the Emperor of the late Ming dynasty. And he was not interested in the 'West Sea Barbarians'. For a century, China's Imperial policy, confounded only by the smugglers, was effectively to seal the country off from the rest of the world.

This isolation from the world had perhaps reached its psychological high-water mark as early as 1423. On Chinese New Year's Day, 2 February 1421, two decades after the construction of the Bloody Tower within the Tower of London and the naves of Westminster Abbey and Canterbury Cathedral, the Yongle Emperor inaugurated not a new cathedral or a new castle, but an entire new capital: Beijing.

Two hundred thousand labourers had slaved for 16 years to build the city you can still see today: a city wall, 10m high, 23km long, surrounds a city at the heart of which lies the vermilion Forbidden City, the gigantic complex of white stone courtyards, marble bridges and audience halls set within a perfect symmetry. Assembled before the Emperor were thousands of ambassadors from Asia to the coasts of the Indian Ocean, all ready to kow-tow to the Son of Heaven.[89] The Yongle Emperor was not simply a builder but also an explorer. And he was fortunate to have within the ranks of his navy the most famous sailor in Chinese history: Admiral Zheng He. Captured at the age of 11 on the field of battle, he was, as was customary, castrated, and sent to serve the Emperor when he was a young prince.

Upon assuming the throne, Yongle entrusted his admiral with a mission to explore the oceans and, in six epic voyages between 1405 and 1424, Zheng He beat a course throughout the seas of south-east Asia, to India, then to Hormuz at the mouth of the Red Sea, and the east coast of Africa, gathering gifts and tribute, including, from the Sultan of Malindi, a giraffe, which was welcomed back in China as the mythical unicorn.[90]

Yet on the death of the Yongle Emperor, China's leaders took a decision that has fascinated economic historians ever since.[91] The voyages were cancelled. Zheng He's records were destroyed. The *haijin* (literally 'sea ban') decree prohibited foreign exploration. In 1500, the building of two-masted ships was banned on pain of death. The Chinese Empire retreated behind its walls. And those walls became higher and grander than ever. The Chinese have been building walls for literally millennia.[92] From the days of the 'Warring States', a 'lattice' of walls or 'earth dragons' began to stretch across northern China.[93] Within 50 years of Yongle's death, under new pressure from the Mongols in the west, a combination of lightning attacks and the renewal of the long wall were agreed; the wall was to be an immense 910km creation, punctuated by 800 strong points, sentry posts and beacon towers,[94] and this would become the foundation for the great bricked border wall built over 150 years which is today such a spectacular sight an hour north of Beijing: an immense physical expression of the splendid isolation in which the Chinese empire had ensconced itself, at once a defence from the outer world and a statement of China's precocious superiority to any civilisation outside it. It symbolised, in Julia Lovell's words, 'the mental wall that the Chinese state had built around itself to repel foreign influences and to control and encircle the Chinese people within'.[95]

By the time the Portuguese arrived off the coast of Canton – today's Guangzhou – in 1535, Pizarro's *conquistador* army had destroyed the Inca Emperor Atahualpa and Hernán Cortés had conquered Mexico. But so powerful and extensive was the throne of China that not even a domestic revolution weakened the Empire's defences against the 'West Sea Barbarians'.

The last of the Ming, the Emperor Wanli, took to the throne in the days of England's Elizabeth I.[96] From the 1580s, he had begun to retreat. He held no audiences, stopped his Confucian studies, refused to read state papers, and slowly power passed to the court eunuchs, a feature of Peking court life for 2,000 years and a political force 10,000 strong. As their power grew, Chinese politics divided, trouble at its borders multiplied, control of the great rural bureaucracy crumbled, and famine and war spread. On 25 April 1644, rebel armies closed in on Beijing and the last Emperor of the Ming dynasty appeared drunk and probably blood-spattered for his final audience. He had spent the previous evening murdering his consorts. Perhaps fortunately, none of his officials presented themselves. The Emperor staggered out of the Forbidden City's back gate, clambered up Coal Hill, and hanged himself with his sash shortly before 1am.

In May, the Qing invaders defeated their competitors outside the wall fortress of Shanhaiguan and trooped, tens of thousands strong, into a burning Beijing through streets lined with stunned surviving ministers and citizens offering flowers and burning incense, before entering what was left of the burnt Forbidden City.[97]

Just three Qing emperors would rule China, from the days of Oliver Cromwell until the dawn of the Industrial Revolution.

They were ambitious and powerful and amid the disintegration of the great Mongol Empire they launched a series of western wars in Mongolia, Tibet and Xinjiang, lands criss-crossed by every major religion and trade routes, to throw back the borders of China to their widest arc and create, in Henry Kissinger's words, an empire 'at least the rival of any Empire on earth'.[98]

It was a Chinese push west across the land, to match the Europeans' push east across the sea,[99] and helps explain why a succession of Chinese emperors had both the strength and the disposition to ignore the 'West Sea Barbarians' of Europe.

In Confucian philosophy, it was understood that the uncultured barbarian would recognise the superiority of Chinese civilisation and 'come and be transformed' once in contact with the Empire. In return, the Emperor was to be compassionate in his 'tendering cherishing of men from far away'.[100] In this tributary system European traders were no different to any other neighbour seeking relations. As such the traders should follow the humble submission required by court ritual, formalised in the Collected Statutes which set out where a 'tribute envoy' could enter China, when they could trade and who they could trade with. Confining trade to Canton was the court's way of keeping the tribute envoys as far away from Beijing as possible.[101] A wall of regulation was built to keep the traders in their place. Trade was circumscribed to Canton. Traders had to leave in the winter. No venturing into China was permitted. No books on Chinese history were to be sold, or the language learned. All trade was channelled through a licensed group of local merchants, the Co-hong, typically restricted to fewer than 12 individuals.

So confronted, the Portuguese settled for establishing a base in Macao with the tacit permission of the Emperor in the 1550s. The Dutch alighted not in China, but in Manila, to where Cantonese silk merchants flocked to exchange their silk, for the silver of the New World and Japan. This was the balance of power that England's traders found and left largely undisturbed for 200 years.

The English arrive

The first Englishman on this new stage was the remarkable Sir Francis Drake. On his extraordinary circumnavigation of the world he landed in 1580 at Ternate, one of the Mollucas, and Java, where he loaded his hull with cloves. The islands were not easy to find. Nestling in the Mollucan triangle in the Indonesian archipelago 500 miles north of Australia, the islands are at the centre of Indonesia's volcanic ring of fire where eruptions every five years or so cover the surrounding islands with a volcanic ash, excellent for nurturing nutmeg groves.

When Drake returned, London's merchants immediately smelled the profit. They were closely connected men linked in a web of family and commercial relations:[102] flexible, ambitious and organised into companies devoted to undertaking the expensive businesses of exploration, trade[103] and, when trade failed, privateering.[104] They made fortunes stealing from the Spanish and Portuguese, and it was in this spirit that the East India Company (EIC) was founded as 'the greatest association of merchants in the universe', in 1600. The Company quickly dispatched east its first commander, James Lancaster,[105] in the flagship the Red Dragon. A 600-tonne vessel built for privateering in the West Indies and armed with 38 guns, the Red Dragon arrived in Ache on 5 June 1602, and immediately led a small fleet fanning out across the straits to attack the Portuguese, stock up on spices and establish a base on the tiny nutmeg island of Pulo Run, which would take the honour of becoming England's first colony in the east. Lancaster's fleet returned home with holds full of nearly 500 tonnes of pepper corns, and the great commander was promptly knighted by James I.

The EIC grew strong on its eastern business. But it was no match for the viciousness and power of its Dutch rivals. After the Glorious Revolution and the installation of the Dutch William of Orange on the English throne, the companies merged and divided the east between them; the Dutch took the East Indies, and the English took China. It would take two centuries, three embassies, two wars and a revolution in English tastes before England's trade with China really took off.

England's traders had not fared well in their first exchanges with the Celestial Empire. A temporary base had been built and abandoned in Japan in the 1620s and ships of the EIC's rival had exchanged fire with Chinese coastal guns in the 1630s. But, by the middle of the century, England's markets were moving.

Tuesday 25 September 1660 was a day like many others for Samuel Pepys. He spent the morning in the office talking over the virtues of peace with Spain and war with Holland and France before heading off in the office barge to Deptford to pay off the good ship Success. Before he left, he wrote later, 'I did send for a cup of tee (a China drink) of which I never had drank before, and went away.'[106]

Pepys was a fashionable man.[107] The first adverts for the national drink had begun circulating in London in 1658[108] and Charles II's Portuguese wife, Catherine of Braganza, had made tea drinking rather fashionable in elite circles. But it was the arrival not of a princess but of sugar that transformed English demand. Sugar became England's largest import[109] from 1750, whereupon in the coffee houses of London Englishmen could mix a cheaper tea with the sugar of the West Indies and sip it while smoking tobacco from the New World. When The Kent arrived in London in 1703 with 65,000lb (30,000kg) of tea its cargo was the equivalent to almost the entire supply of previous years. By the 1740s, tea consumption had soared to 2.5 million lb (1 million kg) p.a.[110]

To satisfy this kind of demand, the East India Company now needed a rather different relationship with the Chinese government to the unsatisfactory relations enjoyed in Canton. By 1777, only four of the Co-hong syndicate could be trusted to trade, and the local official who regulated the business, the *Hoppo*, presided over a fairly corrupt and arbitrary form of local taxation.[111] As English demand for tea rocketed, the regulations began to rub so hard that the EIC decided it was time to spend a lot of money on a large embassy. Britain's best diplomat, Lord Macartney, was dispatched, only to bring home nothing better than notes for a rather good book. Two further embassies followed.

Lord Amherst's embassy of 1816 ended in a physical brawl between envoys and officials outside the Emperor's throne-room. Lord William Napier, dispatched by Palmerston in 1834, did not even make it out of Guangzhou and died of malaria on board his ship after furious rows with the local governor.

By now, the balance of forces was looking very different to the days of the first skirmishes 200 years before. The Royal Navy now boasted 240 ships, 40,000 sailors, and the largest naval base in the world. And England's traders had discovered a rather profitable line of exports to China: opium.

By 1839, the Qing court, like many politicians, had discussed the virtues of legalising opium and then decided to ban the drug. A skilled official, Lin Zexu, was dispatched to Guangzhou to enforce the new policy and on arrival he demanded the surrender of all opium from the traders, writing to Queen Victoria demanding she act to cease the noxious trade: 'May you, O King, check your wicked and sift your vicious people before they come to

China ... to let the two countries enjoy together the blessings of peace.'[112] To prove how serious he was, he threatened to cut off the trade in rhubarb.

In London, the China traders were outraged. Former MPs like William Jardine demanded war. Palmerston, who needed little encouragement on this sort of question, dispatched an ultimatum demanding not just redress for the traders but 'one or more sufficiently large and properly situated islands on the coast of China' as a depot for British trade. To focus Chinese minds, Palmerston ordered a naval blockade of China's principal ports and seizure of Chinese shipping.

Qishan, Viceroy of Zhili (Beijing division), managed to negotiate a withdrawal, and was instructed by the Emperor to play for time. Unimpressed, the British commander, Captain Charles Elliot, started bombarding the Chinese coastline. A deal was quickly secured, including rights over Hong Kong, but Palmerston was furious that the terms were too light. He dismissed the deal and Hong Kong as 'a barren island with hardly a house upon it',[113] and sent Sir Henry Pottinger to blockade more ports, cut traffic on the Grand Canal[114] and surround the ancient capital of Nanjing for good measure. Resisting a heavy shower of blandishments, Pottinger closed a treaty including a $6 million indemnity, ceding of Hong Kong and trading rights in five treaty ports replete with diplomatic missions. The Canton system was at an end.

So began what the Chinese call today 'the century of humiliation' that would culminate in the destruction of dynastic rule in the revolution of 1911. Behind Britain's lead, France and the United States waded in with demands for equal treatment. Huge pressures were now unleashed within and without China. Russia set out to invade China's western regions. A young charismatic claiming to be Jesus's younger brother led the Taipan rebellion and wrestled control of south and central China. The Nian rebellion in the west began a two-decade-long insurgency. Sixty million Chinese died between 1850 and 1873.

When the Treaty of Nanjing came up for renegotiation, France and England raised their demands for full diplomatic relations. In 1856, a minor inspection of the British ship, the Arrow, and the alleged desecration of the British flag, provided a pretext for new conflict.

After a furious debate in the House of Commons, the government resigned, only to be re-elected with a mandate for war. British and French forces were landed and marched on Beijing. The ensuing Treaty of Nanjing in 1858 provided not only for a full-time embassy but more treaty ports and travel rights to the interior. When Britain's ambassador was then blocked in an ambush, Lord Elgin (of Elgin marbles fame) was dispatched to 'bring the Emperor to reason' and in a symbolic show of power he burned down the Emperor's Summer Palace, destroying an invaluable collection of art treasures.

The ensuing 'peace' was not happy. China began a descent into turmoil. In the popular uprisings of 1898, Chinese nationalists fought back in a guerrilla war only to provoke a combined assault from France, Britain, the US, Japan, Russia, Germany, Austria-Hungary and Italy, whose armies laid waste to Beijing. Twelve years later the Qing dynasty collapsed.

With a history like this upon us, Britain and China have done awfully well to build the relationship we have today. At the absolute core of the Communist Party's appeal to Chinese people is their historic aim and role in both preserving the unity of China and expelling the foreign forces that began their incursions with the British at the end of the 19th century and expanded with such disastrous consequences under the Japanese occupation.

But 30 years into the Great Opening Up inaugurated by Deng Xiaoping can we say that we have recovered the past and built the right foundations for the future? I'm just not sure we have. We have made a start for sure. But I have a nagging sense that others are a long way ahead of us.

CHAPTER 5

Is Britain ready?

It was a very practical motive that first took me to China.

The Friday after a tough set of local elections in 2006, I was in my constituency office at the Fox and Goose in Hodge Hill, clearing up the office with my team and nursing some very sore feet. I had spent 14 hours on election day knocking on voters' doors and now I could barely walk. The phone rang and the operators at the famous No. 10 Switchboard came on to the line asking if I could hold for the Prime Minister. Calls like that always made me nervous; I usually wondered what on earth I had done now. But Tony Blair came on to the line to ask if I would move from the Department of Health to the Home Office as Minister for Police and Counter-Terrorism. My staff widened their eyes, and then they cried cheerfully: 'Well, at least it's not immigration!'

The Home Office was not a happy place in 2006. The debacle over the inappropriate release of foreign national prisoners had caused us immense political damage. My new boss, the new Home Secretary John Reid, was one of the greatest people I have ever worked for, but after a fortnight's review of his inheritance, he famously declared it 'not fit for purpose' and decided my tenure as Police Minister must come to an abrupt end. I was sent to 'sort out immigration'.

At the core of the Home Office's problem was that it had simply not built enough immigration detention centres to hold people who needed to be deported but were entitled to a very long-winded judicial process. Added to the problem, large numbers of people who had claimed asylum but lost their cases had destroyed their passports. When we tried to send them home, very often their home country disputed whether they hailed from their shores. Many of these people we believed were from China. Our intelligence service told us that after the terrible tragedy when 58 Chinese nationals lost their lives as they were smuggled through an airless container into Dover, the *modus operandi* of people-smugglers had changed. Overwhelmingly, illegal immigration is in the hands of organised crime. A poor worker typically from Fujian, in the south of China, might pay a Snake-head gang anywhere from £4,500 upwards to organise an illegal passage. This was often a bill that Chinese workers were then practically enslaved to pay off once they got to Britain. Typically, someone would get themselves to a European airport, or to Moscow and then Ukraine, use forged documents to get on a no-frills airline to London, and then destroy their papers before they got to passport control. But the *modus operandi* was changing all the time.

Our challenge was that more people from China were claiming asylum than were being deported. Around 2,000 Chinese nationals claimed asylum in Britain in 2006. Almost all were deemed not to need asylum; but we were only sending home just over 200 people. And so the numbers of failed asylum-seekers from China grew. To break the logjam, I decided in April 2007 that I was going to have to go to Beijing and try and get something 'sorted'.

You might not believe this, but ministers' foreign visits are work, work, work. I was whisked from the airport to the embassy to game-plan for the 'calls' fixed up with He Yafei, the Assistant Minister at the Ministry of Foreign Affairs, and Meng Hongwei at the Ministry of Public Security. I was stuffed to the eyeballs with briefings on the state of Chinese illegal immigration, the number of Chinese failed asylum-seekers in our jails, the state of police cooperation. But I knew next to nothing about the state of the China–Britain relationship. And even less about the challenges facing Chinese politicians and policy-makers. After two days' work I got back on the plane a little shamefaced. The momentum powering China forward was blindingly obvious; the state of things to come was plain to see. I realised it was ridiculous that a British politician, even a fairly new one, knew so little about a nation that set the pace for the world we would live in over the century to come.

Happily, the same cannot be said for our diplomats, who work furiously hard. The British Embassy in Beijing is a complex with two-storey houses set in walled gardens built by the Chinese authorities in the 1st Diplomatic District and occupied in September 1959 when the old British legation building, home to ambassadors since 1851, was surrendered back to the Chinese government. It hasn't the grandeur or scale of many of our outposts abroad. It's a bit hemmed in, close up against the surrounding walls. It has a formality that nods to a grander ambition, a large coat of arms above the front door, and is painted a rather striking shade of yellow, the choice, apparently, of the office staff.

The ambassador Sebastian Wood has a rather good story about one of his predecessors, who went to work in a different era. Her Majesty's ambassador to China would arrive in late morning, check for messages and take his driver out for a long picnic at the Ming tombs. After lunch he would drop back to the office to see if anything had come up. And then he would wander home.

No more. Today Beijing counts as one of the busiest ports in the embassy network. When the Prince of Wales and (now Lord) Chris Patten boarded the gang-plank of HMS *Britannia* in the Hong Kong tropical rain shortly after midnight on 2 July 1997, I suspect there were many who feared for the future of the UK–China relationship. Tony Blair and President Jiang Zemin, senior ministers and some 4,000 guests had watched the hand-over ceremonies, the extraordinary firework display over Victoria Harbour and finally the lowering of the union flag over Government House. But now they needed to craft a very different kind of relationship. And they did. UK–China relations survived what could have been a disastrous, seismic change, and have blossomed ever since.

John Prescott, as Deputy Prime Minister, visited literally every year for over a decade. Very few people realise how much sheer hard work John put into growing our relationship with China – and there are few British politicians who know as much about the country as him, especially about China's green agenda.

One of the key tasks for a diplomat is to think creatively about how to foster the good old-fashioned business of relationship building. Bi-lateral visits by ministers are important – but they can often be 'in and out' affairs where the minister sees very little of the country beyond the car journey between his or her hotel, a few ministries, the embassy and a restaurant or two. Leaders' visits are bigger affairs and crucial to driving forward joint initiatives and deals, and swapping perspectives on global affairs.

But just as important are the structured long-term conversations that build depth and breadth – and we're very lucky that our diplomats in China have consistently proved extremely adroit at creating mechanisms to deepen the relationship. This makes the business meetings between leaders far more productive.

Today, a 'call' by a senior British minister on a Chinese leader in Beijing might open with genuine and polite words about each other's commitments to bi-lateral relations, touch approvingly on some major shared international projects like the Olympics or the G20, move swiftly through a quick exchange of views on what needs to happen next in the global push for growth, a check-in on domestic policy priorities, and then move on to some specific business: some trade deals; a sticking point in a merger; some human rights or judicial cases where a point needs to be registered. Somehow in the space of an hour, despite consecutive translation, a huge amount of ground is covered.

When I got the plane home after my first trip I perused a note from our ambassador at the time: a note – a scorecard – of how well we were doing compared to our European neighbours.

One of the great challenges of British foreign policy is creating some order and a sense of priorities. Every Foreign Secretary has to struggle with it. Fighting wars and maintaining alliances. Fighting terrorism and keeping the borders safe. Countering drugs. Tackling climate change. Halting nuclear proliferation. International aid and development. The scorecard I had to read covered our position on 17 different issues.

On many, we could boast that we were leaders in Europe. Our visa system was swift and secure. We had the most extensive partnerships with the Chinese on climate-change policy – where we were seen as well ahead of anyone else – and international development, promotion of human rights, development of health services, and tackling organised crime.

Crucially, in areas vital to Britain's future economic growth, we had made some good progress. We were, for example, the biggest investor into China of any country in Europe – and the biggest exporter of services. Some $14 billion of UK investment was at work in China – and that excluded banking and insurance.

And we were creating key relationships with China's future leaders, public servants and business figures, of whom we educated more than almost any other country on earth.

The number of Chinese students heading for British colleges and universities was growing at 20% a year, and totalled 60,000. And the UK could boast the only Chinese university campuses of any European country: Nottingham Ningbo and Xi'an Jiaotong Liverpool, and 82 British universities (in other words, about half of them) were delivering education in some way in China. In the field of science, we co-publish more research with Chinese academics than anyone else in Europe (in 2005, we had published nearly 1,600 joint scientific papers with Chinese academics) and, in medicine and engineering collaboration, we were streets ahead of France and Germany.

In other words, we were pretty well-positioned for the medium term.

But even back in 2007, we were behind our European competitors in the areas most important to powering growth and jobs in the shorter term. We lagged behind Germany in attracting inward investment to Britain; there were just 300 Chinese companies operating in Britain and only 50 listed on the Alternative Investment Market (AIM). Worst of all, we ranked just fourth in actually exporting goods. The Germans' economic footprint was far bigger than anything any other European nation could muster. In the field of culture, we were probably behind the French, who had fielded regular high-profile visits by President Chirac and resourced the French Cultural Centre in Beijing and a multi-million pound Year of France in 2005. Chinese tourists were far more likely to visit the Continent than Britain.

If a Chinese tourist wants to visit the great sights of Europe, they need only one visa – a Schengen visa – which allows them to travel unfettered through lots of European nations. But to come to Britain, another visa has to be bought. As a result thousands more Chinese tourists are heading for France than Britain.

But what is more striking is that too many British politicians and policy-makers – and perhaps far too many in the business community – come to China in the way I first did.

How do we compare with Europe?

Today, Britain still ranks pretty well within Europe. But my own sense is that we've fallen some way behind Germany.

May 2012 saw one of those moments that beautifully captured the changing balance of power in the world. In the middle of a giant exhibition space, Premier Wen stood beside Chancellor Angela Merkel on a stage and formally opened the Hannover Messe, one of the largest trade fairs in the world.[115] Founded by Germany's British postwar administrators in 1947,[116] 2012's fair boasted 5,000 exhibitors in the sprawling halls, 500 of which were from China – that year's official 'partner country'. It was a symbol of the remarkable position that Germany has now built in China, a position that is no accident. German companies – and politicians – were in China early. On my first trip from Beijing airport downtown to the British embassy, I vividly remember that practically every car on the road seemed to be a VW Passat. Volkswagen was one of the first major European businesses to set up shop in China, and now its strength in China means the firm can aim to become the world's largest car-maker. Volkswagen sold 2.3 million vehicles in China alone in 2011. Today, VW is not alone. Siemens has been in China since 1872, boasts 64 regional offices and around 29,000 staff. Pharma giant Bayer AG aims to double its sales in the Chinese market to €6 billion by 2015. Insurer Allianz was the first European life insurance company in China in 1999. Bosch had sales of RMB 42.3 billion in 2011.

In 2000, Germany accounted for under 30% of EU exports to China. Today, Germany accounts for fully a half of the EU's exports to China. Although our share of EU exports has been rising since 2009, Britain, France and Italy each hold just a 10% share of EU exports. While the problems bedevilling the Eurozone keep the euro weak, a weak euro has helped German companies profit from an export boom to China.[117] In 2010 German trade with China ballooned by 34% to €140 billion. Exports to China added 0.5% to German growth in 2011[118] — the equivalent of €13 billion. German exports to China have quadrupled in a decade. Société Générale estimates that, by 2020, China will account for about 15% of German exports.[119] Some estimate that BMW and Mercedes were reaping €30,000 ($38,613) in profit per car sold in China, 10 times the margin in Europe. At points, China was making up 90% of BMW's profits.

The relationship is so strong that some foreign policy commentators call it the world's new 'special relationship', an alliance between what Hans Kundnani of the European Council on Foreign Relations calls 'Marx and Mercedes'.[120]

So, Britain is not where we need to be on the starting grid. But nor are we at a stand-still. We are moving in the right direction. Just not at the right speed. The only way to judge one's speed in these matters is really with reference to others. And I feel that when I look at others, they are simply going faster than us.

In the last 10 years America and China's Pacific neighbours have forged a much bigger relationship with China than we have. In the Asian century, I think they have a relationship that puts them a long way ahead of us on the starting grid.

Let's start with America.

How do we compare with America?

Today China and America are two nations like two dancing giants. They can't walk away from each other. But whether they waltz or wrangle will determine how good a time we, as spectators, have over the next century. And clever Americans know it.

In October 2009, I was in Washington for a day of calls with senior White House economic advisors. It was at the height of the recession and we were talking mainly about the G20's response to the crash and the prospects for paying down the new deficits that loomed large. But I couldn't resist asking how America saw its future relationship with China in a post-crisis world. One of the President's senior economic advisors put it rather well: 'Your country and my country have engine trouble and will likely have continued difficulties – but the Asian countries will have healthy growth; their engines will start just fine.'

That's why America works so hard on China – and it is why President Obama led a foreign policy 'pivot', away from the Atlantic, and towards the Pacific. It's a focus that has been sharpening for over a decade.

America's big moves began at the beginning of the century. And it was Bill Clinton who started them. In May 2000, Bill Clinton stepped up his push for one of the most important decisions America has ever taken: to admit China into the WTO and so open a global trading zone that would encompass 4 billion of the world's 6 billion people. Clinton told Congress that if it made the right decision, 'our companies will be able to sell and distribute products in China made by American workers on American soil, without being forced to relocate manufacturing to China …We will be able to export products without exporting jobs.'[121]

Twelve years later his wife Hillary was Secretary of State and making exactly the same case, weathered with a little experience.

Every year, China and America host a Strategic and Economic Dialogue (S&ED). It's a big occasion and, in the press conference that followed the 2012 summit, then Secretary of State Hillary Clinton summed up the 'official' American position: 'what we are trying to do is to build a resilient relationship that allows both of our nations to thrive without unhealthy competition, rivalry, or conflict'.[122]

For most Americans, the swings and roundabouts of that summit between an established power and a rising power are played out everywhere in daily life.

Take the good old American consumer. Its best friend, Wal-Mart, has a store within 15 minutes of 90% of Americans and serves 100 million people every week. Remarkably, 80% of its suppliers are Chinese: over 5,000 of them. Wal-Mart buys more than *$18 billion* of Chinese goods every year. If Wal-Mart were a country, it would be one of the top trading nations with China. That has been good for the American consumer.

Or, take the epitome of American manufacturing: the car. When the WTO studied the 'American Car' back in 2004, they found that very little of the car's value was actually 'American' any more. Indeed, a third of the value was accounted for by South Korean subassembly suppliers; nearly a fifth was provided by specialist components firms in Japan; German design accounted for nearly 10%. Only a third of the value was 'created' in America. America's car makers are today like giant jigsaw-puzzlers knitting together the pieces that are increasingly made in China. Chinese exports of auto-parts to America increased *10-fold* between 2000 and 2010, from $3.9 billion to a massive $41 billion in 2010.[123] That's had a huge impact on America's manufacturing workers. Auto-parts is the second biggest US manufacturing business and 400,000 auto-parts jobs have been lost since November 2000.

Or take the good old American dollar bill – and the rate of interest you might pay for borrowing one. When your currency is the world's leading reserve currency, a lot of people want dollars. Foreign central banks own around 5 trillion dollar bills. This massive demand helps keep American interest rates very low – indeed studies show that US interest rates are anywhere between 0.5 and 0.9 percentage points lower as a result of foreign capital inflows.[124] What's more, Barry Eichengreen estimates that servicing these foreign liabilities costs 2–3% less than America earns on foreign investments. That's a big bonus for America's balance of payments. For the last decade, the biggest buyers of dollars have been the Chinese. Poor Chinese workers have been lending rich American consumers a lot of money for a long time at a very cheap price.

All of this adds up to a scale of exchange that is simply staggering. In 2010, China sold America some $365 billion of goods and bought *$1.16 trillion* of US Treasury bills – that's a quarter of all holdings owned by foreigners.[125] In turn, America runs a trade surplus in services, exported some $273 billion of goods back to China – more than a three-fold increase in just 10 years – and has now invested some $50 billion out of the $1 trillion of foreign investment in China.[126]

Consistently, American politicians underline in public that they are not simply seeking a world of trade with China but a world of trust. Yet, the words cannot belie a state of heightened mistrust that seeps throughout American media almost every day. A recent report to Congress warned: 'The US–China relationship remains dogged by longstanding mutual distrust.'[127] In the year after President Obama's first visit to China in 2009, there were rows about alleged cyber-attacks on US companies (January 2010), US arms sales to Taiwan (January), President Obama's meeting with the Dalai Lama (February), China's refusal to condemn a North Korean torpedo attack on a South Korean ship (March), China's condemnation of US military exercises in the

Yellow Sea (July); an argument about disputed territory in the South China Sea (July); US intervention in a row about a Japanese fishing boat collision (September); more arguments about North Korea in November and about the Climate Change agreement in Copenhagen (December 2010).

There are maritime disputes in the South China and East China Seas; differences over nuclear proliferation in Iran and North Korea; a stand-off over Taiwan and Tibet; simmering discontent about the value of the Chinese exchange rate, Chinese subsidies to companies and human rights; enforcement of intellectual property rights; and alleged Chinese violation of WTO rules. When the Senate Foreign Relations Committee convened hearings on China, they were billed as 'living with friction'. Ten government departments report on China to Congress; three of them are mandated to do so every year.[128] Some 30 pieces of legislation about China were introduced by American politicians in the last Congress.[129]

But for all the friction, I still believe that, on current trends, America is far better placed to profit from the rise of China than is Europe.

Many of the difficulties that cause real trouble for American politicians are more myth than reality. Imports from China are still only 2.5% of American GDP – and nearly 90% of American consumer spending is on stuff made in America. And the figures about America's trade deficits don't communicate the reality of the value of Chinese exports to America because China is often just assembling parts bought in from other countries. A study by the Federal Reserve Bank of San Francisco[130] found that about 55 cents of every dollar spent on something labelled 'Made in China' actually goes on US services, for example the transportation or the retailers' mark-up. What's more, even if the Chinese re-valued their exchange rate, Chinese manufacturing would simply shift to other low-labour-cost countries like Vietnam. American policy-makers often forget that the US runs a trade deficit with not one, but 90 countries.[131]

I've been intrigued by the US–China relationship for years, not least because I slightly despair that Europe's relationship with China is not so strong. Recently a Chinese official told me China and the US boast some 100 different exchanges and dialogues; so many that he had trouble keeping track of them all. But as I see it, here are the two key reasons why China and the US are not going to grow apart, they're going to grow together.

First, America is not going to lose its 'exorbitant privilege' any time soon. China's demand for dollars, which helps keep America's interest rates low, is going to continue for ages. When a nation like China has foreign-exchange reserves of $5 trillion there aren't many safe investments for that much cash; US Treasury bills – IOUs from the American taxpayer – are simply the only products which are safe enough and plentiful enough to park that kind of cash in.

Second, as the Chinese do try to diversify out of Treasury bills, which don't yield very much any more, they are going to buy other more profitable, better-yielding American assets, like American companies or infrastructure. This is going to create a massive surge of desperately needed investment into the American infrastructure and companies over the next 20 years. Today, China invests abroad about the same amount as Denmark. That is set to change very, very fast now. In 2010, Chinese investors spent $5 billion in America. Some 11,500 acquisitions and greenfield investments are now complete, creating at least 10,000 American jobs across 35 of the 50 US states.[132] But China's investment overseas is now doubling annually, and by 2020 some $1–2 trillion will be spent abroad. America is in pole position to catch a big slice of that prize.

China's neighbours

The America–China relationship is really important. But there is someone else who is even ahead of America. China's neighbours.

For literally millennia, that relationship has been very ordered – with China on top. As long as neighbouring kings behaved themselves and paid their tribute to the Emperor they were allowed a good deal of discretion to get on and rule in their own name. On a visit to Fujian province in 2007 (which is where most of the illegal immigration to the UK comes from), I noticed with some amusement that local Chinese politicians had a saying of which they were rather fond: 'The mountains are high, and the Emperor is far away.' The same ethos perhaps held the tributary system together. It was a light-touch system that worked because of China's overwhelming strength. Under the Qing dynasty, foreign kings were equipped with a noble rank in the Qing hierarchy; symbolic gifts of local produce were bestowed on the Emperor to whom the ceremonial kow-tow was performed. The system was not all-encompassing, but it did stretch to Korea, part of Japan, Vietnam and Burma.[133] It lasted 2,500 years.

Since the Great Opening Up, skilful Chinese diplomacy wrought a completely new 'Pacific intimacy' as China began to piece together a rather more modern system of neighbourliness. Their success means that it is not simply America which is ahead of us. It is China's neighbours too. The Chinese live in a neighbourhood of big beasts. America is the pre-eminent Pacific power. Japan is not far behind. Russia and India share a Chinese border. They are all big players. Clever diplomacy would be needed. And China has played a clever hand.

In the early 1990s, diplomatic relations were re-established with South Korea, Singapore, Indonesia and Vietnam. The 'Shanghai Five' – with Russia, Kazakhstan, Kyrgyzstan and Tajikistan – was established in 1994. Then at the beginning of the century, just as China joined the WTO, the stage was set for a dramatic expansion of free trade in China's own backyard.

Drawing on the goodwill among its neighbours which it had built during the Asian financial crisis in 1997, China proposed sweeping reforms in 2001. The Shanghai Five plus new member Uzbekistan would become the Shanghai Cooperation Organisation with a permanent office in Shanghai – and China proposed at the 2001 ASEAN + 1 summit (Association of Southeast Asian Nations plus China) to create an ASEAN–China Free Trade Area by 2010, bringing together 2 billion in one free-trade zone. In 2003, China formally agreed to accede to the basic principles of the ASEAN charter, and the Chinese premier, Wen Jiabao, proposed exploring an East Asian Free Trade Area to be implemented before 2020.

Collaboration is now multiplying at an unbelievable pace.[134] Between 1991 and 2001 intra-regional trade in East Asia more than tripled. China is sucking in 30–40% of imports from other ASEAN countries every single year as China becomes the assembly plant for components made all over the region. Let's take our humble iPhone, for example. China might be the final assembly plant. But the flash memory, display module and touch screen come from Japan. Processors come from South Korea. These bits and pieces make up around half the estimated $172 building cost of an iPhone. China is at the hub of a production line that stretches across East Asia and the Pacific. That makes China very, very important to its neighbours.

The first time I went to East Asia was back in 1995 to spend six months as a young consultant working for Hong Kong Telecom. I lived in a hotel downtown in Hong Kong, worked all hours, and was absolutely mesmerised by the speed of change, bustle and energy all around me. On my first weekend off, I caught the boat to Lantau Peak. It's a steep climb to the top. But as you gaze out over the harbour and the South China Sea, you see the lines and lines of container ships anchored in neat order. Even back then, half of the world's shipping passed through the sea lanes of South East Asia.

China is now locking the links with the neighbours gently but tighter. Some 60% of China's overseas direct investment heads towards its neighbours. Its international aid programme is growing; Chinese aid is now four times bigger than America's in the Philippines. It gives double what the US provides to Indonesia. It is building the new presidential palace in East Timor. It trains civil servants across the region. Sixty thousand East Asian students study in China.

Naturally, China has interests it wants to advance – and protect. Building cities for 400 million people over the next 18 years is going to need a lot of raw materials. Half of the world's new building already happens in China[135] and China is consuming about a quarter of the world's zinc, iron, steel, lead, copper and aluminium. It is probably the world's largest energy consumer. Nor is it water abundant. This drives China's search for new partners with lots of natural resources. Especially in its own neighbourhood.

One of the most extraordinary meetings I ever had in China was a visit to the vast headquarters of the China National Offshore Oil Corporation. In a briefing on the company's work the scale of China's dependence on foreign energy supplies and the huge investment now under way to secure those supplies quickly became clear. To the west, it is building vast pipelines into the western Chinese province of Xinjiang, one carrying oil from the Caspian Sea across Kazakhstan and the other carrying gas from Turkmenistan.

China needs access to secure ports throughout the Indian Ocean and the South China Sea to guarantee links between the oil states of the Gulf and its own seaboard.

China is the largest investor in Afghanistan, mining for copper south of Kabul. It wants road access through Pakistan to the Indian Ocean. It is becoming more assertive about rights to fishing and natural resources in the East China and South China Seas.

China is also gearing up quickly to armour-plate, with gun-boats, what is, by and large, a soft-power strategy. In April 2010 Rear-Admiral Zhang Huachen, Deputy Commander of the East Sea Fleet, declared: 'We are going from coastal defense to far sea defense ... with the expansion of the country's economic interests the navy wants to better protect the country's transportation routes and the safety of our major sea lanes.'[136]

By 2050, the Chinese navy aims to have a global force. The US Department of Defense estimates that the PLA Navy could have its first home-built aircraft carriers on the water by 2015.

This causes tension. 'Mistrust of Beijing throughout the region', writes one commentator, 'is palpable'.[137] China is in dispute with Japan over the Diaoyu/Senkaku Islands; and with the Philippines and Vietnam over the Spratly Islands.[138] Bangladesh, India and Kazakhstan worry about water diversion projects on the Tibetan plateau. Chinese bauxite mining caused a serious backlash among Vietnamese workers. Indonesia, Malaysia and Singapore have banded together to attack piracy and develop their own ability to work together. Taiwan has bought over $6 billion of arms from America. Russia watches warily the activity of Chinese corporations in Siberia. In 2010, the US and South Korea conducted naval exercises near China's shores, provoking a stiff rebuke. A huge spat with Japan ensued when the Japanese imprisoned a Chinese fishing boat captain whose ship collided with a Japanese coast-guard. China reacted harshly to the idea that neighbours were coordinating sovereignty disputes with the US. In 2012 tension mounted following clashes over the disputed Diaoyu/Senkaku

Islands, and the issuing of new Chinese passports with contentious maps of borders.

But China is an 'über-realist' power.[139] Its leaders know these tensions have to be managed. And the bottom line is that it has just helped create among the neighbours the third largest free-trade area in the world after the EU and the North Atlantic Free Trade Agreement (NAFTA), with the lowest international tariffs anywhere and home to a third of the world's population. China is spending $10 billion to improve its road, rail, air and IT links to ASEAN nations and has on offer a $15 billion credit facility to promote trade links.[140] In the race to build links with China, Britain is a long, long way behind China's neighbours.

Some numbers

This is a personal take on Britain's position. But let me give you some numbers about the 'state of interdependence'.

Chinese investment in Britain

Britain is one of the world's favourite places to invest. By 2010, foreigners had invested about £731 billion in us. Around half of this comes from the US, France and the Netherlands. Around just 0.5% of that money is from China. And while Chinese investment in Britain has been growing at a rapid pace – it's averaged 26% growth for 10 years – others, including Spain, Luxembourg, South Korea, India and Cyprus, are investing in Britain at a faster pace. China is not investing as much in Britain as elsewhere: by 2010, China had invested around $9.4 billion in the UK; but it's invested seven times that figure in Japan; six times more in America; four times more in South Korea and nearly four times more in Germany. France has secured 60% more investment and the

Netherlands 38% more. 2012 saw a flurry of activity. China's Bright Food bought 60% of Weetabix. China Gas Holdings bought out the gas assets of Fortune Oil. China Investment Corporation bought 10% of Heathrow Airport to add to its 10% of Thames Water. The UK, said China's ambassador to Britain, 'is the land of thinkers. Chinese manufacturers could learn a lot when they are here.' But the level of Chinese investment is increasing from a very low base.

British investment in China

Britain is also a big investor abroad. In 2010, we had invested over £1 trillion overseas. Half is invested in the US, the Netherlands, Luxembourg, France and Ireland. China plus Hong Kong received just 3% of this money – and while this investment has grown at 17% a year for a decade, our investments in the Gulf, Russia, South Korea, India, Belgium, Cyprus and Spain have all grown more quickly. We are, however, about the sixth biggest investor into China with about $13 billion invested; but in 2010, Japan's investments totalled eight times greater. US investment was nearly five times as large as ours, and Germany's was twice our size: $29 billion.

Exports of goods and services

Goods exports are also a good measure: here we're ninth in the league table, behind Japan (exporting 17 times more than we do), South Korea (14 times more), the US (11 times), Germany (seven times more), Russia, India, France and Italy.

I think these numbers confirm the thrust of what I'm saying; in the race to prosper in the Pacific century, Britain is absolutely on the starting grid. But we're not at the front. And others are moving faster. Now, in Chapter 4 I said I thought this was fixable. And here's how.

Any politician that does business with China soon gets familiar with a few phrases that Chinese politicians use a lot: 'it's time to drop the cold war mentality'; 'don't offer us zero-sum solutions'; 'we should move forward on the basis of win-wins'. I happen to think there's an awful lot of wisdom in this. So what I want to explore is: where are the win-wins between Britain and China in the decade to come? To answer that question, we have to first figure out: what does China need?

CHAPTER 6

What does China need?

If I learned one thing living in America, it's that the key to the American character isn't found on the coast. It's found in the magnificent interior, beyond the great Mississippi river, where 'the West has grown with the growth of a giant'.[141]

One day we may say the same thing about China. What's for sure is that the best view of China's gigantic potential is not on the coast. You have to go west.

It took me until spring 2011 when I managed to get there with an illustrious group of British high-flyers. A couple of years ago, I suggested to friends in the All-China Youth Federation that a smart investment in the future would be an exchange programme that brought young leaders to get to know each other and each other's country; the Chinese jumped at the idea and in 2010, my friend Lu Yongzheng led a delegation to meet me at the Treasury with a proposal for how we could get going. The 'young leaders' round-table' has been a great success and is now in its third year.

China's former ambassador in London, Madame Fu Ying, a lady who herself hails from Inner Mongolia, had encouraged me. Here I suspected we could see at first hand a new Chinese revolution unfolding, where ways of life thousands of years old are giving way to hi-tech, fast-growth city living. Sure enough

Hohhot, the capital of Inner Mongolia, didn't disappoint. It's a brilliant illustration of how today old meets new.

Encircled by the Great Blue Mountains and the Hetao Plateau, Hohhot was founded at the gateway to the vast Zhaohe grasslands eight years before the Spanish Armada as one of 13 forward defence posts against the Barbarian Huns miles ahead of the Great Wall. Today, you can still see the headquarters of the old generals: 100 huts and rooms in three neat lines arranged in a lovely simplicity around courtyards still guarded by stone lions and now nestling beneath a vast white multi-level expressway. The great azure sky arcs above and, in the summer, a hot dry wind blows in from the west. Great boulevards divide up the town into vast blocks. Great towers are being thrown up everywhere. It reminded me a lot of Texas.

Like Texans, Mongolians are proud of their history. History, tradition, pride are everywhere and all around. In the middle of the town stands the vast statue of Ghengis Khan, the man who built an empire across the grasslands, which is still the Mongolians' spiritual home. An hour out of town over rough roads through dusty little villages you arrive at a rough kind of plateau where the yellow earth gives way to a green sea stretching over hills and mountains amid a stunning stillness like a deserted Lake District thousands of miles wide.

In a vast deserted hunting lodge, the size of a small castle and replete with golden domed roofs, the vice-secretary of the local All-China Youth Federation, Zhao Xiao, once a cavalry soldier and a man steeped in the traditions of his past, boiled up afternoon tea in a vast pot of boiled up milky afternoon tea in a vast pot adorned with a battered gold and stencilled surround and into which wind-dried bits of beef and salty little patties of cheese were stirred, before showing us his mastery of both the unique Mongolian horses that had once carried armies to Europe and the extraordinary Mongolian invention created to fill the vast space of their world, an amazing form of singing that is so unique that the United Nations awarded it world heritage status. After dinner that evening and a very heavy night of toasting with the fiery Chinese *baijiu* liquor, I couldn't help hoping that men like Zhao find a way to protect traditions that remain so life-giving. Because Inner Mongolia is changing fast.

Before I set off on this trip, I found myself one day teaching a class on social finance to a group of Chinese bankers studying at Oxford. They were very pleased to hear I was about to venture so far inland. 'Hohhot', said one,

> is a great example of the property boom. There are buildings going up so fast there's not enough people to put in them. So they employ 'flickers' to switch the lights on and off at night to make them look full.

Quite why Hohhot is changing so fast quickly became clear during a formal call with one of China's most important rising stars, Hu Chunhua, then Inner Mongolia's party secretary and now one of the youngest members of the Politburo. Many speak of Mr Chunhua with enormous reverence. Highly intelligent, calm and with an air of unpretentious humility, it was clear why Mr Chunhua had been entrusted his job by the Communist Party: Inner Mongolia has been absolutely critical to China's future as it sits atop the largest coal reserve in the world. In a few years' time, this one province may generate up to 50% of China's electricity as power stations are built literally on top of the coal seams and great windmills sprout up throughout the 4,000 miles of grasslands which stretch west towards the Himalayas. Like Texas, Hohhot is set to become one of the most important energy capitals in the world.

China needs the new power of provinces like Inner Mongolia to propel the country into an era that will see the largest movement of people in human history: 400 million Chinese citizens migrating from the countryside to the city.

Three hundred million people have already made the journey into 30,000 cities from the farms their ancestors tended since the 2nd millennium BC. Back in 1978, fewer than one in five of China's citizens were urban residents. By 2011, half were city dwellers. By 2030, China's leaders want cities to be home to two-thirds of the population. That demands movement of 13 million people a year for the next 20 years; it means creating the equivalent of a new Tokyo or Buenos Aires every 365 days for two decades.

This revolution in Chinese life has consumed a mammoth amount of thought. For a lot of us in the West, China's arrival on the world stage was really brought home by the stunning opening ceremony for the Olympics in 2008. But for many Chinese the 2010 Shanghai Expo was just as important. If the Olympics were a display for the world, the Expo was a display for China.

The immense World Expo site was built alongside Shanghai's Huangpu river and at the heart of the complex stood the glorious China Pavilion. Designed in a traditional Dougong style the Crown of the East, as it was called, stood 50m high and thousands queued every day for up to two hours to get in.

High in the theatre on the thirteenth floor, The Road to our Beautiful Life, a bravura film by award-winning director Lu Chuan, told the story of the gargantuan migration now under way: a grandfather moves his family from a far-flung corner of Fujian to be closer to town. His son, in turn, moves to the city and his children grow up as citizens of the metropolis. In fast-forward over 30 years, a measureless new urban fabric takes shape around them while shot through the film are the dramatic, appalling scenes of the 2008 Wenchuan earthquake. It ends with a view to the verdant, greener city of the future.

Thirteen floors below, the super-star of the Expo was a colossal 100m long digital animation of the Riverside Scene at Qingming Festival, a thousand-year-old Chinese painting which reinforced the message. The painting, of the ancient city of Kaifeng, was fashioned as an allegorical story of virtue like a stained-glass window in a European cathedral: a vision of the harmony of a city set amid the countryside.

Together, the message of the Riverside Scene and Lu Chuan's film were very simple for every single Chinese spectator. You are part of a monumental and difficult change. Be proud. Bear with it. The prize will be worth the pain.

The end of an era

Just how much pain is what worries China's leaders. For the methods pioneered by Deng Xiaoping in the years after Mao are now almost worn out. An era is closing. When China's new leaders took the stage in October 2012, all of them grasped that they will be the guides on a fresh and perilous path for China. It's a journey that I've been trying to understand for three years.

Barry Eichengreen of Stanford University in California is one of the foremost scholars studying international development in general and China in particular. On a trip to Westminster in 2010, I intercepted him with a cup of tea in the Pugin Room, the beautiful tea-room which sits between the House of the Commons and the Lords, to ask just why China's old strategy now had to change.

Eichengreen's research has helped pin down just when growth in a developing economy suddenly gets much slower. At the end of the day, he says, 'all good things come to an end'. Sooner or later the pool of under-employment in the countryside is all used up. Employment in manufacturing peaks. And as the latest technology gets deployed, countries can't simply keep importing the stuff to win a productivity boost. They have to start innovating themselves. Studying 74 different countries between 1950 and 1990, Barry and colleagues found that, broadly speaking, fast growth ends when GDP per capita reaches $16,740.[142]

This implies a slowdown for China at some point over the next 10 years. That is what worries China's leaders.

Kerry Brown, former British diplomat in China, former head of the Asia Programme at Chatham House, and now Head of the Centre for China Studies at the University of Sydney, has thought about this a lot. Before he left for Australia, Kerry let me interrogate him about what China's leaders were about to go through. His argument is that China's very, very rapid growth since 2000 was in fact not only astonishing but quite unforeseen; and now it has hastened social and political tensions that are proving sharper and sharper.[143] The result is a Chinese society that is far more contentious.

In 2009, some nine million petitions were dispatched by citizens to central government. Some estimate there might be as many as 180,000 'mass incidents' every year, especially about land rights and pensions.

Managing this tension is exceedingly expensive; in 2010, the Chinese government said it spent $93 billion on internal security which is $1 billion more than the official defence budget. That's a lot of money that can't be spent on things like schools or a welfare system.

But, says Kerry, the speed of change means that it's not only China which has now reached a watershed moment. It's the CPC itself:

The Cultural Revolution left a huge stain. China's current leaders have eschewed the taboos of that Maoist era and the things it rejected like foreign capital and the non-state sector ... the key moment was China's accession to the WTO [World Trade Organisation]. No one then foresaw the huge growth in productivity that followed. But that productivity growth has brought forward at great speed a series of social and political issues that now need confronting.

The official history of the CPC was only published last year. It sets out three pillars of the party's purpose; winning the Sino-Japanese war; winning the civil war and reunifying the country and reform and opening up.

But now the party needs a new message. But the class composition of China is far more complex than it used to be. So what's the message that appeals across all this complexity?

Senior Communist officials are an elite caste. And like any elite, they talk to each other in an elite language. Arguments are carefully rooted in Mao Zedong Thought, Deng Xiaoping Theory or 'Jiang Zemin's key points', all of which are written into the party and state constitution and all of which, says Kerry, mean 'as much as a form of medieval Latin. Part of the challenge for China's leaders is to create a new emotional language' coupled with the political will to take on deeply vested interests.

So: what does the challenge look like to China's leaders?

First and foremost, China's leaders know a lot about American and European consumers and they know neither has the same stomach for Chinese exports as they had once. China's leaders have listened carefully to Western politicians speechify about 're-balancing' their economies towards manufacturing and away from services. China's planners expect this may be a recipe for slower growth. That means that the export-led growth that has power-driven China for over 20 years simply isn't going to provide the same propulsion in the future. China must now look to the locomotive power of its own consumers.

The problem is that China's consumers are poor. And the economy around them is stacked with risks.

Tao Ran is the director of China Center for Public Economics and one of the best Chinese economists I have met. On a visit to Beijing in May 2011, I caught up with him over lunch just round the corner from Beijing's Renmin, or People's, University, the first university established by Mao and now one of the top three liberal arts universities in China.[144]

Together with Fubing Su, Prof. Ran has produced an excellent analysis[145] of just how the 'China Consensus' has worked in practice.[146] The 'China Consensus' isn't a million miles away from the 'East Asian' model pioneered by Japan, South Korea, Taiwan, Hong Kong and Singapore. The recipe is pretty simple: authoritarian regimes put a sharp focus on growth, keep a lid on workers' wages and rights[147] and divert resources from consumption to investment. Unable to sell goods at home (because workers lack the wealth to buy much), firms export their way to growth and governments use a combination of industrial targeting, tax rebates and tax breaks to help, plus subsidies for new technology and restrictions on foreign firms to grow the strength of domestic firms. As profits build up, the money is re-invested in capital- or knowledge-intensive industries.

Broadly speaking China followed the recipe – but with two important twists, one of accident and one of design.

With a monopoly on political power, the CPC can ensure that the All-China Workers' Union, created to speak for workers, prevents the creation of independent unions that might cause 'problems'. The result is that in the eight years from 1990, workers' share of the wealth created each year has fallen by 10%.

Without the pressure of rising wage bills, China's companies have had more to invest. As a nation, China invested around 29% of GDP during the 1980s. By 2009, that figure rose to an extraordinary 45.6%. That is twice the level ever achieved in the US (back in 1941).[148] Around half of this investment heads straight into property and infrastructure. So despite the massive construction boom in building millions of city homes, demand is still completely outstripping supply and prices are astronomical. This has fuelled property prices which were already high because of the very low interest rates offered by the People's Bank of China to help keep China's exchange rate low and its exports cheap.

With falling wages and much to save to cover housing costs, Chinese consumers lost spending power. So Chinese firms needed to export to grow. In 1980, China exported goods and services worth 10% of GDP. By 2006, the figure had quadrupled to 39%.

The way this process has unfolded has created huge risks because of the close-knit relationship that evolved between China's banks, local authorities and SOEs.

China is different to other East Asian economies in that the enterprise spirit of local provinces, towns and villages has proved vital. Initially, the Chinese tax system created huge incentives for local governments to borrow money to build industrial zones. But when business taxes were re-centralised to the Beijing government[149] in 1994, local government faced an income crunch which got worse when the capital began loading up local government with more and more spending pressures, like building new schools, immunising children, delivering water and picking up the tab for old state-owned enterprises going to the wall.

Dramatically stretched for cash, local politicians became intensely entrepreneurial[150] and, as leaders of a one-party local state, they had plenty of tools to play with.

Land in China belongs to the state, so local politicians have the power to bump farmers off their fields and hand over millions of acres to developers to build more industrial parks. All over China, local communes competed to draw in manufacturers with tax breaks and new infrastructure to pump up the local tax base. Because local banks too are heavily influenced by politics, local officials had plenty of scope to direct loans and credit to boosting local business.[151] Today, as industrial parks have multiplied, land-lease fees make up about 50% of a province's formal budget.[152] By 2003, there were nearly 4,000 of them. By 2006, the figure leapt to over 6,015.

This has created two big problems: first, nowhere near enough land was allocated to housing, forcing up prices to impossible levels. And second, the balance sheets of Chinese banks may be loaded up with some pretty iffy loans. This weakness is one big reason why China has been so cautious about revaluing its exchange rate. Lifting the exchange rate means putting up interest rates. And higher interest rates may knock over an awful lot of dodgy loans. If a slowdown hit China hard and property prices started to tumble, banks would be hit hard by loans that suddenly were not getting repaid. This could be a very big problem because of the massive amount of credit extended to Chinese investors; in fact Chinese banks have either formally or informally offered loans totalling 1.8 times the size of the economy.

Round the corner from Prof. Ran, Fu Jun, Dean of School of Government at Peking University, gave me the fact that sums up China's quandary: consumer demand is not going up; it's going down.

Household spending has *fallen* as a percentage of GDP from 50 to 36%. China needs its consumers to play a bigger role in the economy. But right now, their role is not growing. It's shrinking.

China's leaders know this. Since at least 2008 they've been busy trying to grow consumer demand. But when the global economy crashed the Politburo knew that the fastest way to pump money into the economy was not by handing back money to Chinese consumers, who would have saved it; the fastest way to reflate was by boosting investment. So money was poured into the SOEs and local government to invest, which simply added to the overloaded investment system.

So the challenge for China's leaders is not simply shifting an economic strategy that's nearly 40 years old; it's unwinding the emergency measures from the crash.

Over breakfast one morning in Beijing in 2012, I was appraising China's economic reforms with a British businessman who helps lead a British firm that's been doing business in China an awfully long time.

'There's basically nothing wrong with the Chinese economy', he said; 'the real risk is, can they summon the political will to put in place the social reforms that are going to stop the place exploding'.

He's right. China's economy has miles to go down the road to prosperity. The question is whether it can carry its citizens on the journey.

I find that the difference between the optimists and pessimists in China is that the optimists feel the country's leaders get these problems – and are able to do something about it. The pessimists feel their leaders face trouble – and vested interests – that are just too big to solve.

On balance, I'm an optimist.

My conversations with China's leaders – especially younger ministers – tell me that China's next generation of leaders are not only smart, but are well aware of how their country needs to change. And the roadmap for that change is now becoming clearer.

To the west of Beijing, the rich green forested Western Hills rise from the floor of the North China plain and stretch out beyond to the continental scarp that divides the rich coastal zone from the Tibetan plateau beyond. For centuries, the hills have been a haven for Chinese emperors and their courts fleeing the roasting summers.

Nine hundred years ago, the first emperor to live in Beijing, Wanyan Liang, built a summer palace on Gold Mountain Hill where he could marvel at the view and, just north of the Summer Palace walls, the CPC has built its Party School.

It is hard to overstate the importance of the Party School. It reports direct to the Vice-President. Every senior leader must be trained here – leaders may spend a year of their lives here over the course of their career. And it is here that China's party elite are coached, examined, debate and bond the relationships and networks that last a political lifetime. Over a large lunch in downtown Beijing, a senior professor now teaching elsewhere chuckled: 'the teaching was good, but most important of all, we had a *very* good time there'.

Everyone eats in the same campus canteen, a vast three-storey Chinese restaurant, at the centre of a huge campus around which are arrayed modern buildings, a lake and a training ground. Even the most senior leaders come here for two months' study before moving on to perhaps their last and most senior post; like everyone else, they're barely allowed off campus. It is part boarding school. Part seminary. And part Kennedy School of Government.

On the fortieth anniversary of Britain's resumption of full diplomatic relations with China, a group of the School's faculty and students came together with the Wilton Park think tank and a European delegation, which I was very grateful to join, to talk about 'Prosperity in the New World Order' – not a small subject. Centre-stage in the talks was a ground-breaking new report that was provoking fierce debate among China's policy elite.

At various points over the last 30 years, China's leaders have used collaboration with the World Bank to foster some impetus for change. In the 1980s, Deng Xiaoping used a World Bank report to accelerate the process of 'opening up'. In the 1990s, Jiang Zemin hosted a slightly strange five-day conference with the World Bank, on a boat meandering down the Yellow river.

So when the new president Xi Jinping announced with World Bank president Robert Zoellick new work on China's roadmap to 2030, there was close interest in the results. Months later, the 468-page China 2030 report, replete with hundreds of policy recommendations, was launched by the World Bank's president and Xi Jinping at a press conference in the Fragrant Hills.

For the first time, a report of this type was produced by a joint team from the World Bank, China's Ministry of Finance, and the Development Research Center, which is part of the State Council and provides key policy advice to China's leaders.

The report's starting point is pretty blunt: after more than 30 years of rapid growth, China has reached a turning point when a shift is needed of the same size and scale as China's decision to open up to the West, 30 years ago. China's 'export-led' growth plan is running out of road. Slow growth in Europe and America means Western consumers simply won't be buying as much from China as they did in years gone by. That means China has to fix the foundations that it built on. If Chinese firms can't sell internationally, they need to sell locally. And that means Chinese consumers need more spending power. Equipping Chinese consumers with bigger wallets is going to take two things: fatter pay-packets at work plus a raft of changes that encourage Chinese consumers to stop putting so much cash under the bed or in the bank, and to spend more of it, proverbially, in the shops. 'China', says the report in stark terms, 'needs to implement a new development strategy in its next phase of development'.[153]

This debate has been coming for some time. One of the most influential advocates for change is the former Chair of China's

International Finance Forum, and Vice-Chair of the National People's Congress (NPC) Standing Committee, the Hon. Cheng Siwei. Now in his eighties, he is clearly influential and with a complete grasp on China's challenges. In 2010, I dropped by for a cup of tea in Beijing and he pointed me to an extraordinary lecture he had delivered to the Pacific Economic Cooperation Council the year before.[154]

'According to ancient Chinese philosophy', argues Siwei, 'the best strategy is balancing and compromising. So a good thing will turn to bad by overdoing it.'

Siwei set out six new balances for both the West and China. Spending less and saving more in the West – but saving less and spending more in China. That in turn would unlock a new balance for China: stronger domestic demand and fewer exports as a proportion of the economy.

This isn't just good development theory. It's one of the most important ways China reduces the risk of being hit by another shock. 'But', warns Siwei, 'this is not an easy transition because the most important thing is to increase the purchasing power of the people'.

Chinese politics must be the most carefully choreographed business in the world and the publication of the five-year plan is a very important part of the sequence. It too is used to help ensure a careful continuity, order and predictability. So, the plan is published a year before any leadership change to make sure everyone has a sense about just where that new leadership is to head.

The twelfth five-year plan was duly published at the NPC on 5 March 2011. It was quickly clear that the watershed moment alluded to by Cheng Siwei was on its way.

'I suspect', says Stephen Roach, a highly experienced China-watcher, and head of Morgan Stanley's Asia division, 'history will judge the twelfth five-year plan as a watershed event in the development of modern China', as significant as the fifth plan, produced by Deng Xiaoping, and the ninth, which ushered in huge changes to SOEs.[155]

The plan's starting point is a bleakly realistic view of the post-crisis world in which China now lives, and a recognition that the world economy will recover only slowly. China must therefore look to its *own* growth and that means stronger consumer demand, delivered through rising employment especially in the service sector, rising wages from a boost to the national minimum wage and a shift of 300 million into better-paid jobs in the city, plus a shift from savings to spending fostered by creating a welfare state strong enough to give Chinese citizens the confidence to save a little less than 30% of their wages currently squirrelled away.

How reliable is the five-year plan as a pointer to where China's next generation of leaders will go? I think China's leaders know they have no other choice.

Both the Soviet Union and Japan illustrate a very simple point about the rise of nations. It's the point Barry Eichengreen made to me in the House of Commons. Developing countries – especially those with lots of people – can grow fast when they start to concentrate capital, move people from the countryside and into the cities, and foster industrial revolutions of their own as workers shift out of farming and into factories.

But a quick start might grab the world's attention and provoke a geopolitical question or two, but it is rarely a guarantee of a sustained rise. In fact of the 101 countries which made it to 'middle-income' status in 1960, just 13 became 'high-income' by 2008.[156]

So, how difficult will China's leaders find the business of changing course?

Building the safety net

Let's start with how we persuade China's workers to become China's consumers. In parts of China, it is hard to believe that this is any problem at all.

Drop by for cocktails at any nice bar in Shanghai and you'll pay more than you pay in London. It is not a surprise. The city is now home, amazingly, to 132,000 dollar millionaires – and 350 RMB billionaires, including 30-year-old basketball star Yao Ming. Yao Ming is young. But then so is your average Chinese millionaire. According to the Hurun Rich List, the average age of the Chinese millionaire is 39. Over half made their money in private business, a fifth are property speculators and 15% are 'stock market gurus'. Nearly a third are women.

Yet only a fraction of China's millionaires live in Shanghai. There are now a million millionaires living all over the country. Between four and five hundred dollar billionaires now call China home, more than anywhere else in the world.

Top of the pile is 65-five-year-old Zong Qinghou – or 'Drinks King Zong' – worth some $12 billion and the man who has built Wahaha into a huge drinks combine earning $1.5 billion in profits. The average wealth of China's super-rich has grown by an astonishing 64% in two years, largely as a result of the property boom. But most make their money not in the export trade but the new boom sectors: IT, healthcare, retail. Of the 20 richest self-made women in the world, over half are Chinese. And in case you're wondering, the most popular star-sign for the super-rich is the rabbit.

This vast new wealth is making China one of the world's leading markets for luxury goods. Ferrari now confidently expect China to become their number one market.[157] For Rolls-Royce, China is their second biggest market, accounting for fully one quarter of sales in 2010. Lamborghini say that China is for them already number one. Nine out of ten customers pay in cash. 2011 saw the first ever Asian venture for the Monaco-based Top Marques show. Dealers at the four-day show in Macau were hoping to sign deals with 20,000 customers.

The problem is that China's super-rich won't rebalance China's economy on their own. That's why a senior Chinese minister in the CPC said to me in conversation, 'We know we have to create more socially inclusive growth.'

China needs richer middle and working classes with the money and confidence to spend, and that means they need social security.

Once upon a time, it was China's vast SOEs and the villages that looked after the workers: the so-called 'iron rice bowl'. The passport to what's left of the rice bowl is the *hukou*, or household registration system.

Established in the late 1950s to control internal migration, the *hukou* is a small red passbook with key facts and figures on every family: birth, death, marriage, divorce and city or village of origin are all recorded here. For every Chinese citizen it is the key that unlocks access to the stuff of daily life, from education to healthcare, the right to work, marry or enlist in the army.

The problem is that workers cannot readily transfer their hukou *from where they were born to where they might want to go and work.*

In Mao's China, the policy was workable. In 1978, SOEs employed 60% of China's non-farm workers. But the creation of the new economic zones on the coast in the 1980s sparked the movement of 250 million Chinese to the cities. Now only 20% of non-farm workers work for the large SOEs[158] and while the rules no longer stop workers moving from the countryside to the city, many do not register with the authorities in their new homes because to do so would be to surrender their rights to farm land back at home.

Others simply cannot register because cities can't afford the support costs of incoming workers. Even in great cities like Beijing, migrant workers have ended up forming unofficial cooperative schools to teach their children because they are not part of the formal system of public services.

Hukou reform has now become one of the country's top reform projects. Migrant workers will total 400 million by 2025 and the system has become highly unstable. During the global financial crisis of 2008/09, for example, 23 million rural migrants lost their jobs and had no protection or access to welfare. But change is crucial too for younger migrants born after 1980 – the so-called *ba-ling hou* – who now number 60% of migrants. They don't have much of a connection to the farms of their ancestors. Unlike their parents, they have no intention of returning 'home'.

The iPhone challenge

The second great challenge for China is how it makes its business community more productive – and more innovative.

Now, to anyone who has been to visit some of China's leading businesses, this might come as surprising news. In 2009, I was exploring opportunities for closer economic ties between north-east China and the West Midlands, and found myself in Qingdao. Many people in Britain will have heard of one of Qingdao's most famous exports, Tsingtao beer, produced in a splendid brewery built by the Germans back in 1903.

Rather fewer people, I suspect, have heard of Haier, China's leading white-goods manufacturer, headquartered on a vast industrial park of over 1 million sq metres on the city's outskirts. From a standing start in 1984, the business now turns over $17 billion and is the only Chinese brand in the global top 100. It started by building fridges. Now it takes globally leading positions in white goods, digital technology and home appliances. It claims to invent two products a day.

Haier is a great example of a Chinese business phenomenon; hi-tech at low cost. The strategy is simple: very cheap, very high tech and very wide choice. It is a potent and very Chinese approach to business. Business academics Ming Zeng and Peter Williamson put it like this: 'Forget the idea that the rise of Chinese competitors simply means cheap, low quality imitations flooding world markets. Chinese companies are starting to disrupt global competition by breaking the established rules of the game.'[159]

Chinese computer maker Dawning, for example, puts super-computer technology into low-cost computer servers. Vimicro Corporation helps set the standards for multi-media chips: it has 60% of the world market for multi-media processors in cameras in PCs. CapitalBio's biochip technology has helped revolutionise biotech R&D. Goodbaby offers parents 1,600 different types of buggies and car-seats – four times the range of its competitors.

Many of these companies were forged in the heat of China's great opening up. Forced to adapt, they grew as massive levels of foreign direct investment (FDI) from the West surged in; by 2005 some $60 billion had been invested in China by over 500,000 foreign companies. Chinese companies then profited from the huge new links to overseas markets provided by Western companies and Chinese ex-pats. There are for example, 45 million Chinese living in Taiwan, Hong Kong and south-east Asia. Two million live in the US. Half of the Chinese hi-tech companies listed on the Nasdaq stock market were started by returnees. By 2004, China had set up 70 venture parks for returning entrepreneurs, who established some 5,000 companies.

The great change in Western companies has also helped. Over the last 30 years, thousands of Western firms have turned their products into giant jigsaw puzzles composed of components made all over the world. This created huge opportunities for Chinese businesses to start supplying a small piece of the puzzle and then grow. Wanxiang is a great example. It started as a repair shop for bikes and tractors, became a supplier of universal joints, and survived the 1990s to capture 70% of the Chinese market. Following small orders in the US in 1984, it grew so fast it took out its key US competitor in 1998. Then it bought a chunk of a US brakes manufacturer. Then a chunk of a powertrain supplier. Then auto-component distributors. The company has taken complete control of its business from raw materials to distribution. Its sales are $3.2 billion and now it's setting out to build a complete car.[160]

This is a pattern for lots of Chinese businesses: start with a piece of the puzzle. Grow fast and buy companies with helpful technology or market share. Shift production to China. Innovate like crazy and offer the world hi-tech, low-cost products. The same pattern is repeated in a host of industries. In mobile phones, for instance, Chinese companies broke the hold of Alcatel, Philips, Siemens and Sony with a similar strategy: starting small and expanding fast. In 2000, Chinese handset makers had just 8% of the market. By 2006, companies like Ningbo Bird were selling handsets globally.

The problem for China, however, is the 'iPhone problem'. If you take up an iPhone and turn it over, you can see on the back the words: 'Designed by Apple in California, Assembled in China'. The manufacturing costs of an iPhone are only $6.50, under 4% of the total value of the product. The rest of the cost is Apple's profits (about 65% of the price-tag) and the cost of components, largely from Japan and Korea. In other words,

China is not taking much of the pie. That's why China wants to 'move up the value chain' fast.

But there are simply not enough Haiers or Wanxiangs or Ningbo Birds. China is just not yet producing enough truly innovative companies because far too many companies prosper through hidden subsidies, political connections and a licence to trade on terms that suit them. At the top of the pile are China's vast SOEs, which control over 40% of China's fixed assets.

Protected from competition, they enjoy cosy deals with state-backed banks (which in turn are allowed big margins between the rate they pay savers, and the rate they charge borrowers). They are able to borrow on the one hand at below 6% – but enjoy returns on investment averaging over 14%. With a profit margin like that, there's plenty of incentive for SOEs to invest hard.

The twelfth five-year plan therefore aims for a truly seismic shift in China's vast manufacturing system up the value chain in seven 'strategic emerging industries': IT, high-end equipment manufacturing, advanced materials, green cars, energy-saving and environmental protection industry, low-carbon energy technology and bio-tech. Today these sectors make up perhaps 3% of China's economy. By 2020, China's leaders want to increase these sectors to represent 20% of output.

A surfeit of dollars

Problem number three for China's leaders is harder than it sounds: just how to begin channelling the fruits of its labour into more sensible investments abroad. Over the next 10 years, China has to find a new home – or new homes – for anywhere between $1 and 2 trillion of cash that it needs to invest abroad to avoid overheating its own economy.

Today, China invests abroad about the same amount of cash as *Denmark*. The challenge for China is this: it wants to keep its exchange rate fixed or fairly fixed with the rest of the world. This provides stability and, because the RMB is still a little undervalued, China's exports are cheap to buy for foreigners.

But to sustain this system, China demands that companies paid in dollars for the things they sell abroad do not simply bring home those dollars and sell them for the best price possible. Instead companies have to sell the dollars to the central bank at a fixed price. Some of these dollars are then in turn bought by companies who need to pay for imports from America, to pay their bills to the Americans. But because China exports so much more than it imports from America, vast quantities of dollars are piling up in the central bank reserve.

When you have as many dollars as does the People's Bank of China, there aren't many things you can invest in; lending to the US government – basically buying US Treasury debt – is about the only risk-free product available in the sufficient quantities.

This poses two problems: the interest rate China earns on those Treasury bills is very low (and getting lower, the more the Federal Reserve prints money to deliver quantitative easing). But secondly, if the dollar depreciates against the RMB, the value of China's dollar holdings takes a hit. There is an added problem. When a Chinese company sells its dollars to the central bank and gets its RMB in return, the company then parks this cash in a bank. Banks then lend out these savings many times over. This means the amount of credit – the money supply – circulating in China is burgeoning, and this is driving up inflation which causes a political problem in a country where pay-packets aren't growing fast. The People's Bank of China is constantly having to tighten the rules on how much banks can lend.

China therefore needs its successful exporters to stop bringing so much cash home and start spending that cash abroad on assets that yield a sensible return, like companies. Buying companies abroad comes with the bonus that it brings market share and access to new technology.

In an ideal world, China would also allow more foreign companies to raise money in China, selling their shares or debt on China's exchanges. This would help soak up huge amounts of the excess cash swilling around with few places to go, which is why so much is parked in property, driving local prices sky-high.

The great hub of this new financial exchange will be Shanghai, which has become quite simply one of the greatest cities on earth.

Before I visited, a friend of mine shared some pictures he had taken of the city in the 1980s. He had been an engineer designing engines and was put up in the only hotel in town, the Friendship Hotel, which you can still see on the Bund. He couldn't recognise the picture of Shanghai that I brought home. The pace of change in the city is awe-inspiring. On the east side of the Huangpu river, which twists through the city like the Thames through London, was once a vast expanse of swamp land. Now, Pudong is a bustling jungle of gigantic shiny sky-scrapers dominated by the 88-storey Jin Mao tower.

I was in town the same day as a visiting delegation from the City of London Corporation. Every year, the Corporation has fielded a delegation for two weeks to help lubricate trade talks, and they have an awful lot to offer in what is fast becoming a fundamental shift in the balance of power in the world's financial markets.

Back in 2008, China's State Council broadcast an audacious new target. The Shanghai Stock Exchange (SSE) is one of only two in China. It only opened in 1991. But by 2020, just 30 years later, China's leaders want Shanghai to be one of the world's leading financial centres, a home exchange to Chinese businesses which may by then make up one fifth of the Fortune 500. Today, only 840 companies are listed on the SSE. But that could grow to 60,000 over the next 10 years.

SSE's chief executive, Fang Xinghai, is an incredibly smart man with a PhD from Stanford and experience at the World Bank. When I dropped by to say hello in 2010, Xinghai explained that Shanghai was in fact on track to become the world's number three, *five years early*, in 2015.[161] Today, most of its business is domestic; domestic businesses raising domestic money. Only 100 foreign companies were allowed to invest and the quota for investment was capped at $30 billion dollars, and even this was restricted to certain shares and ceilings; so, for example, foreigners cannot buy 'A' shares, and indeed foreigners cannot buy more than 33% of a particular company.

Opening up the financial market is one of the ways China can begin to liberalise the freedom to trade the RMB more freely. This is a good thing for China. Allowing foreign companies to list on the SSE would help soak up a lot of the excess cash and credit swilling around China. And just as important for the long term, making the RMB an international currency is a very, very good way of guaranteeing openness.

But, opening financial markets and freely trading a currency is not something that can be especially rushed; basic things need to fall into place. Standards of English-language skills need raising. China needs better – and more – lawyers and a stronger legal system. But if China gets this right, it could massively help the task of raising living standards.

Today, most Chinese companies finance their expansion by saving up their profits and not paying dividends. But if companies had the freedom to raise money from investors, more of these profits could be paid out in wages, helping raise the share of national wealth spent on wages and thereby helping raise consumption.

China's challenge

On my way to meet Mr Hu in Hohhot, we received a very timely reminder of the tensions that China's leaders have to govern as they set about reform. Protests had broken out following the killing of a Mongolian herder who tried to stop a convoy of coal trucks from trespassing on the grasslands.[162] Anger had grown at both the incident and the prospects of justice not being done. Here were two Chinas in conflict: the interests of the mining country – and the interests of traditional farmers. The week after I left, the largest protests for 20 years in Inner Mongolia escalated and para-military police were mobilised.

China's leaders know that in the next stage of its development conflicts like those between the miners and the farmers are bound to grow and future leaders need to know just how to manage these growing pains, not least as the new inequality between China's super-rich and ordinary workers grows starker.

If you talk to many younger politicians they express a real disdain for the *nouveaux riches*, flaunting their wealth and arrogantly throwing their weight around. This wealth was new to the plutocrats; they were not used to it and hence they are prone to behave like a new elite beyond the realm of justice and politics. It is an invitation for trouble. Justice for the rich coal owner who murdered the Mongolian farmer, I was assured, would be swift.

In the months immediately following the Eighteenth Communist Party Congress in November 2012, I think it was fair to say that it was the style of the new leadership rather than the substance which caught the eye. But the style was carefully calculated to send a message. Xi Jinping struck a populist pose. He smiled. He told officials to dispense with the usual endless monotonous reading out of prepared remarks. 'I've read your report', he said at some of his first audiences with officials. 'Just give me the bullet-points. And then I want to ask you some questions.' Red carpet, it was said, was to become altogether rarer. This was not business as usual. Significantly, Xi chose to make his first visit to Shenzhen, the place where Deng Xiaoping started his 'Southern Tour' in 1992 in the wake of the Tiananmen Square protests, in order to breathe fresh life into the 'opening-up' and reform policy which has transformed the country. Back at base, Vice-Premier Wang Qishan, promoted to lead the Party's Discipline Committee, was beginning a new Domesday survey of precisely what China's vast SOEs actually owned; in the media a series of stories emerged of highly visible crackdowns on corrupt officials, many of which first broke the surface as photos or allegations in social media.

To reinforce the message, Xi Jinping made a high-profile visit to the National People's Museum on Tiananmen Square in December 2012, to see the hugely popular exhibition 'The Road to Rejuvenation'. Arranged over three floors of the elegant cream, marble and glass museum, the exhibition opens with a magnificent 20ft high terracotta frieze illustrating the achievements of ancient China, before plunging visitors through the sorry detritus of the nation's 'century of humiliation' – the opium pipes, the memorials for Imperial officials under British bombardment, the photos of American troops lolling on the Imperial throne in the Forbidden Palace – and then telling the story of the Nationalists' revolution, the rise of the regional warlords, the emergence of the CPC, the alliance against the brutality of the Japanese occupation, the CPC's eventual triumph and the great postwar modernisation. Xi's message was, for many Chinese, inspiring: we are about to write a new chapter in our country's long struggle.

China's ambassador to the United Kingdom, Liu Xiaoming, wrote a very good piece for the Daily Telegraph[163] when he got home from the Party Congress in December 2012. The 'China Consensus' which emerged from the Congress, argued the ambassador, put the accent on boosting living standards, but with a new model of growth that entailed 'heavy investment in education and science', an acceleration of 'opening up', reform to strengthen the rule of law and a drive against corruption, and crucially a unique Chinese path, system and theory. 'Innovation', he wrote, 'will be the order of the day'.

My take is that the new Politburo is a self-confident group. James Kynge, who runs the Financial Times's China Confidential research team, has a nice phrase for it: the 'three mores' – 'more powerful, more purposeful and more reform minded'. Every great reform moment in China has unfolded in response to some great crisis. Deng's Southern Tour followed Tiananmen Square. The push to join the WTO followed the Asian financial crisis. Now China is reacting again to the crisis of the West that has been such a good customer for so many years, but now finds itself on its uppers. Comprehensive frameworks are something of a hallmark of Chinese politics but there was at the Eighteenth Congress a real attempt to unite and interlink economic, political and social reform plans.

Informed opinion in the UK suggested that the new Politburo was not a break with the past but a very carefully choreographed and quietly determined change of gear that will put a much bigger push behind economic rather than political reform. Almost all of the new Standing Committee have run major coastal provinces like Zhejiang and Tianjin. Li Keqiang drove through the World Bank China 2030 report.[164] There was no sweeping elevation of the so-called fifth generation – what emerged was more 'Generation 4.5'. Five of the seven new Politburo Standing Committee were born in the 1940s and will retire in 2017, while Xi Jinping and Li Keqiang, both born in the 1950s, will carry on. That gives Xi and Li a huge influence over the next five-year plan due in 2016, the next Politburo reshuffle in 2017, the celebration of the CPC's 100th anniversary in 2021, the shape of China's 2022 Politburo and the ideological modernisation of 'socialism with Chinese characteristics' as the country races towards the new target which has become the lodestar of policy for the new administration: doubling Chinese living standards to $8,000 per capita by 2020, creating, in the Chinese phrase, 'a moderately prosperous society'.

At Wiston House, in December 2012, I was fortunate enough to catch up with a visiting team of senior Central Party School leaders. Nestling between some very agreeable South Downs, Wiston House was built in the 1570s by Queen Elizabeth's Treasurer-at-War, Sir Thomas Sherley, and is today the home of Wilton Park, a unique foreign-policy think tank founded in 1946 to host discussion, debate and dialogue on the most pressing foreign-policy issues of the day.

Our debrief opened with the vision that Xi set out for the Chinese people at the Party Congress: the 'Chinese dream', an idea every bit as evocative as the 'American dream'. It's the idea that hard work plus better education, social security and housing will unlock a much better standard of living for ordinary Chinese families and, just 'as the streams and rivers come together to become a great river', better-off Chinese families make for a better-off and stronger – and revitalised – China.

'The Congress', said our Chinese colleagues,

was a decisive moment. A five-in-one development plan, aimed at transforming the model of economic development, reforming politics to maintain the CPC's leadership but within a stronger framework of rule of law, and a social revolution with the extension of comprehensive medical insurance and a stronger safety net.

New priorities have clearly bubbled up to the top. I've not heard Chinese friends talk so urgently before about the need for a 'culturally strong nation' that fostered creativity and innovation or the need to foster entrepreneurship. But that's clearly part of the new lexicon.

Two months later, I was in Beijing for the annual UK–China Leadership Forum. Throughout two days with Chinese colleagues we could hear loud and clear how the gears have shifted: 'we have turned a new page on China's economic development'; 'we're accelerating reform and pursuing a strategy of innovation'; 'in the future the CPC will put more emphasis on human development'; 'we should respect more the role of the market'; 'we should accelerate the role of innovation and strengthen intellectual property rights'; 'we will work faster on going global'; 'we want to unleash the consumption potential of people'. It was all very, very clear-eyed.

While I was in town, I took the chance to head off and see some of the officials with the best take on what's happening in the Chinese economy. China's national bank, the People's Bank of China, is housed behind a monumental semi-circular cream and black edifice just west of the Forbidden Palace, on the gigantic Chang'An Avenue, a road as wide as the Thames, alongside the vast headquarters of what are now the biggest banks in the world.

It quickly became clear that the new leadership is very wary about any big economic slow-down – and is ambitious to crack on with vital economic reform. 'My expectation is that economic growth will speed up', said one Bank official. 'If you look at the history of leadership changes, you always see a bit of speeding after the new team takes over.'

Last year, vital changes were made to the regulation of interest rates, giving banks much more freedom to set the interest rates they offer on deposits and loans. This is important because artificially low rates have helped create huge excess capacity in the iron and steel, shipbuilding, machine-tool and solar-panel sectors and the risk of huge 'non-performing loans', otherwise known as 'sub-prime debt'. The risk is that big loans to these companies could go bad, with huge consequences for the banking system. Hence the very clear focus on pumping growth back up a bit: 'There is excess capacity in these sectors but we're urbanising fast – at 1% of the population a year – so I think these sectors will be OK – if growth stays above 8%.'

I can see the concern. The next few years are critical years for China. China has to hit the growth targets set out in the current five-year-plan if it's to stand a fighting chance of hitting its goals for 2020.

So there's an ambition now to speed up regional free-trade agreements. Huge thought and planning are clearly under way on how to create comprehensive social security, uniting the rudimentary systems in place for rural residents, city dwellers and migrants. There's a clear sense too that things are now changing for the better for China's hundreds of millions of migrant workers:

If you look at the salaries of migrant workers, they're up around 50% in recent years. The starting salary for a migrant worker might be 2,000 RMB a month. It easily might be as high as 3,000 RMB. If there's three people working in a family (a parent and two children, for instance) that's a family income of 8–9,000 RMB. Given the numbers of social homes we're building they now cost say

4–500,000 RMB. That's just five times the family income so they are affordable.

It now means a young woman working as a nanny in Beijing can afford a flat of her own in a county-level town, 100km from Beijing, which, thanks to high-speed rail, you can get to in half an hour.

On the thornier stuff, like the future of intra-party democracy, reform of the bloated SOEs, or reform of the tax system so that local government has money to pay for new social-security systems, there is far more caution; but I sense a determination to push through a minor revolution in transparency and accountability with what officials call 'more emphasis on consultative mechanisms and more channels to air opinions and complaints with the system', especially before policies are set.

At a dinner for the British community in Beijing in January 2012, one Chinese businessman working for a British business put it like this:

> Will big reform happen? The balance of views is that it's now that there's need for transformative change. If left too long it'll be a matter of compulsion not choice. The sense I've got is that time is running out. In the next five years, if there is no SOE reform, land reform, *hukou* reform, they'll be a big problem.

As you might expect the Chinese who are pushing hardest for change are China's younger leaders.

Just north of the Forbidden Palace and the Zhongnanhai district, home to China's leaders, is Hou Hai, a corner of the old city where the Zhuyuan hotel offers a little glimpse into life in Imperial China. Built around inter-locking four-sided courtyards, the single-storey red and green pavilions were once home to a corrupt 18th-century official, who was Minister of the Post. Here in January 2013, we re-grouped with some old friends from the All-China Youth Federation for a first-hand account of the Eighteenth Party Congress from youth delegates. And what we heard was startling. One, a prize-winning young journalist, put it pretty bluntly: 'If the CPC does not fight corruption, it will lose its grip on power in the next five years. If there is no anti-corruption drive, there won't be a Congress in five years' time.' He showed us slides of journalists trying to cover a big fire incident being carried away by security guards, and shared with us how at the Party Congress, in the small discussion groups, corruption came up over and over again:

> In each meeting room, we had 20 delegates to discuss the [Party's] report [the bulk of which was devoted to democracy issues]. All deputies were allowed to speak freely and many mentioned corruption. My work involves exploring complaints from the common people. They share a similarity: [personal] rights are violated by the abuse of power. We have to face up to the reality and hold on to our ideals,

he concluded. It was perhaps the most striking presentation I've heard from a Party member. Ever.

But the basic argument was something a senior Chinese politician confirmed for me:

'On democracy there is a much bigger emphasis on transparency and accountability now. There is a clear edict for senior party leaders to spend time visiting places and listening to concerns and leading problem solving.'

Key to this is reform of the 'letter and visit' system. In the past, concerned citizens could post or petition their concerns to officials. But local leaders worried about criticism would often react by sending a team to visit and 'persuade' the good citizen to withdraw the concern. No more. Now, every complaint has to be logged and receive a substantive reply. More surveillance of system-wide issues would be boiled out of this. What was fascinating was the way my Chinese friend now put the need the need for political reform in its Marxist context: 'Marxist theory demands the "superstructure" change in line with change to the economic base. Now the economy of China is changing so fast, the "superstructure" of democracy and politics has to change too.'

The question is, how can Britain contribute in our own small way to the right kind of change in China – and how, as we set about this task, can we better *our* future by winning a successful interdependence with a nation that will soon be the largest economy on earth?

Three win-wins

I think we've got an awful lot going for us.

Despite the huge interdependence of China and America, the world's two new super-powers are, as the Americans say, 'living with friction'.[165] China's neighbours will always be careful.

Britain remains a small, cool interesting place packed with innovation, a post-Imperial power that doesn't constitute a threat and yet is still an influential member of some of the most important clubs on the planet from Nato, to the EU, to the UN Security Council.

Now we can never fail to advance our arguments about the vital importance of human rights, stronger rule of law, a free media and democracy. But as I said before, Chinese politicians like talking about 'win-wins'. I think it's a good way to think about UK–China relations, and I think there are now three great win-wins within reach.

Win-win 1: Safety nets and market access

First, we have to contribute in a couple of ways to China building its social safety net so that Chinese consumers get stronger. If we can combine this with better access to China's markets then this gigantic change will be a *massive* shot in the arm for Britain's exporters.

In 2011, the Chinese passed the ground-breaking National Insurance Act. In 2012, we celebrated the seventieth anniversary of the Beveridge Report, the blueprint of our welfare state. Published just as the Allies won the battle of Egypt, turned the tide in Guadalcanal and held the line in Stalingrad, the Beveridge Report was the foundation stone for the Britain's welfare state; its cornerstones were the National Health Service and the state pension system that today make up around a third of public spending. These are systems that we know an awful lot about how to build and how to reform. Together with our European neighbours, who have as much experience as we have, we should share that knowledge, expertise and passion with the Chinese. That would be good for China and China's consumers, and stronger Chinese consumers are good news for us. I know it from first-hand experience. Just outside my constituency lies the great Castle Bromwich plant of Jaguar Land Rover, the place that built the millionth Land Rover that drove from the Geneva motor show to China. It's a firm taking on thousands of new workers to satisfy demand from China and India.

Hitherto, our exports to China might have grown fast but relatively they are tiny. Exports this year are some £50–60 billion in value – just 3% of the UK total. We trade four times more with Ireland. Over the last decade, exports to Europe have grown nine times faster.[166]

We can't separate this question from the debate about market access, which remains thorny. In the European Chamber of Commerce some say they have never been so vexed about the difficulties of doing business. But views are mixed. Others say foreign small and medium-sized enterprises are doing well. The truth is, the business of 'opening up' is stuck in what one leading regulator described to me was China's 'slow-motion' reform plan. We need to think more creatively about how we get over the wall, and through the gates. Crucially, we need to use our membership of the world's biggest free-trade grouping – the EU – to advance our cause.

Win-win 2: Partners in pioneering

Second, we have to find many, many more ways of collaborating with China in the innovation business. The creation of a more innovative economy is *one* of the key priorities for China's leaders. Talk to many great British exporters, and one of the first things they say they worry about is losing intellectual property to businesses that will then out-compete them. There is not an easy answer to this.

But better orchestration of business and university could make a really big difference. On my trip to Qingdao in 2008, I stopped by for the afternoon at Qingdao University to get a very vivid sense of just how the world's higher education system is now acting as the most astonishing international ideas exchange. I was there as the regional minister for the West Midlands to help launch Coventry University's Soft Landing Zone for new West Midlands firms seeking to start up in China.

Over lunch, the University's president, Linhua Xia, couldn't speak highly enough of the venture. His message was that universities are now creating a global network of knowledge capital *and* translating ideas into businesses. As Chinese businesses go in search of hi-tech, new businesses are starting on science parks next to universities every day. It's no coincidence, said Prof. Xia, that Win in China – a sort of Chinese equivalent of Dragon's Den – is one of the most popular shows on TV.

In Britain, too, we think we're a pretty innovative bunch. But we need to hold on to a new truth: innovation is not a one-way street. Every day, we have more to learn from Chinese businesses and researchers. Lots of UK firms are already successfully partnering Chinese firms in their international expansion. Shell is partnered with China National Petroleum Corporation (CNPC) in Australia. Rio Tinto's international partnership with the Aluminum Corporation of China (Chinalco) is getting deeper and deeper. HSBC has a strong relationship with the Bank of Communications (BoComm), in which it has a 19.7% equity stake, with great mutual benefits. We need many, many more such.[167] What we learn in China will help us do well in China. We can't just ship the same old products that do well in Europe and hope they fly off the shelves. We have to adapt, and what we learn from adapting are lessons that will help us improve elsewhere.

Coca-Cola, for example, has done well not by shipping in endless cans of fizzy drinks but by tapping into the Chinese love of milk drinks; Coca-Cola's new product, the Minute Maid Pulpy brand, was developed entirely in Coca-Cola's innovation and technology centre in Shanghai: it's now a hit all over Asia and worth over $1 billion.[168] Not everyone can build a research centre like Coca-Cola. Buying or partnering a Chinese company is another approach. Or, at a minimum, building relationships with academic institutions and private start-ups; Nestlé's Research Center in Beijing, for example, collaborates with Jiaotong University in Xi'an to conduct research on metabolic health.[169] Finding ways of encouraging UK companies and UK universities to develop partnerships and sales together with Chinese partners is one of the key ways in which we can innovate together. This is good for UK exports and jobs. And it is good for fostering innovation in China.

Win-win 3: Money

Win-win number three is helping China with the business of diversifying its foreign earnings. What does that mean in practice? It means that we have to be fairly relaxed about a world which moves from 'Made in China' to 'Owned by China'.

The truth is that Britain faces an investment crisis. We need new investment from abroad in everything from infrastructure to commercial development of new ideas.

This can be painful. I've felt that pain at first hand when I watched the remnants of manufacturer Leyland DAF Vans (LDV) being bought up and shipped out from my own constituency. But I've also seen in my home town of Birmingham the positive difference foreign investment can make.

Every year, in Crofton Park, in the south of Birmingham, there takes place an immense celebration of one of Britain's proudest engineering traditions. 'Pride in Longbridge' was the brain-child of community activist Gemma Cartwright, her husband Andy Cartwright and friends, hit hard by the closure of MG Rover. 'Pride in Longbridge' now brings together over a thousand of the finest MG cars to roll off the production line in Longbridge before it closed in 2005.

But behind Crofton Park the Rover site is humming once again, and there are so many guests who want to visit that MG is building a visitor centre to host them and its fantastic collection of magnificent cars from Austin Healey 100s to the Mini Coopers that starred in the Italian Job. At the heart of the new centre is Herbert Austin's original wood-panelled office. One of the greatest British entrepreneurs, Austin helped create the British car industry. Here in the office are the guest-books signed by kings and queens, the coin he flipped when he had to decide whether to carry on in business, and a sign that I guess he looked at every single day, emblazoned with the words 'All great things are born of some dreamer's dream.'

Today, the people investing in those dreams are the Chinese. When Rover closed in 2005, Shanghai Automotive Industrial Corporation (SAIC) and Nanjing Automobile Corporation (NAC) eventually came together to first rebuild MG production facilities in China and then rebuild design and production facilities at Longbridge. The first MG TF roadster car rolled off the line in May 2007; today there are another seven brand new vehicles in the pipeline. When Premier Wen visited the plant on his visit to the UK in 2011, he declared

> I think in future more Chinese investment should fit the local needs of the British side … You may know China has strengths in manufacturing and infrastructure development. When we enjoy each other's strengths, we will enjoy brighter prospects in our cooperation.[170]

I suspect there's an awful lot more win-wins like Rover.

In our own small way, Britain can help solve many of the problems that China's leaders are going to wrestle with over the years to come. I think we can turn our country, our society and our economy to face east. And if you're ever in any doubt, think about a simple question: if we turned the clock back to 1870, to that magic point when the American economy began to overtake us, what would we have advised Britain's leaders to do?

Surely we would have said three things. We would have urged our leaders to foster better links between British businesses and their fast-growing American cousins – I think we would have been less worried about what the Americans were going to 'steal from us' and more concerned with how we put in place links that would help us learn from them. I am sure we would have urged our university leaders to connect rather better to the burgeoning universities of the New World and which are now the best on the planet. And we would have invested more in understanding American politicians – politicians who played such a decisive role in every important decision in the 20th century. The question now is: where do we start with China?

CHAPTER 7

How we boost exports to China

Standard Chartered Bank has been trading in China for a very long time. Its founder, James Wilson, was one of the most extraordinary Scotsmen of the 19th century. Born in 1805, he was the son of a wealthy textile mill owner and went on to become a Member of Parliament, founder of The Economist and the architect of the Indian currency, tax and trade system. When he died, aged just 55, the flag of Fort William in Calcutta was lowered to half-mast and guns were fired from the fort's ramparts for 15 minutes in a final salute.

Wilson spotted that burgeoning trade in the east needed trade banks and, in 1853, he was granted a Royal Charter by Queen Victoria to found the Chartered Bank. After the Suez Canal opened in 1869 and the telegraph reached China in 1871, his business boomed. The bank's former chief economist Gerard Lyons is for my money, one of the best thinkers about the future of the Chinese economy.

Gerard has a nice phrase about the world we're moving into: the world of 'Made in China' is about to become the world of 'Sold in China'. I think British firms need to be leading the charge.

Sold in China

When I came out of business school in 2000, I had a sneaking suspicion that the classmates who would make the real money were those who went to China. I wasn't wrong. On a trip back to China a couple of years ago, I caught up with a classmate of mine who is building a huge cosmetics business in China's coastal zones. Over a rather good dinner in 1931, a swish restaurant in downtown Shanghai, my friend Jeremy explained his target market: affluent young women working in white-collar jobs on about €300 a month. Because of China's one-child policy, these young women might have six 'parents'; her parents plus two sets of grandparents. Her parents and grandparents have saved all their lives; they own their houses and they're keen to spoil their only daughter. That means Jeremy's customers can spend all of their salary as disposable income. Jeremy's aim is to open 1,000 stores in the next five years and then float on the Shanghai stock market.

This one story is a simple snapshot of how consumer markets in China's great cities are booming as China's citizens join the great global middle class. Standard Chartered has thought a lot about this and their conclusion is staggering. The middle-class revolution that is coming could push *three billion* people into the middle class over the next 20 years. Most of this 'burgeoning bourgeoisie' will live in Asia.[171] In fact, the OECD calculate that, between now and 2030, 80% of the growth in middle-class spending will unfold in Asia and, by 2040, China and India alone will account for half of what the global middle class spends.

This should be excellent news for UK plc.

To get a feel for why, I stopped by the City office of one of the oldest 'British' businesses trading in Asia for a cup of tea with one of the firm's managing directors. I wanted to know why he thought British business had such potential. The answer, I was told, was simple:

> Unbeknownst to people in Britain, we have some extraordinarily large firms that have been trading for years all over Asia and are doing remarkably well. The first thing I tend to do when I touch down in an [Asian] market is go and see the local manager of HSBC or Standard Chartered because firms like these have simply been trading in Asia for a very, very long time.

He was absolutely right. Our trading history, good and evil, is actually a heck of a headstart. It's not just Standard Chartered with a long history in Asia. Jardine Matheson was founded in 1832. Now it has sales of $57 billion. It employs 320,000 people running everything from Hong Kong Land to Mandarin Oriental to KFC and Pizza Hut in Vietnam to the gigantic Dairy Farm retail giant which boasts 5,500 stores across Asia, including IKEA. HSBC was founded by a Scot, Thomas Sutherland, in 1865.[172] Today it's one of the largest foreign banks in China with 120 branches, 5,000 staff and Asian profits of over $12 billion. Swire Pacific was founded by John Swire and his sons and boomed when the family started using Mississippi-style paddle-steamers up the Yangtze river in the 1860s. Today, the firm employs 127,000 people, runs a huge shipping business and the airline Cathay Pacific. And alongside these older businesses are now new adventurers: 2011 marked the point when supermarket Tesco's trading profit in Asia outstripped profits in Europe.[173]

On any measure, many of these great trading conglomerates are not British but Asian. Jardine Matheson pays its taxes in the markets where its money is made. Its executives and frontline staff are overwhelmingly Asian. But these businesses are led at the top by Brits who see 'British' values as key to their success. And lots of Chinese consumers agree.

To try to understand why, I tracked down the director of one of the best brand research firms helping business tune in to Chinese consumers. Alex Wilson runs Flamingo Research office in Shanghai and I asked him just how British business was likely to fare as the Chinese consumer grew richer.

For Alex, 2011 felt like *the* year when suddenly everyone set up shop, especially in the pricier end of the market. Alexander McQueen, Burberry, Moncler, Marni and Versace all opened flagship stores in Beijing and now quick-fire expansion is under way in Shanghai and the vast 'second tier' cities like Chengdu, Shenyang, Hangzhou and Tianjin. In Shanghai, LVMH are actually opening not just a shop but their own luxury *mall*. Prada brought The Pet Shop Boys to Beijing to open a replay of their Milan fashion show. Bulgari, Chanel, DVF, Louis Vuitton and Zegna all staged exhibitions of their history.

'It did feel like a bit of a casino mentality', said Alex.

Lots of companies were putting all their chips in and no one really quite knows what will happen.

Let me give you one story about why British firms can do well. I bumped into a former ad exec from Britain not long ago who had basically set up in China to look at ways of bringing the kind of British firms with a shield next to their name to China. Businesses like Savile Row firms, or Loch Fyne. And basically that optimism is right. Credentials which combine craftsmanship and authenticity are really appealing to Chinese consumers.

There are broad trends in luxury; shifts from status to knowledge with less flashy labels. Overly bling is going to go down.

There are a lot of entrenched old-fashioned views about Britain; high society, top hats, Victorian society. But that's counter-balanced by people's sense of London, which is seen as a cool city, cosmopolitan and a centre for music and fashion.

This is the strong potential for British companies and brands. It's a challenge for how this is leveraged. We might see it as a bit kooky and old fashioned but here it has a richness and appeal. Why? Because it helps fill in a gap, a void which is the cultural abyss here.

Partly our brand strength is that we're seen as high quality and, crucially, 'safe'. And this is a big issue. Alex gave me a good illustration. Food-safety scares have bedevilled China for some years and the Chinese media has now decided the problem has to be confronted not hidden. In 2011, the problem literally burst on to the streets when water-melons started exploding outside shops in the summer heat. They had been injected with rather too much growth hormone. When they got hot, they blew up. Nor have Chinese mothers forgotten the scandals of contaminated baby milk. So much powdered baby milk is now imported from Japan that when the Fukushima nuclear reactor went wrong baby-milk stocks were swept off the shelves as Chinese parents started stock-piling supplies they trusted.

'There is a presumption that a Western brand is safe', says Alex. 'On market entry people assume safety. That's a very strong, national brand credential. We're seen as people who make things well; we're seen as people who are fussy about doing things well.'

The mistake British firms have to avoid is assuming that a good brand means they can simply ship in the same stuff they sell in Europe, and Alex had a tale of two great British brands to make the point.

Burberry arrived in China in 2011, and landed with a perfect blend of cutting-edge cool and tech, allied to the firm's heritage. The Burberry 2011 show was spectacular; the world's first holographic fashion show replete with digital rain staged in the vast stage hall from where Beijing Television beams its shows. British band Keane closed the performance. It was rated by many the fashion show of the year.

Marks & Spencer had a rather less happy arrival. Long in Hong Kong, they opened in Shanghai with a very expensive bit of real estate including a food hall replete with oven dinners and Chinese-style rice. Here were two problems. Shanghai residents don't really have ovens; they cook with heat rather than pop a lasagne in the oven. Second, a Shanghai worker was never going to go to an expensive store to buy rice that was almost free in China and loaded with vast cultural symbolism.

So to do well, British firms are going to have to learn a lot more about the Chinese consumer,[174] their habits, differences and trends. For example, growth in spending on luxury skincare and SUVs is twice the rate for cosmetics and cars. The younger generation is far more likely to spend on more expensive, branded stuff than the generation that lived through the Cultural Revolution. Impulse purchases are less common. Brand loyalty has yet to take hold. Chocolate was once bought in China largely as a present but since Mars launched its new chocolate bar, Dove, chocolate consumption has doubled. Demand for the luxuries of middle-class life seems to 'take off' at different levels of wealth.[175] In Beijing, for instance, spending on eating out seems to 'take off' once a family reaches $3,000 a year. Wine, chocolate and fruit juice demand take off at $17,000. Spending on tourism and bank accounts takes off at $18,000 a year.

Understanding the mindset of China's consumers is going to be really important if UK plc is to do well. But just as important as understanding the mindset of China's markets is understanding the new map. Because the map is about to change out of all recognition.

When President Hu bowed out of the Politburo in 2012, he confirmed China's new goal of doubling Chinese living standards by 2020. If that is achieved, it will create a consumer market second only to the US, nearly $5 trillion in size.[176]

But this wealth won't be evenly spread. Its home will be the incredible new cities multiplying all over the country. Some of the best work mapping this revolution has been undertaken by McKinsey & Co. Their new work on the future of cities has just brought the future into a much sharper focus.

McKinsey estimate that one billion people are going to join the urban classes by 2025; 600 million of them will live in 440 cities across the developing world. These new citizens, it is forecast, will generate *half* of the growth in world wealth, adding an immense $10 trillion to worldwide consumer spending. Over half of these cities – 242 to be precise – will be in China. These Chinese cities alone will contribute over a *quarter* of the world's $50 trillion of economic growth between 2010 and 2025;[177] nearly three times the value of North American cities, and seven times the value of west European cities.

Now, if living standards do double by 2020 then the wealth of the average Chinese city-dweller – all 850 million of them – will rise from $4,000 to $8,000, which is around the standard of living enjoyed in South Korea. But beneath the mask of averages are some important differences. By 2025,[178] half the citizens of the 'Emerging 440' – 400 million people – will boast incomes of $16–34,000. Sixty million will earn over $34,000.

The map of these new cities is something British business – and politicians – will need to learn quickly. For example, by 2020 the wealth of 29 cities around Chengdu, in western China, will be as big as the entire economy of Austria's in 2010. I suspect rather more of us could pinpoint Austria on a map than Chengdu.

Serving this new consumer market could transform Britain's wealth in the years to come. But so could helping build these new cities. China wants to build 100 new airports in 10 years. Cities need office space, ports, roads, broadband networks, power stations, power grids, water supplies. That's all good news for UK plc. But only if we play to our strengths.

The opportunity for Britain

One of the most important conversations we have with China is the annual Economic and Finance Dialogue. From its polite and rather scripted beginnings in 2008 the dialogue has evolved into a really productive conversation. In April 2008, I joined the British team of ministers at the Great Hall of the People for a day of talks chaired by Alistair Darling, and then by Vice-Premier Wang Qishan. As is so often the case, the most useful bit was the gossip over lunch, but the summit was also the occasion to support a big delegation of business leaders dominated by financial-services firms.

Financial services are, of course, among our most important exports. We are a world leader. The knowledge we have to share about how financial markets work – or don't work – is still critical to China's development. But the fact that we have a special space for financial services reflects the truth that Britain's financial-services industry is not just 'first among equals' in the sectors we promote abroad, it is overwhelmingly the sector that we push hardest. I think we need to reflect on a bit of a rebalancing.

Ever since I've been travelling in China, I've been fascinated by the question of which British businesses – and sectors – have the potential to do well. As I've interviewed economists, busi-ness leaders, thinkers and politicians for this book, it's become clear that there are at least 10 major sectors where we have huge potential to grow as China grows.

Economists Gerard Lyons and Jim O'Neill, for example, had a similar take. As Jim put it:

> Well, not to be corny about it, but we can do well in the kind of things that are linked to the Olympics. Civil engineering. Healthcare. But I wouldn't be dismissive of no-go areas like Rolls-Royce, or the automotive sector or life sciences.

Gerard Lyons added: 'I think there's a long list of sectors where Britain can do well: nanotechnology; high-end manufacturing; high-end creative industries; financial services outside of banks.'

One way of thinking about this is to look at where the UK now has a global edge, and one of the people who have thought about this hardest is Peter Nolan, professor of Chinese develop-ment at Cambridge University.

I waylaid Peter with a cup of coffee at my favourite coffee bar in the House of Commons, in the atrium of Portcullis House, to ask him about UK potential. Peter pointed me to an interesting phenomenon. Over the last 20 years, huge new businesses have now grown to dominate their sectors by pouring vast resources into the R&D needed to stay a step ahead of the game.

Indeed, the world's top 1,400 companies now spend a combined total of £545 billion on R&D. They have become the locomotive for the world's innovation. Britain does not have many businesses on the list. But the companies people told me would do well in China are all in sectors where we have a good share of the world's R&D spend (see Table 7.1): advertising, aerospace and automotive; branded consumer products; civil engineering;

education and energy; financial services; life sciences, and to a degree, retail.

Now some of these firms will find it very hard to break into China; telecoms is a sector barred to outside competition; media too is hardly open. Some of the sectors listed here – like mining – have British firms merely headquartered in London with operations far away.

But our R&D giants – aerospace, banks, food production and retail, oil and gas and above all pharmaceuticals – all have immense potential, and they nail the idea that somehow manufacturing should not be a key part of our offer.

First, it is actually quite hard to separate manufacturing and services in the way we used to; half of Rolls-Royce's sales, for example, are classed as services, with the firm selling 'flying hours', not engines. Second, the UK is still the world's sixth largest manufacturer and, since 2006, around 25% of the UK's exported goods have been defined as hi-tech.[179] That is a higher proportion than in the US (22%) or France (15%).[180]

During the first days of the financial crash, I was working for Gordon Brown, based at the Cabinet Office as Chancellor of the Duchy of Lancaster. It was my first cabinet-level job and one job I helped with was thinking anew about policy for rebuilding the country after the crash. To assist, the Prime Minister's Strategy Unit did a first-class piece of work unpicking how a decade of globalisation had changed our economy.

The team concluded that the UK had delivered the fastest growth in wealth per head of any country in the OECD and had basically evolved into three broad sectors:

- Our 'leading-edge' economy, which was highly innovative and more productive than anyone else's. This bit of our economy – high-value services, science-based industries and advanced manufacturing – was producing about a third of our output, and employing around a fifth of workers.

- Then we had a 'specialising' bit of the economy, largely manufacturing, where employment was shrinking but firms were becoming much more productive to compete against fierce international competition.[181]
- And then we had a chunk of the economy employing over a third of workers, where productivity growth was slow but lots and lots of jobs were being created in sectors like retail, hospitality and construction.

I then discovered, at the Treasury, that this story of a pretty diversified economy also showed up in tax receipts. If we take 2006/07 – the year before the boom really spiked – and add up personal, consumption, property, environmental and direct business taxes paid by a range of sectors, you find financial services paid £44 billion to the government. A lot of money. But business services paid £46.5 billion; that's over £2 billion more. And manufacturing paid £36 billion,[182] just £6 billion less.

I think all this points to one conclusion: that instead of just focusing on the 'jewel in the crown', as we used to call the City of London, we need a strategy for China that promotes the 'crown jewels' – the best of British from every sector where we're strong. These are all sectors which are forecast to boom in China.

Ageing wealthier Chinese families are going to demand a lot of life science, like pharmaceuticals and healthcare. Britain is Europe's most popular location for investment in pharmaceuticals.[183] Our pharma sector is the one of the top seven biggest R&D spenders, and British companies – GlaxoSmithKline, AstraZeneca, Shire – have a significant share of it.

Any aerospace executive will tell you that demand for planes – and therefore aero-engines – rises broadly in line with GDP growth; that's good news for British companies like Rolls-Royce. Our domestic aerospace industry is the second largest in the world with a turnover of £20 billion.[184]

Growth in the energy sector will be gigantic; China is probably the world's largest energy consumer already. Yet per person, China consumes only 20% of an American. That points to huge growth ahead. Despite its push into renewables,[185] oil demand will grow and pressure will continue to exploit new finds and pipe new supplies. Coal will in fact provide China's principal energy source (not least because it is 85% cheaper than oil)[186] and demand is likely to double. That means clean coal technology will be vital. The UK's low-carbon and environmental goods and services sector is the sixth largest in the world and worth some £107 billion, and our energy giants Shell and BP are among the world's biggest. The vast growth in cities will also mean demand for civil engineering firms like Ove Arup will boom. As Chinese businesses grow, diversify and enter world markets, they need business services. Britain boasts great strength in professional services, including legal, financial, management and consultancy. Exports of 'other business services', for example, increased from £17 billion in 1997 to £40 billion in 2007.[187]

As China's middle class booms, demands for services like advertising multiply. That's good news for companies like WPP.

China is poised to reign as the world's largest market for luxury goods by 2020, when sales are expected to exceed $100 billion;[188] that's good news for UK luxury brands like Burberry.

China is devoted to education. As living standards rise, many Chinese are postponing marriage and family to invest in education and get a decent job; today about 25% of high-school students enrol in college. By 2020, that may rise to 40%. China is going to educate tens of thousands of its citizens to tertiary level. Back in 2000, China boasted perhaps 41 million graduates; but over the next 20 years, two million Chinese will graduate from university *every year*.[189] By 2030 Asia, excluding Japan, will be home to half of the world's graduates. Britain is world renowned as an education leader.

And as China's middle class grows richer, it will ask its banks to do more; consumers will not simply want cash deposits, but sophisticated services such as unit trusts, pensions, life insurance, mortgages and credit cards. Because of China's 'one child' policy, the country is ageing. That means that, along with education, China will prove a huge new market for *pensions*. Chinese cities like Beijing, Shanghai, Tianjin, Nanjing, Guangzhou, Wuhan, Shenyang and Chongqing will become 'silver cities' with lots and lots of well-off older residents. There will be more than 126 million more Chinese citizens over the age of 65.[190] Our financial-services industry is well known. The UK has become a world leader in financial services, which made up around 8% of GDP in 2007. It is one of the sectors where we dominate global R&D. Financial institutions based in the UK account for 18% of cross-border bank lending, 70% of the international bonds market, 11% of the asset management market, and 20% of the global hedge fund market.[191]

So, as China grows, there is a wide arc of business opportunity for Britain if we turn east. There is just one thing that might get in the way.

CHAPTER 8

Building the safety net

Next to the home of traditional Chinese opera in Beijing is a nondescript office block that is headquarters of one of the oldest and most important think tanks in China. The Chinese Academy of Social Sciences was founded in 1977 to rebuild Chinese social science, which was practically obliterated by the Cultural Revolution. The school ranks as a ministry, and its alumni are among the country's most senior leaders, including the disgraced former leader of Chongqing, Bo Xilai.

On a crisp March morning in 2012, as the ice was beginning to melt on the school's lake, I came to visit Prof. Zhou Hong, head of the Institute for European Studies, to ask about what has become the most important policy challenge for the Communist Party of China: how on earth can the country build a social safety net big enough and wide enough for 1.3 billion people?

Prof. Zhou Hong offered a very eloquent outline of the sheer scale of the challenge:

> We're facing a lot of problems never ever before experienced by *any* country in history. We're a huge country moving from a planned economy to a market economy. Planned

is simple. State-owned enterprises can move money from one pocket to another from profits, to pensions or building kindergartens. But a market economy! My goodness! What a chaotic situation.

The first key challenge is pooling. This is not just a social system. It's closely connected to the economic system, to the political system.

The second key word is mobility – mobility of labour.

If we were only facing the need for pooling it would be easy. You just pull together the resources in a city or a village and devote to the needy. But this is too slow. People are moving. Not just moving locally but moving across the country to the coastal areas

Say a worker moves to Guangzhou. By the time they are 40 or 45, they decide they have saved enough and they want to move home. But they go too early. Who then is to pay for their pension? Whose responsibility is this? These people have contributed to the wealth of the coastal areas – but then they move home (where they've contributed nothing).

Before I started visiting China I had a naive assumption that a communist country, if it had anything, was bound to have a welfare state as good as if not better than our own. Far from it. And every summer, in company canteens and community centres up and down the Chinese sea-board there is a vivid illustration of the void as 'summer camps' open for the country's 'little migratory birds'.

The 'birds' in question are the children of China's army of 221 million migrant workers who have left their homes in the countryside to work in the vast economic zones of Bohai or the Yangtze or Pearl river deltas. Every summer the workers' children make the long trek to spend their summer holidays with their parents. More and more companies and non-governmental organisations (NGOs) now help out running activities. All over the Sina Weibo microblogging website, parents post pictures of happy reunited children.

The 'little birds' are migratory because their parents cannot afford to raise them in the cities. In the cities, migrant workers from the countryside have no rights to public services like healthcare or education or pensions or often decent labour rights. Known derisively as *waidi ren*, or outsiders, migrant workers are the backbone of the Chinese economy. In the coastal areas of Shenzhen and Dongguan, rural *hukou* labour (the migrant workforce registered in rural hometowns, or *nongmingong*) makes up 70–80% of the labour force.

Yet they are paid on average three times less than their urban neighbours and have to meet the costs of their own children's education, medical bills and unemployment insurance. Rights at work are poorly enforced; half of all migrant workers at sites in Beijing in 2007 and 2008 state they did not receive their monthly wage but had to wait until the end of the year, which is illegal under Chinese law. These huge migrant communities have to find their own solutions for social problems; in cities like Beijing, unofficial cooperatives have sprung up to organise basic needs like schools for children.

The sheer scale of the task means that has been handed to the local government to get on with. Some cities like Chengdu are pioneering models that are closely watched; Chengdu has allowed more than two million people to become urban residents since 2003 without relinquishing their rural property rights. But many local governments that can afford to make the changes won't because of the cost and the hit to local budgets in which they may have some financial stake of their own.

But within China's great coastal plains, the strains are very, very difficult to manage. Shanghai is a good example. The city of so many billionaires is also home to 500 people over the age of 100 and a million over the age of eighty. People generally don't move out, they stay put, or move in to take advantage of the system. But the city authority is simply not rich enough to support the non-working population. Beijing has reached for the logical solution. It is simply controlling the number of people moving in.

China is moving as fast as it can to solve some of these problems. A basic National Insurance Act is now in place. Pilots are under way for the medical system in provinces like Anhui. Here villages are testing wide-ranging reforms to its 'grass-roots' medical system that will eventually cost $125 billion and offer new access to drugs and basic insurance. In February 2012, new laws allowed migrant workers to apply for urban *hukous* (registration documents) in small and medium-sized cities, to encourage workers to stay closer to homes and develop new cities inland. But the law does not cover either provincial capitals or tier-one cities like Beijing, Shanghai, Tianjin and Guangzhou, where most migrants currently work.

Even when systems are put in place China faces a real problem convincing its citizens to trust them. At Renmin University, a senior professor explained it to me like this:

> In rural areas, many are worried about paying in. Usually peasants say, 'I don't know what will happen to the system if we pay in.' Worries about local corruption – a village official or leader with his hand in the till – don't help.
>
> Or take the challenge of the urban areas and the state-owned enterprises. Recently a friend was doing a consulting project for a firm that wanted to make its (pensions) annuity clear for senior managers. But when we conducted the interviews, people said they wanted the cash now, not an annuity in the future. The issue is in China, cash is king.

This challenge is now becoming a serious block on China's economic development because it stops would-be workers, including well-trained young graduates, from moving to where the jobs are, unless they go to work for the government or utilities or universities: 'In fact we've just interviewed some people for a job here because they can get a *hukou* for Beijing with a right to education, healthcare and pensions.'

This is a problem in which we all have a big stake. Because China's new consumers will only be free to spend if China's government builds a welfare state so its citizens earn more and don't have to hoard their cash for a rainy day.

Despite the gigantic economic advance of China over the last decade, the rising living standards and the huge achievement of lifting 400 million people out of poverty, workers' share of China's national earnings – the money that shows up in pay-packets at the end of the week or month – is not going up, it is going down; down to just 47% of GDP. And more of the money earned is saved, not spent. In fact, Chinese workers are now saving not less but more of their pay-packets each month than a decade ago.[192] The workers who save most live in cities.[193] Back in 1995, Chinese urbanites saved around one RMB in five. Now, almost a third of earnings are squirrelled away. The biggest savers are in their late twenties and early fifties. Younger workers are saving up for a home. Older workers are building a fund of their own for a health emergency and a pension. If this carries on, there's not going to be the consumer boom that there could be in China – and that means an export market for us that is much smaller to aim for.

I've worked with enough young Chinese leaders to know they see the current system as too complicated and unequal. Much of future world growth hinges on how China's leaders crack this challenge over the next 20 years. So when the UK–China young leaders' conference came together at Lancaster House in 2012, I was keen to debate it.

Lancaster House is one of the grandest houses in government. Tucked away at the end of Carlton Gardens, with borders on St James's Park and five minutes from Piccadilly, it is the last of the extravagant private palaces that were the hub of Victorian and Edwardian political society. The Grand Old Duke of York started the Louis XIV-style house in the 1820s, but he died in debt and the Marquess of Stafford's family finished the house and made it an epicentre of Whig politics. In 1911, Lord Leverhulme acquired it, rechristened it, and donated it to the nation as a home for the London Museum and venue for international talks.

I suggested we started by peering into the future and pondering the kind of change that might unfold. Some things, we all agreed, were predictable.

People are getting older; illness and disability will rise. Demand for social benefits will rise. There will be fewer workers to support the retired. The broad trends affecting China are the same as those affecting us.

But the more important stuff is far less certain. How fast will economic growth unfold? How sharp is inequality likely to become? What's the prospect for environmental damage, pollution and congestion? How will disability, obesity and non-communicable diseases develop? How are governments and politicians likely to perform, safeguarding against social unrest? And, crucially, how cohesive or fragmented are families and communities likely to become? Building or maintaining shared systems like a welfare state is far harder when neighbours don't trust each other.

When you look at the list of risks that lie ahead for China's leaders you're struck at just how hard it is to govern China. The good scenario for China in 2030 might entail slower growth, inequality held in check, a far more environmentally friendly way of life and a far stronger shared sense of solidarity, perhaps sparked by social media and shaped positively by politicians. Migration to the cities might slow, social links between the city and the countryside might strengthen, especially across the generations, and older people's health might be maintained by a mixture of culture (avoiding diseases of affluence) and a good healthcare system. That's the nice story.

But if things don't go well, growth may falter and leave very little money to pay for the safety net. Pollution may grow, thereby increasing health costs; fights over energy and water might proliferate; migration to the cities might accelerate beyond cities' ability to cope; inequality might multiply, fracturing any sense of solidarity and, worse, traditional family structures may begin fall apart, leaving the vulnerable alone to fend and fight for themselves in a less sympathetic, more confrontational society.

There's a real lesson that emerges about the absolute centrality of family in keeping China together. If you read Confucius, you get a flavour of this; the first few chapters are all about the importance of filial piety. What shapes the plans of most Chinese families is thinking ahead about their family obligations in a country that is both ageing and where the one-child policy means that any one worker may have to support not one, but several, older people. The family unit in China still plays an absolutely crucial role in the welfare of its members; the state far less. At the end of our exercise a Chinese friend I've worked with a lot said she'd decided that she was now going to start investing in a private pension – because when he was older her son would be responsible for four parents: his own parents plus the parents of his wife.

What's impressive is that China's leaders see the challenge as, yes, a Herculean task, but they remain undaunted. To illustrate the point, a friend told us a very famous story in China, of the old man and the mountain.

One day, an old man called Yugong (literally 'foolish old man') looked out on the two mountains before his home and was troubled that they blocked his view and forced him to take a roundabout route whenever he went out. He gathered his family together to discuss the matter and proposed that they work together to flatten the mountains. His wife voiced her doubts about his strength and where on earth the rocks would go. But the objections were swept aside, and Yugong took his sons and grandsons and started digging up the earth and rocks and carrying them in baskets to the edge of the sea. Nearby lived a wise old man who chastised the foolishness of the project; but Yugong replied: 'You are so obstinate that you do not use your reason ... Though I die, my son lives on. My son produces a grandson and in turn the grandson has a son of his own. Sons follow sons and grandsons follow sons. My sons and grandsons go on and on without end but the mountains will not grow in size. Then why worry about not being able to flatten it?' Impressed, the gods eventually intervene and finish the job.

The point is that no matter how great the task, with patience and application in time it can be achieved. And that is how Chinese leaders see the task of building a welfare state. Their target for completion is 2049. This is a country that thinks and plans for the long term.

China's policy-makers have studied this question a lot. In private they talk fondly about the systems they admire in Scandinavia or the personal accounts system in Singapore. If the CPC is to maintain its monopoly of power amid this change, reformers know they must create a safety net that is strong.

Over a cup of tea at the House of Commons, Rana Mitter, professor of history and politics of modern China at Oxford

University,[194] reminded me that this debate is not in fact new for the CPC. It stretches right back to the party's earliest debates during the second world war, when the CPC's leaders wrestled with the basic question of 'What do we have to do to ensure the people are happy?' This is the key question in Chinese political history. Why? Because 'every major crisis of the last 150 years in China has had social welfare at its root'. Leaders ignore it at their peril. That's why the 'recalibration of the social contract', as Rana puts it, will be at the core of the next decade of Chinese politics.

Before it produced its twelfth five-year plan, the CPC decided to undertake large-scale consultation online with China's 500 million plus online citizens. Calls to reduce income disparities and strengthen the social safety net topped the list of ideas. Two years later, during the NPC, the same kind of concern was all over the Weibo microblogging website.

How can we help China wrestle with this giant challenge? In the West we know lots about building welfare states. Here in Britain, we have just celebrated the seventieth anniversary of the Beveridge Report, which set out the blueprint for Britain's welfare state. We have a huge amount to gain if China's welfare state builders are successful. Is there a win-win to be had?

I think there is.

Parts of the challenge we can't help with. We can't help create the right incentives or tax system to foster more social housing getting built. Unemployment insurance too is basically a matter of Chinese policy.

But, the absolute backbone of any welfare state is a healthcare system and a pension system – and it's the lack of both that is causing older workers to save so much. In Western countries this is where most of public spending goes. In Britain, for instance, we spend over £200 billion a year on state pensions and the National Health Service; that's about a third of all public spending.

China's healthcare and pensions systems are weak. We should think far more about what expertise we *can* contribute in both fields, bilaterally and through the European Union.

China's pension system is massively underfunded. In 2009, total assets under management for the national fund, local government and private sector totalled just RMB 2.4 trillion – that's about $470 of lifetime retirement benefits for every Chinese worker. It's not a lot of money. Yet in Britain, we know a huge amount about long-term asset management and we have firms that are good at it. Crucially, our expertise in the City of London means we are experts in the 'soft infrastructure' that countries need to build and regulate financial-services markets, and we are wiser in fact following the recent crash.

Healthcare is an even bigger opportunity for collaboration.[195] The UK's National Health Service, so prominently advertised in Danny Boyle's marvellous Olympic opening ceremony, is seen as offering a good model. But, more important, we have world-leading health scientists and one of the world's leading pharmaceutical industries; indeed it is the only major global R&D sector where UK firms control a significant amount of global research budgets.

China faces a major disease burden that is costing and will cost its economy a fortune. Cardiovascular and chronic respiratory diseases plus cancer kill 85% of Chinese; that is 25% higher than the world average. 130 million people carry the hepatitis B virus.[196] It has the largest population of diabetics (10% have diabetes, around the same as in the US). Mental health problems are escalating; more than 227 million suffer some kind of mental health issue; perhaps some 287,000 a year kill themselves. More than 300 million people smoke, more than the entire US population. Pollution in some parts of the country can be life threatening and food and drug scandals are now widely publicised by the state-controlled media. An ageing population poses new risks; one study forecasts that, by 2040, China may have as many people with Alzheimer's as the rest of the world combined. A study in 2011 by Chinese economists found ill-health in 2005 cost five billion working days and $296 billion.[197]

Under Mao, China had by 1959 built a system of country hospitals, commune healthcare centres and 'brigade' clinics in villages. During the Cultural Revolution, hundreds of thousands of 'barefoot doctors' – peasants with informal medical training – served the countryside; cooperative medical care spread and life expectancy almost doubled to 65. But during the 1980s, both fell away. By 2000, the World Health Organisation (WHO) ranked China's healthcare system as 144th out of 191 countries.

In 2009, China's leaders pledged a three-year $173 billion spending boost for healthcare to widen medical insurance and dramatically change availability in the countryside; overwhelmingly the money is spent in the city (by 2004, 80% of health spending was urban – and the overwhelming majority of that is spent on 8.5 million government officials).

But medical insurance is thin: in 2010 it was worth just $19 per person; thus in rural areas, the vast majority of a medical bill is paid by the individual. Between 1990 and 2008, healthcare spending by urban residents leapt from 2% of spending to 7%.[198] The target for universal access to primary health care is 2020. Furthermore, public hospitals are often loaded up with obligations they can't afford to service. So they make lots of their own money prescribing drugs. Nor does anyone in China look awfully determined to face down major businesses like the tobacco firms that constitute a public health risk.

There have been programmes that pointed the way; the UK's Partners in Health project has seen the Department for International Development (DFID) work on healthcare in China for over a decade, and crucially some of Britain's leading universities now have big life-science programmes under way. Oxford University is helping run some of the world's biggest medical field trials in China. In my home city, Birmingham University has ground-breaking research initiatives with the Guangzhou Institutes of Biomedicine and Health exploring stem-cell therapy. Cohort studies with local hospitals are under way. There's collaboration on life and environmental sciences on going with Sun Yat-sen University.

Given our troubled past in China, I think there is a big offer we could make to the Chinese government and Chinese people: an ambition to share what expertise we have in building insurance and pensions markets, and much bigger collaboration in health science and health-service management. One day, we should host the kind of Dialogue on health science to match the scale of the Economic and Finance dialogue we began in 2008. Together, the UK and China could launch a major initiative to share knowledge in life sciences and building health systems. That would be a great cause to fight together. It would be good for China. And good for Britain. The health and wellbeing of the Chinese worker is in our interest.

CHAPTER 9

Opening the oyster

The new growth in the Chinese consumer market is not going to do us much good unless we can actually get into it. And we need to think a lot harder about how we organise the business of opening the oyster of Chinese trade.

On one of my first visits to Beijing, the leader of a major British manufacturer explained the gateway which allows entry to British businesses. It is a 24-page official document[199] that is in effect the border control for any foreign firm. If you're not on the list, you don't get in:

> Any business that wants to come to China has to specify exactly what it wants to do; and this is then rigorously checked against the Catalogue for the Guidance of Foreign Investment and Industry. This is basically the long list of which businesses are prohibited, restricted or encouraged.
>
> This says when you can and can't invest, and says when you have to set up a joint venture with a local business. So for example, if you want to set up a telecoms business, you can't. If you want to set up an automotive business, then you need to set up a joint venture.

The Catalogue is quite simply one of the keys to understanding the Chinese economy.

Published by the Ministry of Commerce (MofCom), the Catalogue sets out China's control of the commanding heights of its economy and all points in between. It says in which industries foreign competitors may compete, which industries must remain under state control (monopolised by state firms), in which strategic industries (defence, aviation, mining, energy, telecoms) the government wants to see 'national champions' dominate (again state firms), which industries are targets for making or buying new technology (like high-speed rail) and in which industries the state must own over 50% of any business. Even in sectors controlled by the government there might be competition but not quite as we know it. Telecoms, for instance, is dominated by China Mobile, China Telecom and China United. In 2010, the CPC decided to simply rotate the chief executives of each business around.

One of the people who have thought a lot about cracking this challenge is Lord Mandelson, twice our Secretary of State for Business and Industry and a former EU Trade Commissioner. I've worked a lot with Peter over the last 20 years, and in recent years we've worked together in exchanges and calls with senior Chinese leaders. He's someone with the best perspective in Britain on where the treasure lies in UK–China relations – and how we unlock it. Like me, Peter thinks there's actually a broad range of sectors where UK plc can prosper: 'Anywhere where we are at the higher end of the value chain. So in addition to legal and financial services British business can do well wherever we're creating great value.'

But the challenge of securing free trade in return is hard:

Every year, the EU Chamber of Commerce, which is a well set-up, well-resourced outfit, produced this amazing volume,

an audit of the problem standing in the way of trade – I think
it was first produced when I was the Commissioner and I had
to sort of bless it. It calculated the cost as €20 billion of lost
trade opportunities.

Indeed the last EU Chamber of Commerce report found, in 2011,
that 43% of managers of companies established in China consider
themselves to be discriminated against by measures taken by the
Beijing authorities, compared with 33% in 2010. The situation
may be getting worse.

Given the size of what is on offer, therefore, should we not
contemplate a free-trade agreement between Europe and China?
After all, Europe has now embarked on such deals with South
Korea and Japan. But battering open the doors to Chinese
markets with an EU–China free trade agreement is hard:

> The problem is that there's too little complementarity. It
> would mean that the EU becomes absolutely swamped with
> Chinese manufactured goods in return for some theoreti-
> cal opening of markets to services. But what we might find
> is that licensing or procurement or other non-tariff barrier
> obstacles are still in the way.

Indeed, the lack of enthusiasm for an EU–Japan free-trade agreement is a good illustration of how hard it might prove for Europe
to agree a much bigger deal with China. Peter again: 'The problem
is that you're comparing apples and pears. They're a state capitalist
economy with subsidies operating, more or less openly, on a huge
scale. Production is still governed by non-commercial decisions.'

In part, the global crash rather muddied the water; in the
dark days of 2008, the whole world was looking to China to help
pump some air back into a fast-deflating global economy. And

the fastest way for China to act was by pumping investment into the bloodstream, using SOEs. Chinese businesses were the politicians' spark-plug of choice. But at the time, the world wasn't angry, but grateful.

Reversing that surge-tide and making progress on trade is therefore, in Peter's view, going to take a long, slow patient slog. So if an EU–China trade treaty won't fly, what's the alternative?

> You can make progress with evidence. But it is a long, slow, painful slog. Trade is all about reciprocal concessions. You have to find those areas where China wants help and structure a few win-wins. But remember, the Chinese think very much more long term than we do.

Trade is and always has been a negotiation, a process. And we mustn't be too sanctimonious about it. For long stretches of our own history we sheltered 'infant industries' behind protectionist laws like Cromwell's 'Navigation Acts'. The 'American System' championed by US statesmen like Henry Clay demanded a national plan for a network of canals and turnpikes, support for manufacturing and tariff protection.[200]

In reality, access to China's market is of a different order to just 10 years ago, when the world took one of the most important economic decisions of the century and admitted China to the WTO.

Negotiations began in July 1986. After 15 years of discussion, concessions and commitments were hammered out and new tariffs set before China was finally voted into the club on 10 November 2001.

The results that followed were, quite simply, spectacular. Two decades ago, China and Europe traded almost nothing. Today, China and Europe boast the second biggest economic relationship in world.[201] Since 2001, US exports of goods to China have increased by 380%, from $19 billion in 2001 to $92 billion in 2010; China is the United States' largest goods export market outside of North America and US exports of private commercial services totalled $21 billion in 2010.[202]

Everybody knew that moving what is now the world's second largest economy from a state of isolation dating back millennia to a nation fully incorporated into the global marketplace would not happen overnight. But crucially, China is now locked in to a system of international rules, with a 'court' – in the shape of the WTO – that can issue binding judgements based on China's 'Protocol of Accession' and agreement to Goods and Services Schedules. These signalled agreement to the obligations of more than twenty existing multilateral agreements, including most-favoured nation treatment, national treatment, transparency and the availability of independent review of administrative decisions, agriculture, sanitary and phytosanitary (SPS) measures, technical barriers to trade, trade-related investment measures, customs valuation, rules of origin, import licensing, antidumping, subsidies and countervailing measures, and trade-related aspects of intellectual property rights and services.

As the sun set on China's first decade of membership, officials, ambassadors and politicians in Washington, Brussels and Geneva offered their opinions on progress.[203] Here in the thousands of words of the US Trade Representative's Report to the US Congress, speeches to the WTO General Council and motions in the European Parliament we can read what's gone well, what hasn't, and what should happen next. It is a little like wading through treacle.

No one really disputes the scale of the transformation China had to effect. 'We must acknowledge', said the EU's ambassador, Angelos Pangratis, that China faithfully implemented its tariff reductions according to the schedule [and] used the WTO preparations and the first years after its accession to pursue ambitious domestic economic reforms, which have allowed it to take off the way it did and record the most impressive growth in history.[204]

I've lost count of the number of times I've heard Chinese ministers and officials say, 'China has honoured its WTO obligations.' Experts in Europe and America would not put it quite like that. Indeed, the European Parliament concluded: 'so far [China's] efforts [respecting] WTO rules ... have not been satisfactory by any means'.[205]

Having ploughed through the reports and speeches, I think a rough summary of the state of play gives us a list of seven big worries.

First and foremost is the concern that China's 'state capitalism' is if anything accelerating. The government is basically turbo-charging a host of national champions that are now so big they will be world-beaters. This entails a mixture of market protection plus hidden subsidies to Chinese firms, which is prohibited by the WTO because it gives Chinese firms an advantage over foreign firms, creating an uneven playing field. So, state banks provide SOEs with cheap credit, and Chinese authorities grant special export credits to preferred businesses.[206] WTO rules say that these subsidies need to be declared[207] and in China they typically are not. Indeed, the WTO's China report noted: 'In many cases there are no figures on the magnitude of support provided, and no information is available on subsidies and other government assistance provided at the provincial level, which are believed to be considerable.'[208]

For instance, America recently brought a case to the WTO which forced China to remove large subsidies to wind-turbine manufacturers that appeared to be tied to using Chinese-made components rather than imports.

Second, the Catalogue enshrines a host of restrictions on foreign investment or foreign trade in China's 'pillar' industries (what we used to call the 'commanding heights' of the economy), which generally include those industries like banking, insurance, automotive and telecoms where the US and Europe has great strength. China can for example use its process for screening foreign investment to block deals, using what are quite vaguely defined powers granted to regulators. China maintains investment and ownership caps in banking, construction and telecommunications. In some sectors, it is just not possible to do business. In others, foreign firms have to sign up to joint ventures, which historically have entailed rather a lot of 'forced' technology transfer.[209]

Adding to the difficulty are complicated tariffs and the need to pass the technical standards of the Chinese Compulsory Certification (CCC) system, which are not very clear and which diverge from international standards; only 46% of the more than 20,000 national standards in force in China are adopted from international or advanced foreign standards.

Or there are industry regulations which just block foreign entrants. Only 23 of the 22,000 telecommunication licences granted in China since 2001 have gone to foreign companies.

Foreign law firms in China are currently not allowed to employ Chinese lawyers and are not permitted to participate in bar exams to gain Chinese qualifications. There are severe restrictions on foreign suppliers of electronic payment services like credit card companies. Foreign suppliers can't handle typical payment card transactions where a Chinese consumer is billed and pays in RMB. Instead, China's national champion, China UnionPay (CUP), has a monopoly. Foreign presence of online retail continues to be 'restricted' in the 2011 Catalogue for the Guidance of Foreign Investment.

Third, the US and Europe argue that export restrictions, especially on rare earths, are a major problem. China controls 97% of the world's supply of rare earths, which are a crucial ingredient in most hi-tech equipment.[210] If these supplies can't be exported, then hi-tech firms based in China have a major competitive advantage over firms based in the West. This is not the first time the problem has emerged. Back in 2009, the US and Europe brought a case to the WTO challenging export restraints on nine raw materials vital to the steel, aluminium and chemicals industries.

Fourth, worries about intellectual property rights (IPR) are widespread.[211] In 2010, over 103 million items of counterfeit goods, to the value of over €1 billion, were seized at EU borders; 85% of them were made in China, and seven out of every 10 European businesses operating in China say that they have been the victim of IPR violations.[212] In 2007, European manufacturers estimated that the loss of intellectual property costs them 20% of their potential revenues in China. In May 2011, the US International Trade Commission estimated that US businesses suffered a total of $48 billion in lost sales, royalties and licence fees owing to IPR infringement in China in 2009.[213]

Next on the list is government procurement. Europe – and to a lesser extent, the US – have open markets which let foreign firms bid to supply government contracts. China on the other hand does not. Big government contracts can help firms compete, because they provide a big base-load of demand which enables firms to drop their marginal costs and therefore prices in international markets, and contracts can be used to drive demand for local suppliers. And so China is being urged to sign up to the WTO's Agreement on Government Procurement.

Then there are the rules of the game which, for most businesses, is the crunch issue. It was the number one concern posed by the EU's ambassador to the WTO. Indeed, the WTO found China's trade and investment policies were 'opaque and complex'.[214] Few laws and regulations are available in foreign languages. If a business is to make a big investment trying to trade in China, it needs a degree of certainty and predictability. And in China that is often too hard to come by. Nor is commercial law well tried or tested – or predictable – in the courts.

Finally, and just for good measure, the US and, to a far lesser degree, some in Europe would add China's exchange rate policy, which has kept the *yuan* undervalued. This is not something that gets negotiated in a trade agreement and is, of course, hotly disputed. To this list of 'big stuff', negotiators would append pages of little things on products from blockbuster films to beef.

In crucial new industries, these issues can come together with some power. Take the market for electric cars, which will soon become a vast new global industry. The US argues that Chinese state-owned industries were gaining special subsidies, foreign investors were being blocked, or forced to join technology transfer agreements, and export quotas on rare earths – which are vital to technologies like electric batteries – were damaging foreign companies' ability to compete.

Some might be drawn to conclude there are more stumbling blocks than building blocks on the field. But, if there is not going to be an EU–China free trade agreement soon, we're going to have to find a pragmatic way forward. And I think that for Britain there are two pragmatists to learn from. The Americans. And the Germans.

Lessons from America

Let's start with the Americans.

Each year, the US Trade Representative (USTR) Ron Kirk has to publish a report to Congress setting out the trade picture in China with a plan for what the US government plans to do next. Ambassador Kirk's office dates back to the 1960s, when Congress demanded a special figure based in the President's office to drive forward trade negotiations. President Kennedy beefed up the role, and today the USTR is the president's key advisor on trade and coordinates policy across the US government for advancing America's trade interests.

Mr Kirk's report is prepared by a Staff Committee, which draws together reports from experts in the Departments of Commerce, State, Agriculture and Treasury, the US Patent and Trademark Office, and US officials in China. A subcommittee then meets, in the words of its report, 'to evaluate, coordinate and prioritise the monitoring activities being undertaken and to review the steps that China has taken to implement its commitments'.

The USTR then calls for written evidence and organises hearings, before publishing a report that crystallises America's agenda. Working through that agenda day to day is the US–China Joint Commission on Commerce and Trade. Founded in 1983, it brings together the US Department of Commerce and MofCom[215] in an annual summit chaired by a Chinese vice-premier and the US Commerce Secretary, but it oversees a host of working groups exploring everything from 'industrial policies, competitiveness, intellectual property rights, structural issues, steel, agriculture, pharmaceuticals and medical devices, information technology, insurance, tourism, environment, commercial law, trade remedies and statistics'.[216]

Finally, the US–China Strategic and Economic Dialogue, the S&ED, created in April 2009, represents the highest-level bilateral forum between the United States and China. The S&ED brings together the Secretary of State and the Treasury Secretary with their Chinese interlocutors and includes a big economic and trade dimension.

In Europe, we simply don't have a battering ram that good. We have lots of different teams milling around with small sticks. It's time to build a better battering ram.

The challenge for the European is that we're lobbying for market access piecemeal. Every country has its national effort, its 'special relationship', despite the fact that trade is actually an EU 'competence'. American states might have their own lobbying efforts – but the real heavy lifting breaking open the Chinese market is done by the US Trade Representative, reporting regularly on progress to Congress.

If trade is all about concessions, then let's remember we hold some great cards. China wants 'market access status' as soon as possible; that would mean easing up restrictions in a host of markets. We could set out a route-map to rapid agreement, so at least China knew what we were asking of it. Second, lots of EU countries find reasons to block Chinese investment; the rules of the game are not very clear. In the US, there's a clearing house for new investments called the Committee on Foreign Investment in the United States (CFIUS). We could create one in Europe as part of a new investment agreement which monitored Chinese investment and any blocks put in place by EU countries.

Third, the Chinese rightly complain about European trade barriers like the EU's vast agricultural subsidies for European farmers and agricultural tariffs. We should commit to simplifying them in return for trade concessions. Fourth, the EU needs to rationalise the endless number of dialogues on this and that and make sure there is a clear, powerful, single official leading on trade negotiations plus a political summit each year to break through the deal blockers. That's how the Americans do it, and it's a pretty good model.

Our model would need to be different. But, frankly, if the quartet of the President of France, the German Chancellor, the British Prime Minister and the President of the European Commission found one day a year to sit down together to talk about European access to China and then take the conversation to their Chinese counterparts: we would move an awfully long way.

Finally, all of this needs reporting to national and European parliaments along with a report on Chinese compliance with WTO obligations, just like that produced by the US Trade Representative, so that we debate this stuff far more frequently. When the report comes to the UK, our own government should publish a position statement and lead a debate in the Commons.

Lessons from Germany

But in our pursuit of 'cracking China' there is one case-study that we should study much harder: Germany. The great surprise of writing this book has been the discovery of the extraordinary relationship now unfolding between Germany and China. A Chinese economist working in London put it to me like this;

> When you listen to Chinese officials talk about Germany they say: 'We have this history of investing in Germany. We understand Germany. We understand German labour laws.' In Britain, the lack of understanding cuts both ways; Chinese don't understand Britain and Britain doesn't understand China. In Germany and America people not only keep up

to speed, but they keep ahead. They analyse where things went wrong in the past, and how to do things differently in the future.

The German success in China is simply mind-blowing: fully 47% of European exports to China are from Germany.[217] Whereas our Prime Minister has set a target of increasing UK–China trade to £60 billion by 2015, the German target for 2015 is *three times* that figure: £180 billion.[218] In think-tank land they talk of a German–China 'special relationship'.[219]

Now, Germany does happen to make the kind of stuff that China needs. In 2008, China imported $1.13 trillion of goods: 78% ($880 billion) was machinery and electrical and hi-tech products.[220] These imports were either sophisticated machinery to upgrade its production lines or high-end components for its huge machinery and electrical exports. These are markets where Germany is strong.

But we would be deluding ourselves if we thought German success was an accident of its industrial structure. The Germans have quite simply invested harder and longer in building relation-ships abroad and making changes at home to position themselves for China's advance.

For instance, in June 2012 Chinese Premier Wen Jiabao came to Berlin *with 13 ministers* to hold what was in effect a joint cabi-net meeting with Germany.[221] China hasn't done this with any other EU member state.

To understand this better I took a detour in Berlin to go and meet the people who toil away in the engine room of the German–China relationship: the German chambers of commerce.

Visiting the Deutscher Industrie – ie. Deutscher Industrie-und Handelskammertag, the Association of German Chambers of Commerce and Industry, in its magnificent polished granite, glass and steel headquarters on Breite Straße in Berlin is like step-ping into a huge, modern government department. Indeed, my contact welcomed me with a laugh as we crossed the huge atrium behind Reception: 'this is a little like stepping into a ministry'.

Every German business has to be a member of a chamber of commerce and the national association pulls together 80 local chambers, representing millions of members 'from the kiosk owner on the corner to the international automotive group'.

I wanted to pin down some of the secrets of the German–China relationship, and it quickly became clear that the relationship today is the fruit of an awful lot of work over a very, very long time. The instinct to export is part of German business DNA. Open the business pages of a paper and you'll see sales reported at home – and abroad – as a matter of course.

'We were very lucky', said my contact, who helps run the Asia-Pacific team. 'We've had a number of Chancellors – Kohl, Schröder, Merkel – who all took the relationship incredibly seri-ously and devoted time to it.' That has helped build not only a reputation as a serious partner, but serious institutional relation-ships with China's powerful National Reform and Development Commission and Ministry of Commerce, MofCom. MofCom's director for Europe used to be stationed in Berlin.

The long engagement of German leaders reflects a high German comfort level in doing business in China. 'We have a tradition of being there.' It's a cultural affinity that German busi-nesses don't share with, say, India or Japan.

Nurturing this relationship today is an incredibly well-or-ganised business of exchange. In many towns and cities across Germany, the great physical symbols of the export culture are the *Messen*, the trade exhibition halls in which German export-ers show off their wares. German chambers of commerce have worked hard to make sure that plenty of Chinese buyers flow through the *Messen*, and Premier Wen's opening of the great Hannover Messe in 2012 was a great coup.

The Germans work hard at the business of trade representation in Asia too. Germany's chambers of commerce fund three offices in China, which provides a first port of call for advice for visiting German exporters, whether small or large. Every two years, the two-day Germany–China business conference brings together over 700 chief executives and decision makers. 'It's a must to be there', I was told. In the break-out sessions and lunch-breaks, German industry leaders and Chinese ministers get an awful lot done.

The visits of Germany's chancellor then provide an extra push. But what's striking is how much preparation goes into them. Months ahead of time, a call goes out to Chamber members for issues to raise and applications to join the trip. The Chamber's Asia-Pacific team then carefully winnows down who might have the most to gain by joining Germany's leader; issue papers are commissioned and then boiled down to a series of one-pagers for the chancellor to negotiate with China's premier. At the core of it all is the Chamber's Asia-Pacific team with a governing committee run by some of Germany's most senior business people: Siemens, Bosch, BASF all provide chief executives or chairmen who are seriously engaged in the committee's work, give it serious time, and lever in resources and networks to advance its work.

I'm afraid it knocks our efforts into a cocked hat. The sooner we study just how Germany has succeeded, and bring our own efforts into line, the better.

But this is merely the first part of our work. There is a second win-win that lies open to us. To become China's partners in the pioneering business.

CHAPTER 10

China's innovation challenge

Monday 25 June 2012 was a remarkable day for China's booming science scene.[222]

Miles above *the surface of the planet, the crew of the Shenzhou-9 sp*acecraft including Major Liu Yang, China's first female astronaut, executed their final routines and docked with the Tiangong-1 space lab module, completing China's mastery of the three key space procedures needed to launch a moon mission in 2017 and a space station in 2020.

Meanwhile, over four miles below the surface of the sea, the crew of the submarine Jialong reached the bottom of its fourth dive, deep into the Mariana Trench in the western Pacific to complete a feat surpassed only by the US, Japan, France and Russia. Between space and the ocean depths, the crews of the Jialong and the Shenzhou exchanged messages of good luck and congratulations in a wonderful – and very public – demonstration of China's determination to become one of the globe's leading science powers.

But the best pointer to China's tech leadership isn't in space or the deep ocean. It's in Zhongguancun, the university quarter in north-east Beijing now home to malls of electronic and big-tech businesses, research centres and hundreds of start-ups.

Back in 1997, Zhongguancun's 'technology park' was a village with a couple of buildings and some entrepreneurs hustling for government contracts and hiring students from Tsinghua University, China's equivalent of MIT. Today, thanks to its close links to government, media, and the best universities, Zhongguancun is a boom-town. It's home to R&D centres for every major global tech business: Nokia, Ericsson, Motorola, Sony, Microsoft, IBM, Sun and Oracle. More and more believe this could be the world's next Silicon Valley.

Annual conferences like ChinICT, founded seven years ago by French technologist Jules Quartly, are now showcases of not foreign but Chinese talent, including China's three tech giants – Baidu (China's Google), Alibaba (eCommerce) and Tencent (social networking) – collectively known as BAT. During Bo Xilai's downfall, the best source of gossip and rumour became Sina Weibo, China's equivalent of Twitter. It boasts 140 million users and is aiming to be China's Facebook by creating a social networking platform that is host to hundreds of third-party applications from online gaming to messaging to virtual currency.[223]

China's tech sector now sends businesses to float on America's Nasdaq stock market faster than anyone else. There are more Chinese companies listed on Nasdaq than companies from any other nation bar America.[224] Renren (another Facebook wannabe) raised $743 million last year. Jiayuan, a dating site, raised $80 million days later. Many of America's leading venture capitalists now hang out on college campuses in China, much as they did at Harvard and Stanford at the end of the 1990s. China's domestic venture industry is growing fast and invests in US ideas to re-import. Chinese venture firms backed 28 US start-ups in 2011 – double the number of the year before[225] – and Chinese-born entrepreneurs are creating incubators like Inno-Spring in Silicon Valley.

China's tech boom has now convinced the world's tech industry that something big is afoot. In a recent survey of global technology executives, nearly half (43%) said they believed the tech innovation centre of the world will move from Silicon Valley in the next four years; nearly a third (30%) said they expect it to move to China.[226] KPMG's Head of Technology, Tudor Aw, explained why: 'China today has a highly competitive education system which produces a vast pool of talent. It has fostered an environment which encourages the development of disruptive technologies and we simply can't ignore any more what's coming around the corner.'

The country's software sector has grown over 20-fold since 2000. It already exports $14 billion of software.[227] By 2015, the goal is $60 billion.

And Zhongguancun in Beijing is but one of China's tech hubs; Shanghai, Dalian, Hangzhou, Xian and Chengdu can all boast big tech sectors. Shenzhen is home to Tencent, China's largest social networking site with some 450 million registered users and number five in the world for hours spent on a website. Hangzhou is home to Alibaba, China's eCommerce empire.

China's 'Steve Jobs problem'

Yet for all the advances online, in space, or under the ocean, China's leaders know their country has got to become more innovative still.

To grow long term, a country has to be home to innovators. The Nobel laureate Michael Spence recently explained it like this: 'Innovation is new knowledge that is applied to add value by creating new products, by creating new production techniques or by lowering costs. It doesn't just appear magically out of the blue. It has to be created.'[228]

But China has an innovation problem.

One of the people who have thought about this a lot is Will Hutton, who pointed ahead to the change of course now under way in China in his book The Writing on the Wall.[229] Will and I discovered our mutual interest in China when we wound up in a bar together at Oslo airport waiting for a delayed flight back to London along with Will's excellent research assistant, Philippe Schneider.

Will's argument is simple: good institutions are vital if China is to become a truly innovative country. In the West, we have them. In China they don't. And that's a problem for China. For us in the West, these institutions – 'the rule of law, the independence of the judiciary, the freedom of the press, the scientific and research processes in independent universities, or the very idea of idea of representative, accountable, checked and balanced government', and above all an idea of a public realm and tradition of debate – 'all these flowed from the great intellectual, philosophic and political wellspring that we call the Enlightenment'.[230] For 'Decision making needs the grit in the oyster – the passionate dissenter who with institutional safeguards can oppose an emerging consensus and force the group to re-evaluate what it is doing. It needs, in short, genuine pluralism.'[231]

This emphasis on good 'institutions' is perhaps the most important lesson that development economists and economic historians have drawn from, on the one hand, the catastrophic failure of 'shock therapy' in Russia and eastern Europe, when a brand of market fundamentalism was rapidly introduced to former communist countries, and, on the other, the study of why over the last 300 years the West appeared to industrialise first.[232]

When Dani Rodrik and Arvind Subramanian[233] explored the role of geography,[234] trade and institutions (especially property rights and the rule of law) in explaining income differences between countries, they found *institutions* are the key – the 'only positive and significant determinant of income levels'; indeed, 'once institutions are controlled integration [into the global economy] has no direct effect on incomes while geography has at best weak direct effects'.

The lessons of history appear even starker. Good institutions are critical to good science – and rapid innovation. It is not simply the case that 'necessity is the mother of invention'.[235] Traditional societies might produce an inventive individual, but, as economic historian Joel Mokyr put it, 'what makes ... [innovators] implement, improve and adapt new technologies or just devise small improvements in the way they carry out their daily work depends on the institutions and the attitudes around them'.[236]

When societies lack effective institutions, then innovation and invention fail to flourish, or the pace of change slows to a snail's pace – as it did in Islamic societies after the golden age of learning (750–1100), pre-Tokugawa Japan (before 1603), or China after the advent of the Ming dynasty (1368–1644).

China today is wrestling with an innovation – and institution – problem that is not new or a simply a symptom of one-party rule. It is arguably 500 years old. By the end of the 1700s, astute Western observers were noting that while China was mighty, it was also mightily undynamic. In 1776, Adam Smith wrote 'China seems to have been long stationary', and pin-pointed China's isolation as the force that had cut off the nation from innovation. Smith was right. Economic historians today now point to the crucial years after the Yongle Emperor's death as a turning point in China's history.

By the end of the 11th century, China's technology was prodigious. It had produced an astronomical clock and 150,000 tons of iron – as much as all of Europe five centuries later.[237] When the Yongle Emperor took the throne in the early 15th century, he not only built Beijing, he dispatched his admirals to Africa and commissioned a compendium of Chinese learning so great it filled 11,000 volumes, an encyclopaedia unsurpassed until the advent of Wikipedia in 2007.[238]

Yet after his death, the foreign expeditions were forbidden; the iron foundries, once among the most technologically advanced in the world, were left to rot; the records of foreign ventures were destroyed; conflict and epidemics multiplied.[239] China wasn't standing still; it was marching west:[240] great swathes of today's western China were brought into cultivation, paved roads and iron bridges were driven through the southwest; Tibet, Nepal, Burma were added to its dominions.[241] No other empire – not the Moguls in India nor the Ottomans in the Middle East – had the same scope for 'internal' expansion. But the effect was to cut the country off from sources of invention and innovation overseas.

The phenomenal growth of the last few decades has not come about primarily by unlocking the institutions of science but through radical liberalisation of the market economy on the one hand and, on the other, through what Will Hutton called, in a phrase I rather like, 'Leninist corporatism': the use of state control to direct vast amounts of savings into business investment in infrastructure and SOEs.[242]

As China moves into the next stage of its economic development it desperately needs its economy to become far more innovative and productive. Today, China's patent record is thin. Two-thirds of China's 800,000 research scientists and researchers work in government laboratories, and research spending is characterised as 'rule by man rather than rule by merit'.[243]

But the bigger challenge is a huge state-owned sector which has become a drag-anchor, burning cash and delivering a pretty poor rate of return.

Between 1995 and 2005, the number of SOEs in China halved from 300,000 to 150,000 as smaller firms were gobbled up into bigger, more powerful outfits. A strategy of 'grasp the big and let go of the small' means the state's share of manufacturing is lower than its share of other strategic industries (e.g. IT, transport, energy, mining, telecoms, construction) but those in state hands enjoy a myriad of advantages: preferred access to bank loans and below-market interest rates from a banking sector dominated by state banks, favourable tax treatment, public investment and big government contracts.[244] Sinopec (petroleum), China Telecom, China Southern (airlines) and Chinalco (aluminium) are all good examples of giant firms enjoying huge loans, capital investments, tax savings or priority access to resources.[245]

Figures are hard to pin down, but a study for the US–China Economic and Security Review Commission concluded that nationalised firms probably make up *half* of economic output and employ perhaps a third of the urban workforce.[246] About 300 great holding companies (90% owned centrally and 10% owned locally) own and control some 100,000 subsidiaries plus many more shareholdings in listed companies.[247]

These nationalised firms are, by and large, nowhere near productive enough, hog bank lending, thereby keeping it from small, entrepreneurial firms, and hoard cash rather than invest it. At least one in five lose money. Total factor productivity growth is only about two-thirds of the rate of the private sector; little is spent on R&D and these firms' labour productivity is 4% that of the US.[248] One in three of their workforce is estimated to be structurally idle.[249] Some estimate that these 'market distortions' cost the economy 10% of GDP in lost efficiency.[250] Overall, they are now only making (after-tax) returns of 3.2%, which is less than the cash would make parked in a bank. The result, according to some economists, is that the additional output produced by investing one extra dollar is now lower than it was in the days of Mao.[251]

Nationalised firms, however, are now more, not less, important than they were ten years ago because they became the saline drip which the government used to pump investment into the economy during the global crash. Investments by centrally controlled firms went up *42-fold* in the last four years to more than $1.7 trillion in 2011.[252] Government researchers now admit that the massive expansion has concealed poor-quality assets. When I stopped off at an expert economics think-tank in Beijing in early 2012, they were absolutely damning. They refused to be quoted publicly, but they were absolutely clear that nationalised firms were becoming a dead-weight.

By contrast, the 'free market' bit of the equation is roaring ahead; China's 431,000 small and medium-sized enterprises generate two-thirds of industrial output, pay two-thirds of taxes, and employ three-quarters of the workforce.[253]

This innovation crisis is a huge opportunity for an innovative, entrepreneurial nation like Britain. But we need to get our act together. Fast. Because the Chinese super-tanker is starting to turn.

If Adam Smith were writing today he wouldn't be exploring the magic of the division of labour in pin factories. He would be studying 'Foxconn City' in Guangzhou.[254]

Employing 230,000 employees, many of whom work 12 hours a day, six days a week, Foxconn City is the hub for Foxconn's business manufacturing some 200 million iPhones and iPads. Indeed, the company now assembles 40% of the world's consumer electronics devices.

When Apple was refining some final improvements to its ground-breaking technology in mid-2007, including scratch-resistant glass, Foxconn assembled thousands of workers to start putting the products together. In the middle of the night.

Engineering teams to guide 20,000 assembly workers that Apple's analysts thought would take nine months to assemble in the US took Foxconn in China just 15 days.

For all the challenges China wrestles with around innovation, we have to wake up to the innovation juggernaut that is coming our way.

It is true that Chinese R&D is still a state-dominated affair. But it is vast. The Chinese Academy of Sciences (CAS) sits at the top of the tree, overlooking research universities with more than one hundred national research institutes, each of which might contain dozens of labs. Together these organisations employ some 60,000 people. Individual ministries like the Ministry of Industry and Information Technology sponsor another 658 industrial or military–industrial laboratories. Regional government controls a further 3,000 industrial bureaux.

Together this created a system that didn't encourage much diffusion until it was somewhat marketised in the 1980s. Now, these changes have created a mixed R&D economy employing around 1 million people spending approximately $136 billion – the second highest figure in the world.[255]

The system is still fraught with inefficiencies and 'stove-piping'. Critically, it has not been able to solve what some Chinese call their 'Steve Jobs problem'. On the occasion of Mr Jobs's death, many in China asked themselves, 'Why don't we have our own Steve Jobs?'

Leading this critique, however, is none other than the leader of China. On the launch of China's twelfth five-year plan, Premier Wen hardly pulled his punches when he wrote in the party journal Qiushi that

Chinese capacity for indigenous innovation is weak, that Chinese industrial technology is at a low level and that both Chinese basic and cutting-edge research are relatively unimpressive … the Chinese science and technology system is incompatible with the needs of economic and technology development.[256]

When President Hu recently spoke to the country's two top think tanks, the Chinese Academies of Sciences (CAS) and Engineering (CAE), he said the key to fostering economic growth was nurturing 'home-grown' innovation, and called for 'more scientific, vigorous and efficient' methods for fast-tracking innovative ideas into business.[257]

Be under no illusions: China is now squarely focused on a shift from manufacturing products invented elsewhere to becoming a country with an integrated economy that can invent, develop and manufacture products based on Chinese intellectual property.

The twelfth five-year plan, published in 2011, identified weak innovation capacity, loose links with industry, a shortage of high-level personnel, poor allocation of resources and a 'disorder in the prevailing institutional mechanisms'. But it also set out an ambition to master seven strategic industries[258] where Chinese leaders believe there will be revolutionary change within the next decade, with a goal of tripling, from 5% to 15%, the contribution these industries make to Chinese GDP by 2020. China now wants to become an 'innovation nation' by 2020 and a global scientific power by 2050.[259]

The five-year plan ambition was then followed by the medium- and long-term plan published in summer 2012, which I think history might prove to be as seminal a reform as the abolition of the Corn Laws in England and the advent of the American System in the early-19th-century United States.

China's goal is now to 'create an environment for encouraging innovation independently, promote enterprises to become the main body of making technological innovation and strive to build an innovative-type country' in which China will 'master core technologies'[260] in a shift from the *shanzhai* economy, which basically mimics foreign technology, to the *gongjian* economy, where China conquers, as in battle or conflict, on its own terms.

Right now, the US remains the world's leading science and innovation nation. America spends some $400 billion a year on R&D. China's budget of $141 billion in 2010 (about 12% of the world's total) is a long way behind. But China is aiming for a *gigantic* leap in spending, from 1.75% of GDP to 2.2% in 2015. What's that worth in real money? $2.16 trillion over five years. Business R&D intensity already surpasses EU-15 levels.[261]

Adding booster rockets to the power of this spending is a huge push in engineering education: 30% of Chinese students graduate in engineering; that compares to 4% in America. China now produces more first university degrees in natural sciences and engineering than Japan, South Korea, the US, Taiwan, France and Germany. Put together.[262]

The results are already extraordinary. In 2008, China was ranked fifth in the Science Citation Index. China now accounts for 19% of the world's hi-tech manufacturing, up from 3% in 1998. Its trade balance in hi-tech goods was $155 billion in 2010 and it boasts as many offshore R&D centres for US multinational firms as Europe: 1,300 of them. It is already the world's leading producer of solar panels, wind turbines and, soon, lithium ion batteries. Surveying China's low-emission coal-energy plants, third- and fourth-generation nuclear reactors, high-voltage transmission lines, alternative-energy vehicles, solar- and wind-energy devices and high-speed trains, all more advanced than those in the US, Energy Secretary Steven Chu said it was a Sputnik moment for America.

Crucially, China's leaders have recognised the limitations of state-sponsored 'centrally planned' research. Far more money is being moved directly into the market or to local and regional government. In 2010, over 50% of money for science and technologies was placed with local government[263] – and now 70% of national R&D is undertaken by around 36,000 industrial enterprises.[264] The 'enterprise sector' now employs nearly 1.5 million R&D experts. Ten universities are targeted to become 'world class' early in the 21st century, with 100 institutions raised to international levels.[265]

What's more, China's leaders have available some tried and tested methods to develop the strategic industries they've prioritised.

Take telecoms equipment. Here China provides two global leaders, Huawei and ZTE. Both grew over the years by being allowed to compete with China's state firms; to develop partnerships with government R&D labs; to secure low-interest bank loans (for example, in 2004, a $10 billion credit line from the China Development Bank and $600 million from the Export–Import Bank of China to support 'going out' – i.e. 'going global') and contracts from Chinese telecoms providers.

Or take solar energy. Chinese panel manufacturers received $20 billion in 2010 in loans from the China Development Bank; have been offered tariff and tax incentives and support from 16 R&D centres. China is now a leading manufacturer of renewable-energy equipment, and the industry's sponsoring ministry is about to invest $14.7 billion in electric car-makers.

This progress should tell us that it's complacent for us to think 'We don't need to worry. We're great at inventing things and the Chinese aren't.'

The US Congress does a far better job than Parliament, in my opinion, of studying events in China, and a brilliant report to Congress published recently summarised China's strategy: 'speeding up the construction of an innovation system that takes enterprises as the centre, the market as guide, with commercialisation and research interwoven'.[266]

That is going to have profound consequences.

Robert Atkinson is an expert in the evolution of Chinese business. In his testimony to Congress in spring 2012,[267] he put it like this:

> The Chinese are practicing what would be called absolute advantage. They want to be good at everything and they have a conscious strategy to do that.
>
> The Chinese aren't very good at first-to-world innovation. They didn't invent the iPhone. They don't invent a lot of brand new things. We do ... But I think there is a second component of innovation which is equally if not more important and that's what you would call 'innovation adaptation', taking something and then adding to it.

His colleague Danny Breznitz, Associate Professor at the Georgia Institute of Technology, again testifying before Congress in spring 2012, takes up the argument. Chinese firms, he argues, have become masters of 'design for production'.

> By mastering this skill, they have ensured a continued advantage in manufacturing unrelated to low cost labour ... China's capabilities in production and large markets as well as political commitment afford it strong advantages in deploying new technologies developed elsewhere at scale ... It is in deployment stage, especially large-scale deployment that many of the most important opportunities for innovation, improvement and learning occur ... Chinese technology companies shine by developing quickly enough to remain at the cusp of the global technology frontier without actually advancing the frontier itself.[268]

Sometimes that innovation might follow breakthroughs in the West within a matter of weeks – and in fact American venture capitalists investing in China are one of the fastest routes for innovation transfer.

This scale of investment and ambition is already completely changing the competitive environment of major innovation-based businesses.

Take aerospace. The head of Boeing is very blunt. China's efforts to build aircraft means the end of the old duopoly between Boeing and Airbus.

Or take the automotive business. Kevin Wale, president of GM China, recently argued: 'What China does better than any place on earth is to innovate by commercialisation, as opposed to constant research and perfecting the theory like the West.'[269]

Or take advanced IT manufacturing. Andy Grove, the founder of Intel, now argues that countries which are good at production technologies soon become good at innovation.[270] And indeed it isn't always innovation which commands the premium; novel innovation might one day become another commodity bought and sold in the global marketplace.

He's right. Lots of the innovation into different parts of an iPhone is now conducted in China. This is the point that struck me. Henry Ford didn't invent the car. But he built a pretty incredible business figuring out how to make them. Foxconn didn't invent the iPhone. But they're building an incredible business building them.

This point was underlined for me by the leader of a very large UK business with first-hand knowledge of growing the firm's business in China:

> People investing in China purely to export are getting it wrong.

For our business it is the absolutely critical market. It's all about the demand growth and it's where the innovation is going to be.

We would be in China even if we didn't sell anything in China because we're going to learn more there than anywhere else. There is just such change under way; for example, with the growth of the new middle class who have to live somewhere and move around and consume things, China has to solve a series of problems at a speed and on a scale that no other country is going to experience. And we want to be part of solving those problems.

The key question is how we partner with China globally. We have then to do it and we have to be clear about how we're going to continue to compete.

So we have to think: What is our competitive advantage? What does China really need, and then how are we going to sell it? There's a side to China that would wipe us off the earth and that would be bad for them. But to figure this out and get it right, Britain has to be far more joined up.

So what are our competitive advantages? I don't think that we have many. Education is one; healthcare is another. We're good at building a services economy. We're a post-colonial power. We're not the US and we're not a threat. We have both smallness and personality. We have a certain creativity. We can innovate: but we have to know how to capture that value for ourselves.

I'm afraid there is a lot of truth in that, as easy as it is for me to say. I think the key is to remember that as the century unfolds we will have as much to learn from China as China will have from us – if not more. Alex Wilson from Flamingo Research said something which I found very striking:

I wrote a big trends report for a Japanese client recently and I tried to explain the difference between invention and innovation. Take the neon sign. Someone recently found a neon light in an American fair from 1904 – yet the technology was not invented until 1910. The French had got the title because they had actually put it into a commercial sign.

This is what we need to understand better in Britain. We invented cricket, we invented football, and we think that gives us some kind of claim to say how it should be done. Actually today invention doesn't count for so much. Of course it's important but just as important is what the Chinese do, which is iterate and proliferate.

Take the example of the Chinese high-speed train. When it was unveiled last year there was a big uproar in Japan, who said 'they've stolen our technology'. But they hadn't. The Chinese train went 100km/h faster than the Japanese bullet-train. If they had stolen it, it would have gone at the same speed.

The Chinese are able to innovate creating things that are faster and operate at scale. You see this in lots of forms of technology. Sina Weibo is a good example. The idea [of Twitter] is mimicked but the execution is better. It's got functional improvements. When you reply you start a conversational thread. It's got video software built in.

We're old fashioned in the way we want to hold on to things. The Chinese have a culture of iteration. We should be learning from the way Chinese work. That'd be a big step forward for us.

The example of the Chinese high-speed train is a fascinating case-study of the dilemma the world's businesses now confront in doing business in China.[271] In 2011, China's state-owned train-maker, CSR Corporation, unveiled in Shandong a beautiful, sleek high-speed train with a design inspired by an ancient Chinese sword. Built in plastic reinforced with carbon fibre and magnesium alloy, it is light and very, very fast.

But the train's launch came amid anger in Japan as Tadaharu Ohashi, Chairman of Japan's Kawasaki Heavy Industries Ltd, threatened legal action if there was any evidence of violation of contracts signed between Japan and China. Back in 2004, Kawasaki transferred technology for its famous Shinkansen bullet train to China to help create a 200km/h train which CSR Corporation built in partnership with them, a train called CRH2. China's Ministry of Railways rapidly – and crossly – dismissed the claims, accusing the Japanese of a 'lack of confidence'. Counter-attacking, Chinese officials argued[272] that China's CNR Corporation Ltd and the China Academy of Railway Sciences had been filing patent applications abroad since 2009 covering train assembly, hulls and bogies. More important, argued the Chinese, their train was just a lot better than Japan's: 'What China did in boosting rail speed from 250km/h to 350km/h is important and similar to progress made when Japan raised train speed, enlightened by European technology, from 100km/h to 200km/h.'

He Huawu, Chief Engineer with the Ministry of Railways, said the organisations and individuals that have participated in the government-sponsored R&D high-speed rail technology include 25 key universities, 11 first-class research institutes, 51 state-level labs and engineering research centres, 63 academicians, more than 500 professors, more than 200 researchers and more than 10,000 engineering personnel in China. China's application and resources is something we're going to find it harder and harder to compete with.

So we need to figure out how we collaborate. And we don't have much time.

CHAPTER 11

How China and Britain become partners in pioneering

The British pavilion at the Shanghai Expo was a stunning production, created by British designer Thomas Heatherwick. When I visited in 2010, I was with a cross-party delegation of MPs and I think it is fair to say the cutting-edge design was not to everyone's taste. A Conservative MP was heard to exclaim: 'Good God! It looks like a cross between a skate park and a stealth bomber!'

He had a point. But the British pavilion was carefully designed to target a big problem that Britain has in China. We are not seen as innovative, creative or entrepreneurial.

As part of their prep for the Shanghai Expo, British civil servants commissioned some very interesting research among Chinese people to explore their impressions of Britain. The results were fascinating. This is what the report said: 'Participants in all the focus groups overwhelmingly saw the UK as a traditional place. Common images described and discussed by groups often focused on tweed-clad people enjoying afternoon tea in beautiful gardens.'

The pace of life was seen as gentle and everyone had a lot of leisure time. Icons that came to mind ranged from the Queen to Big Ben to James Bond to David Beckham to Shakespeare. Older Chinese did tend to see the UK as a leading country. The under-thirties certainly did not. Britain was not associated with new technologies or thought of as a creative or cutting-edge kind of place. Britain's industrial heritage, automotive and arms industries all rang bells. But heritage. Tradition. The past. Well-preserved old buildings, beautiful gardens and people behaving like gentlemen. That was what leapt out.[273]

China's thirst for innovation creates a wonderful opportunity for the UK. It's a win-win like no other. We *are* an innovative country. We're a creative place. We're entrepreneurial. And China's rise creates a huge opportunity not only for hi-tech exports and our education system but crucially for us to develop firms together that combine our respective strengths into businesses that will beat all comers in the huge East Asian marketplace of two billion and beyond.

But it's not going to happen by accident. The invisible hand of the marketplace won't deliver an 'inter-dependence in innovation'. A few 'visible hands' are going to be needed, first and foremost, to foster a lot more demand in China for partnering with Britain. Second, we need more to offer. Here at home we need to do far more to make sure we are absolutely one of the world's innovation hot-spots. And third, we need to radically rethink the way we create new networks between our great city-hubs, with our universities at the centre.

Becoming a partner of choice

It's pretty clear that if we're to become China's partners in pioneering, then we need to work harder on our reputation, and therefore the level of trust between us. Relationships are built on trust and while our 'trust foundations' in China are not bad, they need to be a lot bigger.

One of the people who have thought about this a lot is Martin Davidson, Chief Executive of the British Council and a man with an unusual honour: he was one of the last Colonial Officers recruited by the civil service to work in Hong Kong – in 1979.

Just before the Olympics got under way, I caught up with Martin at the Council's HQ just off the Mall. The idea that the Foreign Office was still recruiting Colonial Officers 30 years ago is perhaps why Martin's starting point was the legacy of Britain's history:

> Don't underestimate the impact of our history. It is still very real. Before the big Tony Blair visit [in 1998], we had to organise a few mega-events and we did some focus groups to help get them right. I'll never forget one young woman who was very positive about Britain but then at the end said: 'But I can't forget that you were responsible for the Opium wars.'

I would hazard that very few people in Britain know much about the Opium Wars. In China, the story is at the heart of the new National Museum. Launched in March 2011 replete with ground-breaking technology and architecture, it opens with an exhibition entitled 'The Road to Rejuvenation' which is all about the British-led 'century of humiliation'.

Yet our history and sense of tradition, argues Martin, represent an opportunity because like the Chinese, we treasure them:

> Some of our history is on the negative side but we're actually hugely attractive in China. They pride themselves on being a 2,000- or a 5,000-year-old civilisation depending

who you're talking to. What they appreciate is a society that renews itself against a background of tradition.

This is the key point: as I listened I realised this explains much of the fascination with Britain that I'd encountered in Chinese politicians. This tradition and the culture built on it, around our language, our education system and our creativity, is what gives us a gigantic opportunity to build trust and, crucially, relevance. Martin continued:

> Look at what China is trying to do with its economy. They're obsessed with becoming IP creators. I think that means there's a range of opportunities for fusion [between Britain and China] – education, skills, creativity, technology. That's part of their ambition, their future.
>
> So the issue for us is how are we going to partner?
>
> One of the things we have to be is attractive. We have to be clear on why Britain, rather than France. What attracts them is our great assets, our language, our education, our way of life. We need to invest much more in attracting and engaging China with this.

The British Council's research has now pointed to just how trust can be fostered through a brush with our language and culture. The deeper the immersion, the deeper the trust.

Ahead of the Olympics, the Council commissioned market researchers Ipsos Mori to explore the question in detail. Mori found that people taking UK qualifications, developing English skills, experiencing UK arts or studying in the UK are *far* more likely to trust the UK and aim to visit or do business with us. The greater the trust, the greater the level of interest in doing business with us.

In China, the UK and Germany both enjoy a strong 'trust' head start over the Americans; asked a straight question about how much you trust someone from the UK, Germany and America, the British Council found that, net,[274] 50% of young people trust people from Britain and Germany; only 10% trust Americans. Chinese who trust the UK are far more likely to have a positive view of our education system, social institutions, scientific research, contemporary arts and culture scene – and opportunities for business and trade. But trust and culture are intimately entwined; nearly 60% of Chinese who have had some kind of cultural contact with Britain trust people from our country. That's 15% higher than those who haven't enjoyed any kind of cultural contact.

The British Council's research pinpoints four key ways in which trust can be fostered: learning English; building friendships and personal connections with people in Britain; gaining some kind of direct experience of the UK, our people and culture through, for example, exchange programmes, especially visiting Britain; and meeting people from Britain who are open and tolerant and respect difference.

And beyond the office, the lab and the classroom are cultural spaces in China which are vastly expanding and which could create a huge new space for China and Britain to foster new connections. Martin again: 'Here they're opening a theatre a week. They're opening a cinema every day. But there's no educational system that educates people in that direction. No means of actually creating content. There's huge demand for this.'

Remaining a place with something to offer

I'm afraid, however, that, as hard as it sounds, relationship building is going to be the easy bit. The harder and far more important challenge is to make sure we remain somewhere with something to offer. I think merely a short introduction to China's ambitions to be a leading science power should be enough to convince us that we need to speed up our efforts to become one of the innovative places on the planet. Otherwise, we're simply not going to have enough to offer. There is no future for Britain as a low-pay, low-skill, low-innovation economy. On the contrary. We have to become one of the world's innovation hot-spots.

How we do this is a book in itself – and the man who has written the best one, for my money, is Lord Sainsbury, Chancellor of Cambridge University and Science Minister in the last Labour government.

David's perspective is rooted in an appreciation of how the world of production has radically changed over the last two decades of globalisation, in particular the way production has 'fragmented' so that for a single company R&D, design, supply management, production, distribution, logistics and after-sales support might all take place in different parts of the world.[275]

As David argues, this change has radically increased the speed of innovation; the Apple iPod, for instance, moved from concept to market rapidly because it integrated components already made by others.

This mega-shift has big consequences for us in the UK and the way we collaborate with countries like China:

> We simply can't compete on low wages and low costs. We have to go upstream and the things that China can't do.
>
> That means competing – and collaborating – on our ability to innovate.
>
> The idea that the world is flat is nonsense. The world of innovation is very 'spiky'. The conditions and environment for innovation have to be right. It has to be supportive

of enterprise. And government has a role. It's not about enterprise zones or reducing regulation. It's about education, infrastructure, investment, knowledge transfer and the quality of universities and science. If you think that the only thing that matters is cost, then you'll be trapped in a race to the bottom.

The right approach will vary by industry – but the basic mindset is simple: compete by innovating.

In every industry we should focus our innovation policies, our inward investment policies and our export promotion policies on those parts of the manufacturing chain where as a country we are most likely to be successful, that is the knowledge-intensive parts. In many cases this will be R&D and design and in other cases it will be the production process itself.

David is very clear about what we do next: we have to make industrial policy – or what David Sainsbury calls 'innovation policy' – a total focus for government.

It's only fair to say that industrial policy has a chequered past in the West.[276] But there are big reasons why, now, we have to embrace the idea.[277] Firstly, the financial crisis revealed we were too dependent in much of the West on taxes from financial services. Secondly, the market alone is not going to fund adoption of the combination of technologies we need to shift gear to lower carbon consumption. But, thirdly, our industries are now competing with the 'state capitalists' of China.[278]

Now Britain has become a far more innovative place over the last 10 years, as public investment in the science base has doubled to £6.3 billion in 2011, R&D tax credits support around £5 billion of spending, and the Technology Strategy Board invests over £300 million a year. Today we are one of the world's greatest science nations. We punch well above our weight. We rank second only to the US both in terms of the volume of research and the frequency of citations. Britons have won 112 Nobel prizes – second only to the US. We have eight UK universities in the global top 50, and our universities turn out more science and engineering PhD awards per head of population than any other country in the G7 group of richest industrialised nations.[279] Our research base is also much better interconnected globally. Far more of our science is produced in partnership with others; between 1996 and 2000, under a third of scientific publications were internationally co-authored; now the figure is 40%.[280] Over a third of science, technology, engineering and maths (STEM) doctorate students are from abroad.

We've also become much better at spinning out ideas from universities. University income from commercialising science doubled between 2001 and 2007 with spin-outs worth some £1.5 billion. Licensing agreements almost tripled between 2001 and 2006, and patents more than doubled.[281] UK universities now rival the best of the US.[282] Half of leading research investors now have R&D centres in the UK – second only to the US – and the UK accounts for around a third of the entire European venture industry.[283]

But none of this is enough to keep us at the world's cutting edge. Our businesses spend less on R&D than the OECD average.[284] We don't train enough scientists or engineers. We don't file enough patents. Venture finance is still too thin between the crucial £250,000 and £2 million level and, if you look at the global R&D scorecard, you'll see that Britain makes a significant contribution to that progress in just *three* sectors: pharmaceuticals, financial services and telecoms. We should be making more of our European culture, which is the origin of all Western science. We should be celebrating and strengthening our education system and elite institutions. We should be transforming the standards of our technical education.

And that's why we need to raise our game. And if we're to become good partners to China, I think there's one other nation where we can learn from what's been a technology miracle in the last 10 years: Israel.

Lessons from Israel

China's relationship with Israel has been increasingly rapidly. Although the countries disagree on some important political issues, the business and technology relationship has been growing fast. The two nations signed an important cooperation agreement in 2011, and Israel's exports to China are growing at around twice the rate of their exports to the US. It's not a surprise. In its search for innovation, China has immense respect for what it can learn from a country where, between 1996 and 2000, technology exports doubled from \$5.5 billion to \$13 billion, and then surged to over \$18 billion by 2008.[285]

Today, almost half of the world's technology companies have bought start-ups or opened R&D centres in the country and it now has the highest density of start-ups in the world (one for every 1,844 Israelis).[286] Between 2000 and 2005, foreign direct investment (FDI) in Israel tripled.[287] More Israeli companies are listed on the Nasdaq stock market than companies from all of Europe and, in 2008, 30 times more venture capital was invested per capita in Israel than in Europe.

In 2012, I was fortunate enough to explore this at first hand with an old friend of mine, Sir Trevor Chinn. Together with Jon Mendelsohn, Ed Balls and the team at Labour Friends of Israel we'd developed the idea of an Economic and Finance Dialogue between Britain, Israel and the Palestinian Authority, and on our first research trip I had the chance to quiz some of those who have watched Israel's extraordinary tech boom unfold.

Saul Singer is one of the authors of the brilliant book, Start-up Nation. A former journalist, he is now in demand all over the world from politicians and policy-makers keen to learn the lessons of Israel. In October 2012, he was kind enough to drop by for a cup of coffee and a chat in the dark-panelled Oak Room of Jerusalem's famous King David Hotel.

Israel now has the largest concentration of start-ups outside Silicon Valley and, per capita, two and half times as much venture capital investment. Now, Singer is the first to point out that there are lots of factors in Israel that are unique. The country itself is, in a sense, a start-up. The wave of immigration from Russia and eastern Europe after the fall of the Berlin Wall provided not only a huge injection of talent – 800,000 newcomers including many well-trained mathematicians and scientists – but a pool of ambitious newcomers who wanted to make the most of their new-found freedom. Immigrants are by and large highly entrepreneurial; half the start-ups in Silicon Valley were founded by immigrants. Second, Israelis share a culture of almost dogmatic questioning of authority inculcated by shared experience of military service in a defence force that of necessity fosters an independence of mind and personal responsibility for decisions. Elite units hire the best talent, invest heavily in training[288] and drum into recruits a sense, as Saul puts it, of 'how to combine a need not to fail and a need to take risks'.

But there's plenty we can learn from Start-up Nation, not least the way the Israelis have organised the root of all progress: money. And the organiser-in-chief of the money has been Israel's Chief Scientist.

Industry House, a rather 1970s-style tower block in the middle of Tel Aviv, is an unlikely epicentre for Israel's technology miracle. But as the home of Office of the Chief Scientist, it houses the institution that has perhaps done more than anything else to spark the start-up nation.

Today, the Chief Scientist is a young and incredibly bright former venture-capital partner, Avi Hasson, who explained to me over a sandwich just how the office has worked. Israel founded the office back in 1969, at a time, as Avi says, when 'Israel was only selling oranges to the world'. Today, the Chief Scientist is chief advisor on science to the Israeli cabinet and venture capitalist-in-chief.

'In the area of innovation, government has an inherent role to play. You can't optimise the role of innovation by leaving it to the market.' Government, argues Avi, has to make sure there's a decent infrastructure – good human capital, research institutes, labs – a sense of the country's social goals and, crucially, of risk-sharing:

> Risk sharing is inherent in the role of the office of Chief Scientist. Most R&D projects fail. It's sad but true. There-fore we've got to have a lot of these projects going on. Venture capitalists don't actually like risk. So we share it to make sure there's the right quantity of projects under way but also the really forward-looking stuff.

Avi's office has some $550 million to invest every year. Projects are put up to the office each month. He never provides 100% of the money – co-investors are important, and he doesn't earmark his budget in advance determining to back one sector or the other; it's the quality of the project, not the sector, that's important. What's impressive is just how much effort goes into making a decision. Over 120 experts are on the staff, screening and evaluating investment opportunities before they get to Avi's investment committee for decision. That must be a big part of why the system works; for every dollar he invests, two dollars of private-sector investment are levered in – and $5–10 of returns are generated for the economy. Some 3,000 companies apply for help each year, and chunks of money head into incubators and accelerators that foster new start-ups. The Chief Scientist always puts in money as debt, not equity, and is repaid by royalties of around 3% of a successful company's sales. About a quarter of the Office's budget is made up of royalties from successful companies backed in the past. In other words, the downside of a company failing is shared; the upside is given away to the private sector.

'If it's working', says Avi, 'we don't step in. We step in where we see there are failures. Risky is a good word in the room. We can handle risk.' If three-quarters of his investments succeed that's a sign that he's not taking enough risk.

A couple of things are fascinating about what the Chief Scientist has achieved. Firstly, 20% of the funds go into cross-national projects: Israel has 50 bilateral agreements with other countries, provinces and cities, and there are four cross-national funds with the US, Canada, South Korea and Singapore. Secondly, Israel has achieved a very clear sense of priority attached to innovation, shared between the parties: 'half of our exports are hi-tech and we're a very trade-orientated economy. If you meet the prime minister, he can talk intelligently about this stuff. I can genuinely say to you there is zero politics in what I do.'

China, as you might imagine, is all over Avi's office: 'China is our number one partner today; not just the federal level, but the provincial level, the city level. We can't contain them', he chuckles.

One of the most famous initiatives of the Chief Scientist's office was the creation of Israel's Yozma funds, a $100-million investment in 10 funds which have now grown to $4 billion and which revolutionised the Israeli venture industry. Yozma's investment brought together a foreign venture capital (VC) fund,

Israeli VCs and investment banks. The government provided a match of $1.50 for every $1 raised by the private sector, and offered pre-agreed buy-out rights. Between 1992 and 1997 $200 million was raised, and Yozma now manage $3 billion and support hundreds of new Israeli companies. Now there are around 45 Israeli VC firms.

Today, the Chief Scientist doesn't need to seed venture funds but is investing in many of the ideas these venture funds are finding, for the Yozma approach has helped fuel an ecosystem of venture funds, incubators and accelerators all over the country that help power Israeli innovation.

One of the best is Jerusalem Venture Partners (JVP), founded by serial entrepreneur Erel Margalit. Erel is an extraordinary guy. He grew up on a kibbutz, earned a PhD and served in the Special Forces before becoming an entrepreneur. Today, his fund is based at a complex of offices in the Old Mint of the British Mandate in Jerusalem, alongside Ottoman-era warehouses – the JVP Media Labs – which are home to a host of new businesses, a nightclub and social enterprise space.

Over a meal in Jerusalem, Erel set out what inspired him – and just why the approach has worked so well. 'I wanted to make a point. Here was this city, Jerusalem, where people came to study, not work. I wanted to change that.'

Back in the early 1990s, Erel had persuaded the then mayor of Jerusalem to create what became known as the 'Silicon Hills', a development park now home to scores of global R&D centres for some of the world's leading technology players. Land was put aside, a development authority set up, tax incentives created and the mayor was put on the road to sell Jerusalem to international investors. The offices for trade were sited next to the mayor's. 'He was', says Erel, 'a fantastic salesman. He could sell you an elephant in Jerusalem zoo. And frequently did. Our rallying cry was to sell all the lots on the mountain.' Seventy lots were sold including to companies like Intel, and soon the first hi-tech incubators arrived, to grow exponentially when the government's Yozma programme kicked in. At first, the funds were run by international VC firms like Advent, but now groups like Erel's have successfully raised round after round of financing – often from major US pension funds.

JVP now manages funds of some $900 million. When it finds a new company it likes the look of, it might give it a home in its media quarter offices and invest up to $1.5 million over 18 months getting it ready for its first proper round of investment; but crucially, in the first six months, the most risky phase of life, it invests alongside a $500,000 grant from the Chief Scientist's office. That's a big bit of risk taken care of.

And it's not just in media and hi-tech that this kind of approach is now at work; businesses like Rad BioMed in Tel Aviv are deploying the same kind of approach in biomedical research. The firm's tech scouts constantly hunt for new ideas in teaching hospitals and universities to find marketable ideas. Firms which might only employ one or two people are created in the accelerator labs. Rad BioMed might look at 150 ideas a year – and fund just two or three of them. Once an idea is tested to destruction, a bid is submitted to the Chief Scientist's fund with an aim of raising around $530,000. Rad BioMed might raise another 15% of that to fund the company getting something ready for market in 18 months. Since 1991, the fund has created some 150 start-ups with sales of over $1 billion.

The US and Israel have one of the most successful innovation relationships of any two countries in the world. There's a very clear value proposition. Israel is a small country. It doesn't have a lot of export opportunities in its own neighbourhood. The US is a world leader in IT and software with lots of customers and investors. But this is not a market operating with merely an invisible hand. The visible hand of government has helped a lot.

The results have been remarkable; of the 300 or so R&D centres in Israel, 80% are American. Saul Singer quotes the head of GE, Jeffrey Immelt: 'You guys are great at innovation and we're good at scaling up. Bring us your innovation and we'll scale it up.'[289]

I think this is an idea with big implications for Britain; we're good at invention. We're less good at start-ups. But we are good at trade, especially in Asia. In the years ahead I think there's big potential for British firms and universities to partner with countries like Israel developing ideas for the Chinese market.

One idea we should study hard is a programme that was incredibly far-sighted. Back in the 1990s, the US and Israel decided to create the Binational Industrial R&D programme – BIRD. Both Israel and the US invested some $30 million into a perpetual fund, and the interest each year was used to fund companies that drew on Israeli and US enterprise.

At dinner one night in Tel Aviv, its then director Ed Mlavsky told me it was at first a disaster. Then slowly but surely the fund began to find ideas that have produced over 300 Israeli–US companies. 'When I arrived', said Ed, 'the fund had been theoretically running for about eighteen months. There was only one problem. They weren't any projects!'

Key to the fund's success, said Ed, was understanding what would make a good marriage between and Israeli and US firms.

The 'recipe' Ed hit on was to find a US firm, publicly listed, with about $2–400 million in sales, that was growing quickly. The trick was to then entice them to engage with the BIRD programme and find them a suitable hi-tech partner in Israel. BIRD would fund 50% of joint project expenses incurred by both the US and the Israeli partner and then recoup the cash as a royalty on sales, limiting any pay-back to the BIRD fund at one and half times what it initially lent. So shared downside, but limited upside, as the jargon goes.

The results have been simply spectacular. By the time Ed left BIRD in 1992, it had invested around $100 million in 300 projects. Half the projects led to sales totalling $3 billion.[290]

To date $250 million has been invested in 780 projects that have produced over 300 Israeli–US companies creating $8 billion in direct and indirect sales[291] (three-quarters of Israeli firms that went public on Nasdaq had BIRD funding).

Hub to hub

Thinkers like David Sainsbury have pinpointed just how we can bring many of these lessons home: helping leading sectors sustain global positions; stimulating training; making sure that emerging technologies become the growth sectors of tomorrow. We often think that we don't have many 'levers' to pull; but we do. Her Majesty's government buys in goods and services each year worth some £150 billion – that's 12% of GDP. Government accounts for 55% of all UK spend on IT and 30% of construction. We spend £9 billion a year on universities and a further £1 billion through the Technology Strategy Board. These are pretty big levers.

Once upon a time, one of the key institutions in British government was the Board of Trade, coordinating policy of a far-flung trading empire. Today, there's a very good case for not a new Board of Trade but a Board of Innovation. Yet I can't help thinking that the epicentre of our new innovation relationship is not actually going to be Whitehall or Westminster; it will be in Britain's regions.

'The locus of innovation', says David Sainsbury,

is at the regional level where workers, companies, universities, research institutions and government meet more directly. Regions are the building blocks of national innovation capacity because they offer the proximity vital for collaborative relationships and can provide the specialised assets such as research institutes that enable companies to develop their innovative potential.[292]

He is completely right. If we are to become *partners* in pioneering then we need to interconnect our universities, cities and regions far better to the great economic hubs of China.

China's cities are powerful economic hubs which account for nearly 80% of China's output. In Shanghai, for instance, a quarter of the population has a college degree and there are half a million foreign ex-pats.[293]

But the same is true in Britain. As you might expect, I feel strongly about this. I was the first regional minister for the West Midlands, I created the Council of Regional Ministers, and campaigned hard to become mayor of Birmingham. I've seen at first hand how important regions and cities have become to fostering innovation. Before I left the Treasury, I had drawn up a plan to create full-time regional ministers to act as real centres of power in government. Here's the summary from my civil servants of just why cities are so vital:

Our core city regions are key drivers of growth and we must avoid any sense that we are turning our back on the role that they play nationally or locally.

Based on current economic and policy trends, Oxford Economics' analysis of the future economy[294] predicts that cities will be important sources of gross value-added (GVA) growth in the medium to longer term. London, Manchester,

Leeds, Liverpool and Birmingham city regions generate 40% of employment in England.

We also expect cities to be vital places in which to adapt to the knowledge-intensive economy and address the unemployment challenges. Knowledge-intensive sectors that will drive future job growth tend to locate in cities – *37% of GB knowledge-intensive businesses were clustered in London and just three other major cities, Manchester, Birmingham and Bristol, in 2008.*

So we need to ask how in each city we bring together the power of business, local councils, universities, our great research hospitals, science parks, colleges, schools, civil society and investment funds and connect to the same kind of nexuses in China.

I think that universities could be the cornerstones of this work. Why? Because culture, language, education and research are the dimensions to the UK–China relationship that came up time and time again as we spoke to people about Britain and China's future. The clear implication is that our universities, colleges and schools are going to be among the hubs for the UK–China innovation relationship for the rest of the century.

Today, one of the universities that is leading the charge is Oxford University, where, on the tennis courts of St Hugh's College, the nets are coming down and one of the country's leading centres for Chinese studies is about to go up.

The £20-million five-floor Dickson Poon Building is the new home to the University of Oxford China Centre and will bring together 45 world-class academics and research projects on everything from Chinese business to ancient history and art, health and environment in the largest centre of its kind outside North America.

The driving force behind the project is the previous warden of St Hugh's, Prof. Andrew Dilnot. I have long been an admirer of Prof. Dilnot as someone who is able to deploy an immensely impressive academic pedigree in pursuit of better public policy, and so before he went off to lead Nuffield College, I met him at St Hugh's to ask why Oxford had committed such an effort to the project. At the core of the Centre's purpose, said Andrew, is a simple insight:

> Only 1% of the world's population is British. We have to think of ourselves as a university of the world. Over the long term, we might produce 1% of the world's innovation – but is that all we're interested in? One per cent of the world's innovation? We're 1% of the world's population. That means there's 99% elsewhere.
>
> One day China's economy is not only going to be bigger than America's, it's going to be four times bigger … Now if you're an economist, then difference is fascinating. We can learn a huge amount more from studying them because it's more variety, more experience. We can also learn a lot from China, because education is so valued culturally; the role of learning is not simply an instrumental good. It's a good in itself.

In particular, we have huge amounts to learn from the astonishing pace of change now unfolding:

> We've never seen sustained growth like this. China's economy has grown eight-fold in just over 20 years. That's an incredible rate of technological progress. We must be able to learn from this. We've never seen a society experience anything like that before. That means that grandchildren are starting off life 20 times better off than their grandparents. That's creating an incredible melting pot.

Initiatives like Oxford's China Centre are precisely the kind of project Britain needs to invest in to drive forward a long-term relationship with China: a genuine two-way relationship from which we learn as much as, if not more, than we teach. But within great cities, the challenge is to create innovation relationships into which we '*spin*' more and more business activity.

Birmingham University is helping pioneer this new approach, and so one afternoon I popped over to the University's campus to quiz Prof. Edward Peck, who leads on the China relationship, for a few thoughts. Birmingham is so interesting because it is developing institutional links rather than simply hosting personal relationships between academics. But a growing relationship is good for the University and good for the city. Prof. Peck:

> We want to be higher in the world league of universities. We're about seventieth out of 150 right now and we want to be higher. We know there are two key drivers of this: one is citations – and internationally co-edited papers get cited more often – and the other is academic recommendations.
>
> We went to Guangzhou because it was our twin city and opted to make a serious investment but to lead with research not teaching. What Guangzhou wanted was relationships in high value manufacturing and engineering and areas of life sciences.

The Guangzhou administration are now co-funding projects where there's economic potential for the city, and Guangzhou is able to bring together research centres, academics and commercial partners. Already, there are important projects under way in stem-cell therapy and mainstream manufacturing with local manufacturing partners. Prof. Peck argues that the future for the university is now to 'spin-in' businesses to the relationship it has built within China's growing bilateral trade links; the university's recent 'Guangzhou Expo' in Birmingham was designed to introduce the local business community to the opportunities now on offer.

The relationship is already rich in diversity. It boasts an engineering and physical sciences collaboration with South China University of Technology (SCUT), with significant projects with commercial partners; an international education centre with Jinan University which is launching an MBA in 2013; a medical and dental sciences collaboration with Sun Yat-sen University; a college of social sciences collaboration with Guangzhou University exploring research into service industries. A joint public services academy is within range.

But where universities like Birmingham need help is in sustaining up-front investment in relationship building and potentially funding ideas which are jointly developed. This is where a UK–China binational fund modelled on the US–Israel fund could make a big difference.

Partners in pioneering

If you put all of this together you can see how, with some important changes, there is a fantastic partnership in innovation to be had with China. A partnership that is good for both of us. But there is a warning too. We should be really clear about what happens if we fail to rise to the challenge. Quite simply we'll find China's great new companies to be not friends but foes. Competition from China itself will simply beat us. China has billions in sovereign wealth funds – and is spending the money on smart graduates, technology and foreign businesses, 400 of them bought up in the last five years. China's productive capacity is expanding fast. But this is nothing compared to what might come. As Brad DeLong and Stephen Cohen have argued,[295] China's sovereign wealth funds are deep and hold the potential to buy expertise from wherever they need to.

Denis Simon, Vice-Provost of Arizona State University, recently argued to the US Congress: 'If we look at the formation of innovation networks and collaborative R&D across borders, across the global economy, increasingly we're seeing Chinese companies be part of those networks.'[296]

If we're not part of these networks, then Britain will cease to work at the cutting edge of global progress and the production systems of the future. And countries which are good at production create a lot of jobs.

Let's finish with a final look at my Apple and Foxconn example. If you just considered sales, you'd see Foxconn well ahead of Apple in the Fortune 500. But Apple is far more profitable. In theory Apple may be paying more tax into the American treasury. Now factor jobs into the discussion and the equation changes. Apple only employs 43,000 people in America. Foxconn employs 1 million people across three continents. In fact, Apple's success has been great for job creation – but not in America: the New York Times estimates the firm has created an astounding 700,000 jobs outside the US.

That's why being good at production is important. That's why becoming partners in pioneering with China is so important. And to make that happen, there's one more thing we both need. Money.

CHAPTER 12

Money is the root of all progress

I never really thought that I would become an entrepreneur.

If it hadn't been for a business plan competition at Harvard Business School, I'm not sure it would have happened. Back in 2000, the dotcom bubble was ballooning at furious speed. I came home with Sarah, who was six months pregnant, and somehow persuaded her that we could live off my credit card while I wrote a business plan with an old friend, raise some venture money, and get started.

Like all start-ups, it was a rollercoaster. Building sales. Building teams. Developing technology. Managing cashflow. Keeping shareholders on board when the tech sector crashed. But we were lucky. Through sheer hard work and some good luck, the business – called eGovernment Solutions (eGS) Group – took off and became in 2009 a top 100 private technology company highlighted by media-tech watcher Red Herring.

When I became a minister I literally had to give my shares away. eGS ran electronic marketplaces for local councils and police forces so they could pool their purchasing power and buy goods and services cheaper to make their budgets go further. But it wasn't going to be possible to hold shares in a business that ran an electronic marketplace for the police and still be a minister in the Home Office.

So, one afternoon I had to all but give my shares away for nothing; the business I had helped start on a coffee table and put everything into for four years was gone. I shuddered to think how much I had lost, but I figured you have to be philosophical about these things and decide what it is you want to do in life. Right then, I wanted to be a minister, not an entrepreneur. I've never regretted a minute that I spent on eGS, but I would never have had the chance to become an entrepreneur if I hadn't been able to raise the money from venture-capital firms who nurtured us through our rollercoaster years, or our bankers who supported us when cashflow was tough.

And one of the key problems in Britain right now is that entrepreneurs and business simply can't get hold of the finance they need to start a business or to expand. When problems like this set in, countries start to become less entrepreneurial and growth rates start to slow down. I can see that's exactly what's happening in Britain right now.

The financial crash has been terrible for investment in Britain. In fact, the collapse in business investment has been the biggest single cause of the recession. But when an economy is starved of investment it's not simply a short-term problem; it causes long-term engine damage.

Right now our banks are 'damaged'. They hold lots of bad debt in 'zombie firms' that they're praying will recover and repay them. Meanwhile, our banks are not in much mood to lend.

That means that the Bank of England's efforts to pump more money into the economy by literally printing money – quantitative easing – is not getting us very far. Worse, bigger UK companies which do hold bucket-loads of cash – there is £733 billion on UK corporate balance sheets, up by £107 billion since 2009 – simply don't have the confidence to invest because the economy is so weak.

The tragedy is that, before the crash, Britain was just starting to escape a long, long history of stubbornly low investment. Duncan Weldon, an excellent young economist at the TUC, has written quite a lot about this. Here's how he explains the problem:

> From the late 19th century until the first world war there was a trend for the City of London to export UK capital overseas rather than increase investment in the UK itself.
>
> The lack of investment in the UK economy 1918–39 was discussed by economists, policy-makers and business people at the time. The Macmillan Committee was set up in 1930 to examine whether the banks were failing to provide the funding. In the 1950s and 1960s the lack of investment was again identified as a reason for Britain's relative decline vis-à-vis the other Western economies. Both Wilson's indicative planning agenda of 1964–70 and much of the original aims of the Heath government (freeing up competition 1970–2) were aimed at raising the level of investment in the UK economy.[297]

So, we've been trying to tackle this for a long time.

The last Labour government was actually beginning to make some progress as we became, quite simply, one of the world's favourite places to invest. We've always had some strong fundamentals. We're in a good spot. Foreign investors like our financial and legal system, the English language and ready access to the neighbouring markets of America and Europe.

But we also made changes that business investors liked. In 2010, the World Bank's 'Doing Business' Report ranked the UK the best business environment in the EU, and the fifth best in the world.[298] Our regulatory environment was judged less restrictive than any other outside the US.[299] Our product markets were among the most competitive in the OECD.

This hard slog had a handsome pay-off. The UK became the most popular place in Europe to invest and the second most popular place in the world. Over $1.3 trillion of foreign direct investment (FDI) is invested in the UK; that is nearly one dollar in 10 of every dollar spent on FDI.[300] For some small islands off the coast of Europe, that is a phenomenal achievement.

But there was more. We began to fix a decades-long famine of investment in our infrastructure. Capital spending on transport quadrupled from £2.9 billion in 1997 to £11.9 billion in 2008/09, including the construction of 69 major trunk roads and motorways (since 2001) and of Terminal 5 at Heathrow Airport, which added capacity for 30 million passengers, and an increase in rail punctuality to 90% – which, though far from perfect, was still the highest level on record. Our digital infrastructure was transformed, as we delivered one of the highest coverage rates for digital subscriber lines in the OECD and gave internet users a faster speed than the US, Germany or France.[301]

But for all this progress, the decades-long famine means our investment rate still lags the OECD average,[302] and this is costing us growth. The World Economic Forum ranks the UK twenty-fourth in the world on overall quality of infrastructure.[303] ONS statistics show that, in 2011, the total value of new orders for infrastructure construction was £8.5 billion, down from a peak of £11.6 billion in 2009.[304] Heathrow Airport is currently operating at 99% capacity. That creates delays. Congestion on our roads will add some £10 billion of business costs by 2025.[305] Our rail network is overcrowded at peak hours, especially in the south-east and north-west. Demand for shipping is forecast to outstrip port capacity.[306]

Economics expert Dieter Helm told the Treasury Select Committee:

The gap between what needs to be done [on infrastructure investment] and what is being done remains very large. It is a good news story that it is finally being taken seriously, but we are not anywhere near closing up those gaps.[307]

Three main barriers hold back private-sector investment: weak demand, tight credit conditions and heightened uncertainty about the economic outlook. And for business investment, the picture is just as bleak. In late 2012, Adam Marshall from the British Chambers of Commerce came to the House of Commons to share some research undertaken by the Chambers into the state of bank lending to the business community. The conclusions were simply awful:

As the Breedon Review, Eurostat and others have noted, the situation in the UK is unique. No other country has seen bank deleveraging on the same scale as the UK. SME [small and medium enterprise] loan rejection rates in the UK are higher than in other European countries. And UK small- and medium-sized companies, unlike those in many other countries, are overwhelmingly reliant on debt when they seek external financing. Breedon suggests that UK SMEs alone face a finance gap of up to £59 billion within five years.[308]

Britain needs investment. And China may be able to help.

China goes global

Britain's thirst for investment is a colossal opportunity for a win-win with China. Over the next decade, hundreds of billions of dollars will flow from China to the rest of the world. If we were wise we would try to make a home for as much of that money as possible.

When developing economies grow, investment is generally sucked in. But when economies reach a tipping point, investment cash starts to flow out; that switch-over is about to happen in China, on an epic scale.

A look at headlines over the last few years might lead you to think that hitherto the Chinese have been busy 'buying up Africa'. And indeed, Chinese investment in Africa has grown.

When the pace of Chinese growth proved rather faster than expected in the early years of the century, China suddenly became the world's biggest consumer of crucial commodities like cement, copper and aluminium. Today China consumes around 40% of the world's supply of copper, aluminium and steel.

Big state-owned commodities firms were caught short of raw materials. China's big oil firms, for instance Sinopec, CNPC and CNOOC, had no foreign investments in the 1990s. As foreign-exchange reserves piled up, China's oil majors became the advance guard pioneering China's 'Going Global' strategy; other natural-resource players quickly followed suit in iron ore, bauxite and copper.

The Chinese investment boom in Africa became, in the words of the IMF, 'phenomenal'; it grew twenty-fold between 2003 and 2009, by which time China had $13 billion invested in sub-Saharan Africa, growing at $1 billion a year.[309]

Pinning down precise figures is hard because of the so-called 'Angola mode' by which China invests.[310] So, the Chinese government might agree to undertake a development project in exchange for rights to local natural resources like oil, or production-sharing contracts, or a mining joint venture. The construction project is then given to a Chinese construction firm and a Chinese firm, perhaps an oil company, starts exploration. At home, a Chinese bank, perhaps the Export-Import Bank (EXIM), provides the construction firm with a loan for the building project.

The whole thing moves forward without the Chinese government actually giving the foreign nation any money. This combination of equity financing for exploiting resources and debt financing for infrastructure build creates a package which unlocks Africa's natural resources in a highly effective way; part of the reason why Africa's natural resources had been left relatively untouched until now was the lack of infrastructure in for example, roads, rails, energy and communications networks.

Around this investment, China has packaged an extraordinary eco-system of political and development cooperation. In 2000, China launched the Forum on China–Africa Cooperation (FOCAC) with 51 African countries. 2006 was declared 'Year of Africa' at the FOCAC Beijing summit, where the China–Africa Development Fund was launched: this is a $1-billion fund to provide equity investment to encourage private firms to invest in Africa in everything from agriculture to energy to industry parks. Chinese investment has helped

- Angola become a logistics hub in south-west Africa with new industry parks and railway
- Sudan create an oil industry, now the third largest in sub-Saharan Africa, where over 10,000 Chinese workers helped build a refinery and pipeline
- Zambia, where China is helping drive the government's efforts to create Special Economic Zones.

And while investment might have started in African natural resources, it has now spread to agriculture, manufacturing and services. China took a big stake in a South African bank in 2005. More and more Chinese firms are investing in African businesses from roads, rail and light vehicles in Angola to agriculture, garments, telecoms and tourism in Zambia. Of the 800 Chinese firms EXIM estimated were operating in Africa in 2006, 85% were private SMEs.

And yet although it has grown so fast, Chinese investment in Africa is tiny relative to that of others. Chinese global FDI in Africa increased from just 0.5% of total FDI in Africa in the early 2000s to around 4.5% in 2007. A small amount has achieved a great deal. And now, China's investment story is about to change dramatically.

China now has so much money to invest that there is plenty to spend on buying into Europe.

China comes to town

François Godement and Jonas Parello-Plesner at the European Council on Foreign Relations are two of the best writers on China and Europe. They've labelled the new surge of Chinese investment into the hard-pressed continent as a 'scramble for Europe'.[311]

In fact, Europe has been the world's favourite place to invest for 20 years; nearly $12 trillion is invested – around 36% of the world's total. But since 2003, China has become a much more significant part of the flood.

Back in 2003, around two-thirds of Chinese FDI headed to Latin America. But by 2009, that figure had fallen to a third and the share of Chinese FDI heading to Europe almost doubled between 2004 and 2008. Europe is now the third most important location for Chinese investment after Latin America and Asia.

Official statistics don't seem to give us a very clear picture. European figures show perhaps $9 billion of Chinese investment. Chinese ministry figures indicate $13 billion. But new analysis by the Rhodium Group of the period 2000–11 uncovers around 570 deals worth $21 billion – and the jump in recent years has been extraordinary. Before I was elected to Parliament in 2004, there were perhaps 10 deals a year, worth an average of $100 million.

In 2010, deal-flow exploded to $10 billion: a tripling of value in just three years. This is now twice the level of Chinese investment into the US, and most of the money heads into Germany, the UK and France. French figures are flattered by a huge Gaz de France deal. Put that aside, and the UK emerges as China's favourite European place to invest with a deal value of $3.7 billion, about a billion dollars ahead of Germany.

But this is as nothing compared to what is likely to happen next.

Today, China has a tiny global footprint. It owns very little of the world's assets – perhaps $300 billion is invested abroad. That's a paltry 1.5% of the world's total asset base. Indeed, China invests less globally than Denmark and is on a par with Sweden, Singapore and Taiwan. America's stock of overseas investment is 16 times bigger. Right now, China invests about 5% of GDP abroad. China's GDP is projected to grow to around $20 trillion by 2020. If it continues to invest 5% abroad, then overseas direct investment will balloon from $300 billion to $1 trillion.

Most 'transitional economies' in fact invest rather more than 5% of their wealth overseas; they invest 15%. If that happened in China, then *$3 trillion* will flow from China to the rest of the world. So the Rhodium Group settle on a forecast of $1–2 trillion invested by China globally by 2020.[312]

If Europe captures the kind of share which we've won over the last few years – around 25% – that will mean $250–500 billion in investment, around $25–50 billion a year. Now over the last five years, the stock of FDI in the UK has increased on average £60 billion a year – around $95 billion at current exchange rates.

If we captured half of the money coming into Europe from China, that could revolutionise foreign investment in Britain, adding between 15% and 25% to the inflow of FDI each year. Over a decade that would make a serious impact on our investment rate in the UK.

This seismic shift from 'made in China' to 'owned by China' is now well and truly under way. In my brief conversations with China's investment leaders at the CPC's Party School, it's become clear that Chinese investors are buying three things.

First, China's sovereign wealth fund, China Investment Corporation (CIC), is looking at infrastructure deals plus stable, long-term investments with a decent yield; utility companies are a good bet. So CIC recently bought 10% of Thames Water, has invested $3.3 billion in France's utility giant Gaz de France and has injected $340 million into Songbird Estates, the owners of Canary Wharf.

Secondly, China's state-owned enterprises have been making investments in natural resources or trade infrastructure. So, Sinochem bought out coal, oil and gas player Emerald. Sinopec bought out Addax Petroleum in 2008 and CNOOC bought Awilco Offshore. COSCO has bought major port businesses in Piraeus, Naples and Antwerp.

Thirdly, China's leading entrepreneurs are pursuing a more transformational strategy. Geely (automotive), Huawei (communications equipment), Lenovo (IT) and Sany and Wolong (industrial equipment) are buying up the pieces of the jigsaw puzzle they need to become world-beaters.

The globalisation of the world economy over the last 20 years means production lines that were once organised within a factory's walls now stretch worldwide. China's leading firms have mastered the art of organising these chains of production to compete with the world's best, becoming global players far faster than Japanese or South Korean firms like Toyota or Samsung. Many of these Chinese firms started with what's been called the 'loose bricks' in Western companies' defences: perhaps a low-value part of the market where they could compete with low labour costs, or a peripheral marketplace in Africa or South East Asia.

Firms like Wanxiang were early masters of the art, buying out competitors and suppliers – like Schiller, Universal Automotive and Rockford Powertrain – to build access to markets, technologies and brands that can operate globally. Now, the same inexorable logic is unfolding in sophisticated industries where Americans and Europeans treasure their edge.

Chery is now one of the world's biggest car companies; its first exports were to Syria. In 2003, it began a push across the Middle East. By 2008, it was targeting 1 million sales a year in the US and had begun to master the business of globalising new product design. Chery's chief executive, Yin Tongyao, has a slogan: 'Learn cost control from the Japanese, craziness from the Koreans, keen pursuit of technology from the Germans and market manoeuvres from the Americans.'[313] The firm only started in 1997, with lessons learned from Volkswagen. But since then it's systematically built its knowledge base worldwide, hiring former Volkswagen engineers when they were laid off in China then buying out two-thirds of design experts Jia Jing. It's built up its engine expertise by buying old Ford engine plant equipment. Now it can produce 500,000 engines a year from a plant employing 200 engineers with experts from eight European countries, the US and Asia. It's just signed a joint-venture agreement with Jaguar Land Rover.

In 1995, Huawei was making most of its $200 million a year selling telecoms kit in rural China. It began its global journey with steps in Hong Kong, Vietnam, Russia and then

Africa. Bigger, tougher contracts with ever more sophisticated technology followed in Thailand and the UAE. Then came deals to build third-generation (3G) mobile telecoms networks in Hong Kong, Mauritius and Malaysia. By 2006, Huawei had won contracts from three-quarters of the operators for new 3G licences in Europe,[314] and beat Motorola and Marconi to win a share of BT's 21st Century Network programme. Now, Huawei is at the cutting edge of China's mergers and acquisitions hunt in Europe. While the firm has been barred from America, Australia and some of Europe, we have welcomed it.

Where industries are most complex of all – say building nuclear reactors or civil aircraft or manufacturing petro-chemicals – China has used huge domestic contracts to draw in leading foreign firms to transfer technology to 'national champions'. Those 'national champions' are now strong enough to compete in world markets – and Chinese overseas direct investment is helping.

In power generation, for example, China insisted the only bidders for its vast Three Gorges Dam project would be a lead foreign firm plus Chinese partners, and technology transfer was part of the deal. The contract was for two-thirds of the value of the total installed base of generators. Chinese firms are now shipping this expertise worldwide.

In petro-chemicals, Sinopec has now grown so huge – $75 billion in sales – that it is now able to muscle in on oil and gas development projects worldwide. The same process is now under way in aircraft manufacturing; Chinese firms are joining in as subcontractors for planes to be sold in China and, as part of its sales deal in China, Airbus agreed to set up an R&D centre with AVIC (Aviation Industries of China). Once they have absorbed the knowledge, Chinese firms 'cost innovate';[315] Xi'an Aircraft Company's regional jets, for instance, were launched 30% cheaper than their rivals.

European investment from these new Chinese challengers shows just how Chinese firms are acquiring the pieces of the puzzle they need to become world-beaters. The communication equipment and services sector has already seen over 100 deals – some 20% of the total; there have been over 60 deals each in the industrial machinery and renewable energy sectors. Automotive components, financial services and IT services have all seen big investments.

Around many of these investments, Chinese firms are ramping up R&D activities. Geely considerably expanded its engineering teams at Volvo in Sweden. AVIC's subsidiary FACC is investing tens of millions in aviation research in Austria. Huawei has a host of R&D centres across Europe.

'There is nothing so hard', said the wise Machiavelli, 'as to try to introduce a new order of things'. As Chinese companies begin to diversify internationally and build up competitive positions in world markets, people – and the media – are noticing.

Is China buying the world?

As Chinese firms go global, there will, I am sure, be moments of hysteria. But let's at least be clear: China is not 'buying the world'. Far from it.

Few people in Britain have studied the evolution of Chinese business as hard as Peter Nolan, professor of Chinese development at Cambridge University, and he has written an excellent book to underline a simple point: China is not 'buying the world.'[316] The book begins with the media narrative now taking hold around the world. In 2009, Fortune headlined its cover 'China buys the world', with an article inside asking, 'Is your company – or is your country – on the list?' The Economist splashed its November 2010 issue with 'Buying up the world: the coming wave of Chinese takeovers'. A month earlier, the Independent headlined 'The great haul of China'.

Peter's key point is of fundamental significance: the last three decades have seen the great giants of the global marketplace take leave of the countries in which they were born. They have re-formed themselves anew into great networks of trade that now span the planet, owing little loyalty or indeed business to domestic hearths.

In fact, the UN Conference on Trade and Development (UNCTAD) estimated that, by 2009, the foreign assets of the world's 100 largest companies totalled 57% of total assets and foreign sales made up 61% of total sales.[317]

Even in America, the majority of large firms now sell more abroad than they do at home. Between two-thirds and three-quarters of sales of Exxon, Procter and Gamble, IBM, Pfizer, Coca-Cola, Schlumberger, Caterpillar and Dow Chemical are outside the US.

Since 2000, some 2,500 $1-billion mergers, worth in total some $7.4 trillion, have created a new global super-league. These firms now dominate global trade. They monopolise competition in globally traded goods and services:

- two great firms control the market for large commercial aircraft
- 10 firms control nearly 80% of the world's auto business; indeed the top five, boasting sales of between $108 billion and $221 billion, sell half of the world's cars
- three firms control nearly 80% of the world's mobile telecoms infrastructure
- 10 firms control 70% of world pharmaceuticals
- four firms control 60% of the beer market
- four firms control 75% of the cigarette market.

In the supply chains of these behemoths is a similar concentration:

- three firms dominate aero-engines
- two firms dominate automotive braking systems
- two firms dominate computer chips
- three firms dominate industrial gases
- three firms control the world's market for 200 billion soft drink cans.

These firms have all created vast defences by spending so much on branding and R&D that no one can overhaul their lead. The world's top 10 companies now spend $2–3 billion a year on branding. In 2008, the Business Department found the world's top 1,400 firms spent an unbelievable $545 billion on R&D – and spending among the top 1,250 rose by 30% between 2005 and 2010.[318]

Eighty per cent of those firms are based in the US, Britain, France or Germany.

As Peter puts it, 'The "commanding heights" of the global business system are dominated by firms from high-income countries.'[319]

Now, in response, China has consolidated a number of big firms in a handful of strategic sectors where domestic champions are strong.[320] Here, the full scope of the 'state capitalism' technique has been brought to bear on tech transfer deals (for example, in high-speed rail), whopping domestic contracts (for example, power generation), cheap access to capital or technology, or just straightforward prohibitions on foreign competition (e.g. banking).

- *Telecoms*: China Mobile; China Unicom; China Telecom
- *Oil/chemicals*: Sinopec; CNPC; CNOOC; SinoChem
- *Aerospace*: AVIC; COMAC; CASC

- *Military*: China North; China South
- *Auto*: Shanghai Automotive; Yiqi; Dongfeng
- *Power*: Shanghai Electric; Harbin Electric; Dongfang Electric
- *Metals*: Baosteel; Wisco; China Shenhua; CMACC
- *Electricity*; China Southern Power Grid; Huaneng; Huadian; Datang
- *Construction*: China State Construction; China Rail Construction; China Construction
- *Airlines*: Air China; China Southern; China Eastern
- *Banking*: Industrial and Commercial Bank of China; China Construction Bank; Bank of China; Agricultural Bank of China; Bank of Communications

Yet despite this,

- Out of the Fortune 500, just 79 firms are from the developing world and they are overwhelmingly confined to oil and gas; metals and mining; and telecoms.
- China has just nine firms in the top 1,400 businesses that dominate global R&D and brand building.

The oil reserves of the six Western oil majors total some 68 billion barrels of oil (BBO) and in total Western firms control perhaps 110 BBO. By contrast, China sits on top of just 1.1% of the world's oil reserves and its oil firms control perhaps 28 BBO – about a quarter of the West's total. When, in 2005, China's oil major CNOOC tried to take over US oil major Unocal, the bid was withdrawn in a storm of controversy. The result is that China has been forced to take minority positions in major firms like BP, buy firms in smaller markets like Angola or Kazakhstan, and expand 'loans for oil' deals in Russia, Brazil, Venezuela, Kazakhstan and Angola.

China's banking firms are strong; but total funds under management by the world's biggest fund managers totalled a mind-boggling $62 trillion in 2009.[321] The world's top 50 fund managers control over 60% of those assets. That is vastly greater than the total foreign exchange reserves of the Chinese government – around $5 trillion, or the funds available to China's sovereign wealth funds.

Or take the tech sector. It's a sector that spends more than any other on R&D. Of the R&D spenders in the top 1,400 firms, 228 are in the tech sector; three-fifths of them are American. Eight of the top 10 firms are the tech sector's super-giants: Microsoft, Oracle and SAP dominate business software; IBM and HP dominate the servers market.

Overwhelmingly, hi-tech manufacturing is monopolised not by Chinese businesses but by Western businesses that have set up shop in China. The US has some 60,000 investment projects worth $100 billion in the country.[322] Chinese sales are worth a fortune for US companies like General Motors (11 plants employing some 32,000 people); Coca-Cola (41 bottling plants employing 48,000 people); Apple (whose key supplier Foxconn employs over 1 million people); Yum! Brands which runs Kentucky Fried Chicken employing a huge 230,000 people in 4,000 restaurants; Wal-Mart (95,000 people).

Together American companies are selling $147 billion worth of stuff, exporting $72 billion worth and turning in a tidy $8 billion in profit. Germany is the next biggest with some $20 billion invested by companies like Volkswagen, Bosch, Siemens and BASF. Together these firms make up nearly one third of the value added in the Chinese economy and two-thirds of the value added in the hi-tech sector, employing 41% of scientists and engineers. Pascal Lamy, Director-General of the World Trade Organisation, put it like this: 'What we call "made in China" is indeed assembled in China, but its commercial value comes from those numerous countries that precede its assembly.'[323]

Investment flowing into China totals a huge $243 billion more than money flowing out. In 2009, China was investing overseas just 14% of what Britain invests globally. And as Prof. Nolan points out, the market capitalisation of the top 34 UK companies in the Financial Times top 500 is around $2.1 trillion – vastly larger than the resources under management in China's sovereign wealth funds.

But even if we can decide to relax a bit about Chinese investment, we still have to face some big questions.

How we do we maximise our share of cash coming into Europe? How do encourage some of that investment to head into areas where it is especially needed, like infrastructure? How we encourage investment that, on the one hand, helps us learn from China and innovate together and, on the other, helps us export more? And what is off limits? How can we ensure there's a process that's open, transparent and predictable for Chinese investors?

Because, rest assured that if a business confronts a process that is about as certain as a lottery then it is unlikely to consider investing a significant amount of cash.

We need to be realistic. Foreign direct investment is not a charity venture on behalf of China Inc. Chinese overseas direct investors are here to make money. Chinese politicians at home are concerned to raise the long-term growth rate of China.

So what we need to fashion is a win-win that works for both of us. And that's going to need some 'rules of the game'.

CHAPTER 13

The new rules of the game

We have a pretty ambivalent attitude to 'foreign takeovers' in Britain.

Generally, we've tended to be pretty relaxed about foreign entrepreneurs coming to Britain and setting up shop. Lots of our greatest businesses have been founded by immigrants. When the Japanese first started to invest in the rather moribund UK automotive sector back in the 1980s, there was little outcry. In fact, there was a sense of relief.

Foreign takeovers are a little more complicated and I've seen that complexity at first hand. Take my home-town of Birmingham. When Tata bought Jaguar Land Rover (JLR) there was a sense of relief, in that what was seen as the dead hand of their former owners, Ford, had been lifted. Tata has invested £1 billion a year in R&D, pioneering, in the words of its chief executive Ralf Speth, 'the most ambitious product development programme in the history of the brand'[324]. JLR now has a workforce of 17,000 staff at three manufacturing plants and has just made £1 billion in profit.[325]

Around the same time Kraft's £12-billion takeover of successful Cadbury, a business that helped shape the very fabric of the city, provoked outcry, and years on remains controversial.

Today, you can hear similar stories all over Britain. In the north-west, for instance, the Stanlow oil refinery, next to JLR's Halewood site, is owned by Indian conglomerate Essar. Tata Chemicals bought Brunner Mond, a chemicals firm started in 1873, in 2006. Blackburn Rovers FC, founder members of the Football League, is owned by an Indian poultry firm, VH Group.[326] Rolls-Royce, Aston Martin, Harrods, The Savoy, Manchester United FC, Typhoo Tea, HP Sauce, Harry Ramsden's, Heathrow Airport, Madame Tussauds, P&O, The Body Shop, Pilkington, Abbey National, O2, MG Rover, The Times, Hamleys, Chelsea FC, Weetabix, Walkers crisps, Beefeater gin – they're all owned by foreigners.

Sometimes, lots of people worry about 'foreign ownership' because they see profits taken elsewhere. The recent outcry about foreign companies like Amazon or Starbucks paying practically no UK corporation tax only adds to the concern.

But in an open economy like ours, overseas direct investment is enormously important in three key ways.

First and foremost is jobs. The Rhodium Group estimated that already around 45,000 jobs are supported in Europe by Chinese investment.[327] But think about how many jobs have been created or supported by, say, American investment: perhaps as many as 4.3 million EU citizens get monthly pay-cheques from US firms. UK Trade and Investment (UKTI) data show that, in 2011/12, overseas investors created 52,741 new jobs in the UK (up 26% on the previous year) and safeguarded 59,918;[328] that's over 112,000 jobs in just a single year.

Second is tax receipts. Most tax in Britain is paid by and for workers in income tax, employers' national insurance – not corporation tax – and VAT. That means that the more people in work, the more tax comes in.

Third is innovation. Over the long term, rising productivity triggers rises in wages and living standards. There's been a one-to-one relationship between rising productivity growth and rising wage growth. Key to productivity is competition – and competition from firms like Huawei in telecoms infrastructure is a good thing; it brings down costs and is ultimately of benefit to consumers. Chinese firms have proved extremely adept at what business academics Ming Zeng and Peter Williamson call 'cost innovation': incorporating hi-tech into new products and producing them at scale and much lower cost than the competition.[329] This is similar to the kind of pioneering manufacturing associated with Japanese firms in the 1980s, whose inward investment helped transform the UK automotive sector.

Inward investment has been part of every European country's make-up for years. The free movement of capital was one of the four founding principles of the 1957 Treaty of Rome. By the late 1980s all the capital controls limiting movement of investment within the EU had been largely abolished. By 2010 an amazing $8 trillion of intra-EU foreign direct investment knitted together businesses, with North American and Japanese firms adding another $4 trillion into the mix.

Nevertheless, for investment from China, there have to be some rules of the game to clear up two important sources of confusion, economic security and national security.

Economic security

China is a 'state capitalist' system: government and business are closely intertwined. China wants to build up national champions and if this book does just one thing I want it to show just how difficult the task ahead is for China's leaders. China's leaders need

China Inc. to succeed. They confront major challenges taking on vested interests in their own country, not least the gigantic state-owned enterprises sector which simply isn't productive enough. They need China's firms to go global.

In Europe, there are plenty of nations, like us, that could use a little more investment. And some argue that the way each of us competes for money is to miss a trick. Thus François Godement and Jonas Parello-Plesner: 'as Europeans compete with each other for Chinese business they diminish their leverage and thus reduce their chances of collectively striking a better deal with China'.[330]

Godement and Parello-Plesner worry that as Chinese firms build up strategic assets from transport infrastructure to industry parks to logistics to sovereign debt, a 'China lobby' will grow within the EU of countries like Cyprus, Malta, Greece, Italy, Portugal and Spain that will alter the balance of China policy within Europe. Already Poland and a host of central European countries hold summits with China in which China has promised infrastructure investment in central Europe.[331] European politicians worry too about us losing our edge: in particular, whether Chinese firms are going to buy up Europe's 'crown jewels' and 'steal' intellectual property or manufacturing assets and ship them off back to China.

Back in 2010, when Chinese cable maker Xinmao launched its takeover bid for Dutch fibre-cable producer Draka, the European Commissioner for Industry Antonio Tajani was prompted to call for a pan-European investment review on the grounds that: 'We have to make sure it's not a front for something else, in terms of taking our know-how abroad.'[332] His fellow Commissioner Michel Barnier supported the call, as did the European Parliament.

I just don't think that a country like Britain, which has gigantic inward investment from all over the world, can really defend this kind of view: not least because it is hardly in the spirit of the rules Europe itself agreed as long ago as Maastricht. Article 63 of the Treaty on the Functioning of the European Union says this: 'All restrictions on the movement of capital between Member States and between Member States and third countries shall be prohibited.'

Because we followed this idea, the EU has pretty much the most liberal economy in the world for foreign investment;[333] that is good for growth, jobs and tax receipts.

National security

The question of national security, on the other hand, is much more important, not least because there is still in place the small matter of the European arms embargo (imposed after the Tiananmen Square protests), and China's record on export control of lethal technology has not been perfect in the past.

Right now, national governments are left to interpret the rules about stepping in to bar foreign takeovers on national security grounds. Under EU law screening is permitted for member states to protect public security and 'take any necessary measures for the protection of the essential interests of their security'. Europeans have taken radically different approaches to this: France specifies 11 sectors for review and rules off limits not just defence, but also aerospace; the Dutch on the other hand have no review at all.

But it's not just about takeovers. What about critical national networks? The energy grid, communication systems, financial systems, transport networks like rail, or gas and water utilities? In both the US and Australia, Chinese firms have been turned back from investing in communication networks. My old friend Nick Butler, formerly at BP and now visiting professor at King's

College London, recently pointed at proposed Chinese investment in the UK nuclear industry and argued:

> Systematic abuse of intellectual property and a series of
> cyber-attacks on UK businesses by Chinese entities which
> could not operate without the approval of the government
> in Beijing have led to a new focus on cyber security in big
> companies and in Whitehall. Jonathan Evans, the head of
> MI5, recently talked of cyber security as one of the four
> greatest challenges to the UK and said that one unnamed
> business had lost £800 million as a result of hacking ...
>
> If the Horizon deal proceeds, the Chinese will not need
> any cyber-warfare technology to understand the UK elec-
> tricity sector. They will be inside the system, with access to
> the intricate architecture of the UK's National Grid and the
> processes through which electricity supply is controlled, as
> well as to the UK's nuclear technology.
>
> Perhaps that doesn't matter. Perhaps a Chinese wall
> exists between the Guandong Holding Company and the
> government in Beijing. Perhaps we have reached a level
> of globalisation in which the nationality of ownership is
> irrelevant.
>
> But even if all those things are true, it seems regrettable
> that in return for this investment the Chinese are not being
> required to halt the cyber-attacks and the theft of intellec-
> tual property in which they are now the world leaders. If
> the Chinese do indeed want to invest for decent commercial
> reasons a degree of reciprocity would be welcome.[334]

There is no black and white answer to this. The UK needs predi-
cable, open rules to assess what benchmarks a foreign company
must meet to be allowed into critical national infrastructure. But

in reality, the only way we're going to secure real assurance on this question is if investment in the UK from China is not seen as a one-way street. In truth, we have to become far more *inter-de-pendent*. We need a two-way street.

Building the two-way street

The real secret to creating a good environment for Chinese investment in Europe – and in Britain in particular – is to accelerate British investment in China.

It's far easier to defend Chinese investment in Britain when it's not a one-way street, but a two-way motorway; when European – and British – politicians can say: 'Look. British firms are able to invest in China with ease; we should allow China to invest in Britain.'

Strategically, I don't think British firms are investing anywhere near enough in a market that will soon be the world's largest. And right now, there is a sense that the playing field is not level enough. The leader of a major British manufacturer trading in China put it to me like this:

> The UK needs to be much stronger on reciprocity. So, China Mobile has just set up business in the UK; Volvo was recently bought out. We don't insist on any kind of recipro-cal arrangements for Europe.
>
> China hasn't offered any further concessions beyond what it set out in the WTO discussion. What we'd find is quite a coalition that would support us; the private sector in the UK; Europeans and Americans.

To check this I looked up some statistics on just where UK foreign investment is heading – and where our overseas assets now lie.

Overwhelmingly, British overseas investment is tied up in our two oldest markets, the US and Europe. In fact, just five overseas markets account for over half of our stock of foreign investment: the US, which accounts for nearly a fifth of all UK money invested abroad, the Netherlands, Luxembourg, France and Ireland. In fact, we have more money invested in Belgium than we do in China (see Table 13.1).

But now look at the markets where British investment is growing fastest (Table 13.2). Again, China is not very high up on the list. Our investment in the Gulf, Russia, South Korea and India has been growing much faster. Indeed, UK investment in China and Hong Kong has been growing at the same average rate over the last decade as our investment in Portugal.

I hope this picture changes fast. And to get a better sense of what we need to do in practice, I thought I'd sit down with the chief executive of the British business that has pulled off probably the largest merger and acquisition of any of our national leaders.

Diageo's £815-million acquisition of control in its joint venture partner, Shuijingfang, in 2011 is not just any deal. The firm is the proud producer of the *baijiu* that is said to be China's oldest, still manufactured today using distilling techniques that go back to the 14th century. It's hard to convey the cultural importance of *baijiu* in China. The 'white liquor' has been distilled using a special double fermentation process for some 5,000 years, usually from sorghum, and rolls out of the bottle at anywhere between 40 and 60% proof. Like rice, the culture of *baijiu*, with its roots in agricultural China, is an intimate part of social, political and economic life. Travelling and negotiating around China, one learns quickly that the civilised banquets of Beijing tend to a get a little racier the further you drift from the capital. The toasts multiply. And so do the measures.

Kenneth MacPherson, at the time Diageo's General Manager in China, recently told a fond story of his introduction to *baijiu* in 2003, when he travelled to Chengdu for the first time: 'It was a beautiful dinner, with fine *baijiu* and performance of traditional Chinese zither. I just instantly felt how *baijiu* stands for something decent in China.'[335]

At most dinners outside the capital, there'll be a toast or two offered with the local fire-water. Descending from a minibus at a function in Mongolia, I was charmed to be greeted with the traditional 'getting off your horse' drink: a large silver dish of *baijiu* that naturally had to be knocked down in one. The training of a misspent youth was suddenly proving an important political skill. But I met my match at a banquet in Qingdao, when my neighbour raised a cocktail combining not only the very best *baijiu*, but the best of the Tsingdao beer and the best local Tsingdao red wine. All in one glass. Down in one. That feat I couldn't surpass. The *baijiu* market in China, by the way, is worth a cool £25 billion.

Paul Walsh, Chief Executive of Diageo, is rightly very proud of his firm's takeover of Shuijingfang in 2011 – and he is full of praise for the support Diageo secured from successive governments, navigating China's political labyrinths. But, he adds, big deals in China are not for the faint-hearted.

> The process for us took five years – and that was with a willing seller. The problem was it was very hard to pin down who exactly was responsible for making a decision. So the file would ping backwards and forwards between the province and the centre. And then all the personnel would change.
>
> Our experience was that no one would say 'yes' and no one would say 'no'. They just asked a lot of questions! There was a lot of getting through the protocol. But what

we found is that there were a few hot buttons. So when we showed them around our distilleries in Scotland, they would ask 'Where are all the people?' They couldn't believe the level of automation and efficiency we'd achieved. That's when they said 'wow'.

But the only thing people wanted was our marketing expertise. We're extremely good marketeers. And one of the things they insisted on – it was a key part of the deal – was that we'd be marketing *baijiu* around the world.

There was a sense of 'I just wish it'd go away' – no one wanted to stick their head above the parapet.

Listening to Paul's story, I couldn't help but remember with a smile the extraordinary memoirs of Lord Macartney, the first official ambassador to the Emperor of China.

Back in the 1790s, as frustration with the slow business of negotiating tea supplies mounted, the leaders of the East India Company prevailed upon the government to send a proper emissary to see what could be done.

The Home Secretary, Henry Dundas, was persuaded to appoint the best-qualified man in England for the job. Lord George Macartney, born in Northern Ireland, had won plaudits as ambassador to the court of Catherine the Great. In 1793, at a cost of some £50,000, he and his entourage were dispatched for China aboard HMS Lion and HMS Hindostan. His party comprised 95 people including a painter, metallurgist, watchmaker, mathematical instrument maker, botanist, and 53 soldiers, sent 'to the most civilised as well as most ancient and populous nation in the world' to impress upon them 'the benefits which must result from an unreserved and friendly intercourse between that Country and his (the King's) own'.[336]

Immediately upon his arrival negotiations began about just how Macartney would traverse to Peking – and to the feet of the Emperor. Chinese officials were very clear that Macartney would need to follow the protocol of the ceremonial approach of the kow-tow: three separate kneelings each followed by a full prostration with the forehead knocking the ground three times to the shrill commands of an usher shouting, 'Kneel, fall prostrate, rise to your knees',[337] intended to dispel any doubt about one's place in the Emperor's world. After being kept waiting for a month and a half in Beijing, Macartney was finally summoned to breakfast at 4am.

The next day, he joined the Emperor for his birthday and finally he was summoned to meet the Emperor at the theatre. There were a lot of gifts. But no negotiating. Eventually, as winter approached, the Chinese officials began to suggest it might be time to go home.

When Macartney protested that his work had barely begun, he received a summons one morning while ill in bed to come in full ceremonial dress to the Forbidden Palace through the spacious courts to the Imperial Hall, where he was led up a staircase to 'a fine yellow silk arm-chair representing the majesty of China and containing the Emperor's letter to the King'.[338]

The letter was then conveyed by 16 Mandarins and their attendants and the now almost fainting Macartney to his chambers. It was a blunt dismissal. Requests for trading rights were dismissed, along with the case for trade: 'Strange and costly objects do not interest me', thundered the Emperor. 'As your ambassador can see for himself, we possess all things.'

The idea of a permanent embassy was poo-pooed as a complete waste of time. China had nothing to gain from links to Britain; England, said the Emperor, was a place trapped; 'the lonely remoteness of your island, cut off from the world by intervening wastes of sea', was a poor relation to China, the capital of which was 'the hub and centre about which all quarters of the globe revolve'. Macartney returned home disappointed.

For centuries, China's leaders were adept at managing the 'West Sea Barbarians' keeping them at bay with a blend of charm, time and steel – as Paul Walsh learned when negotiating the Diageo takeover of Shuijingfang.

Today, when China is changing so fast, it's often hard for British business-leaders to find precisely where in the 'system' decisions actually get taken. Part of the reason that it is so hard is because the Communist Party of China invests so much in generating a high degree of internal consensus about important decisions. So pinning down the Chinese leader who will (a) take a decision and (b) own the decision is not straightforward.

Given this complicated way in which decisions are taken, British businesses need to make sure they approach the business of mergers and acquisitions in a serious and heavy-duty way. Someone who has watched this close up for many years is Stephen Perry.

Stephen has been doing business with China for an awfully long time and is Chairman of the 48 Group, an association of British business people which led the campaign against the British government's embargo of trade in the first days of Communist China. Its motto, 'Equality and Mutual Benefit' – in Chinese 'Pingdeng Huli' – echoes one of Zhou Enlai's 'Five Principles' of cooperation with the outside world in 1953. Stephen has in the past been critical of the way we fragment our trade investment effort in China between UKTI, the China–Britain Business Council, the Confederation of British Industry (CBI), the Institute of Directors (IoD) and, he might have added, the City of London.[339]

Stephen and I caught up at a conference at the London Stock Exchange and I asked him about the traps that British businesses fall into:

Mostly they send people to China and they sort out some sort of joint venture. But it's got to be the top guys who go and get involved. That's the only way to be taken seriously. And you have to structure deals that if they go wrong, then it hits both sides. You've got to have stones that fall on both sets of feet.

And then you've got to feed the deal. Relationships need constantly feeding. You have to think constantly about how the end of one stage is the beginning of the next.

So there is a lot that business leaders need to get right. But I think it's pretty clear that governments can help. Some of that help is the local political support. Helping provide the guide to how decisions are really made, who makes them, and how to marshal armour-piercing arguments that will work in a political system that still prizes consensus.

But crucially, to make it easier for Chinese politicians to say 'yes' we need to put all of our weight behind a new investment agreement between the EU and China.

Given that the EU and China trade so much with each other, it's actually a bit odd that mutual investment is so thin. A new EU treaty could help change this – and deal with some of the growing concerns that European businesses are flagging.

Every year, the EU Chamber of Commerce publishes its annual guide to how business leaders feel things are going. This year's survey was not happy reading. The survey found:

Governmental policies concerning FIEs [foreign-invested enterprises] are still of grave concern to European companies doing business in China. Indeed, 42% of respondents continue to believe these policies are less fair now than they were two years ago, a figure in line with last year (43%).

Only 13% said they perceive policies to be fairer today than they were two years ago. The outlook for the future is not positive either: 43% of respondent companies believe that government policies affecting the business environment will be even less fair for FIEs over the next two years. Only 17% are confident that these will be fairer towards FIEs within two years.[340]

When the firms were asked what their priorities were for change, there were some pretty unequivocal answers:

- Rule of law/transparent policy-making and implementation (71%)
- Promotion of fairer competition (55%)
- Fewer monopolies and implementation of environmental regulations (53%)

Today, for all sorts of economic and political reasons, there is no prospect of a free-trade agreement between China and Europe. But there is a good chance of a new investment agreement that could make a big difference, as a senior EU Commission official explained to me, one afternoon in London:

The European Parliament motion on 'Unbalanced trade' [between Britain and China] was quite critical. It reflected the fears about China which are there in the European Parliament. But from the Commission's perspective it was too strong.

On the free-trade agreement the Commission view is that the time just isn't right for this. The differences are just too great. China wants tariff reduction. We want all sorts of other things; we want progress on the procurement rules, progress on rules around human and social development; I think there are some 11 key demands at the top of the iceberg, so the time just doesn't feel right. We're now waiting for the new administration [in China] to come into place. For us negotiating market access is the key barrier.

On the investment agreement, the time is now right. The Commission is now preparing the impact assessment as a prelude to setting out the negotiating guidelines for agreement in the second quarter of 2013.

The Commission is much, much more positive.

The chief virtue of an EU trade agreement is that it would on the one hand liberalise the environment for investment by, for example, revising the investment Catalogue (the Catalogue for the Guidance of Foreign Investment and Industry, produced by the Ministry of Commerce), and on the other offer more protection for those investments, especially IPR protection that would, crucially, be predictable.

For example, in the manufacturing sector European investors are still frequently prevented from setting up wholly owned foreign enterprises and are required to establish joint ventures with Chinese partners. China continues to maintain investment restrictions on some key industries for Europe such as automobiles, petrochemicals or steel.

China is itself busy negotiating bilateral free-trade agreements with countries like Australia, New Zealand, Japan and South Korea as well as a bilateral investment agreement with the United States. The EU simply cannot afford to get left behind while others strike preferential trade agreements.

Right now there is an extraordinary patchwork of bilateral agreements between 26 EU countries and China. A comprehensive investment agreement offers both the prizes of protection and access to the Chinese market for investors within one single framework.

As the EU Trade Commissioner Karel de Gucht put it in a speech in June 2012, the Investment Agreement

> would help to improve access to the Chinese market for European investors. It would help provide a level playing field for companies, regardless of their ownership structure or origin, in both Europe and China. And it would consolidate our current 26 bilateral investment agreements into a single framework.[341]

I think this kind of investment agreement could have a big impact for British firms in particular. Indeed it is part of the story of how our EU membership is transforming trade access in Asia for British firms. Very few people know that the EU has just opened Korean and Singaporean markets to the UK. A free-trade agreement with Japan will follow soon. In time, a deal that opens service markets, where Britain is strong and China very protectionist, is crucial. Our free-trade outlook is in fact one of the reasons the Chinese want the UK to be influential in the EU: through our influence we keep markets open.

Let's have a look at just how Britain is faring in the race to invest in China (Table 13.3). Again, we're definitely in the starting grid. And again, we're a long way from the front. As you might expect, China's immediate neighbours – Japan and South Korea – have vastly bigger investments in China than we do. But look at the US; it has five times the level of investment than the UK has on the ground. Germany has twice as much. And both are growing at a much faster pace than the UK.

Now think about some of sectors where British firms are the world's innovation leaders – telecoms, banking, insurance and media. Right now, access to those sectors is heavily circum-scribed by the Catalogue. All are sectors where IPR protection is extremely important.

If a new EU investment agreement opened those sectors up a bit more, that would be good for some of Britain's world-beaters. That says to us that we need to be at the forefront of pushing the new EU investment agreement. We ought to be pressing for speed. And, crucially, we need to be pushing for an agreement that helps the sectors where we are strong.

CONCLUSION

How Britain prospers
in the Pacific century

This book is a short and sharp contribution to a crowded literature on China. But it's actually a book about Britain by a politician who has spent most of his career in business. So I know that there are political and business questions that I've left unanswered. What about human rights, the rule of law and democracy in China? Will China's economy slow or not? Where do we go from here? In this conclusion, I'd like to have a crack at answering these questions. But I want to start with a warning.

This book is basically an argument about the next phase of globalisation that is quickly unfolding around our ears. The next stage may prove as bumpy as the first. When John Maynard Keynes sat in Bretton Woods representing Her Majesty's Treasury in 1944, he surveyed the possible results of the agreements on a new world finance and trade system and concluded:

> We have had to perform at one and the same time the
> tasks appropriate to the economist, to the financier, to the
> politician, to the journalist, to the propagandist, to the
> lawyer, to the statesman – even, I think, to the prophet and
> to the soothsayer.

I think even he would have been impressed with what we had fashioned by the year 2000. By the time I left secondary school Deng Xiaoping had led China in its first steps towards 'opening up'. By the time I got to university, the Berlin Wall was torn down. By my second year, Manmohan Singh had begun to dismantle India's 'licence Raj'. By the time I graduated in 1992, President Clinton had set the stage for NAFTA and the admission of China to the WTO. Across a little over a decade, decisions on four continents created a global marketplace that linked six billion of the world's seven billion people. It was quite a *fin de siècle*.

With the long boom that followed, the UK grew faster than either continental Europe or Japan *for the first time in a century*. Productivity rose, wages rose, wealth per head rose faster than anywhere in the G7 group of richest Western nations. The last 10 years have seen the creation of huge new wealth, an explosion in travel and trade, vast new horizons opened wide.

But beneath the wide averages, something else was going on. Long before the great crash, the new age of interdependence stopped feeling good for an awful lot of people. For many, globalisation had become a dirty word. I'm a believer in globalisation. I feel that our natural instinct to 'truck, trade and barter' has been the chief motive force in our economic development. It has driven generation after generation of entrepreneurs to fling back the frontiers of what's possible. I'm proud to have made a tiny contribution to that great movement as an entrepreneur myself.

But as I've served one of the most deprived communities in the country these last eight years, I've seen at first hand how the creative destruction of global capitalism has become the community destruction for local constituencies like mine in Birmingham. The price and the prize of globalisation are quite simply out of balance. The prizes are being carried off by a lucky few. The price is being paid by everyone else.

It's not a surprise then that a lot of people are questioning whether this globalisation business is all it was cracked up to be. Unless we find a better way of sharing the fruits of new trade, then this discontent will only grow, and risk becoming an unstoppable political force expressed at the ballot box as a vote for parties that want to roll back the clock, put up the fences and retreat to the past. In a democracy, anxiety isn't abstract. It shows up on polling day.

If we want to deepen our interdependence with great new markets like China, we have to check and reverse the inequalities of the last ten years. Interconnecting ourselves with a developing economy is not going to be easy. There are going to be some nasty bumps along the way. I know. I've felt the bumps myself.

The fight to save Leyland DAF Vans (LDV), one of the last great manufacturers in my constituency, was the most important fight of my first term in Parliament. The company could trace its roots back to the great automotive business founded in east Birmingham by Herbert Austin, who helped lay the foundations for one of the country's pivotal manufacturing hubs during the late-Victorian boom that powered Birmingham to become Britain's second city. At its peak in 1921, Austin's business employed 8,000 workers.

By the time I was elected in 2004, LDV was, to be honest, a troubled business. But the crash finished it off. For six months I negotiated with Russian owners, Malaysian investors, Swedish managers, British bankers, and agents for Chinese asset-strippers. One desperate afternoon in the Prime Minister's study in 10 Downing Street, I finally persuaded Chancellor Gordon Brown to underwrite a local buy-out with £5 million in loan guarantees.

But the business was closed: agents for a Chinese firm bought the assets and shipped them out of the country. It was a heart-breaking moment. And a classic example of how fast capital, creativity and culture now blow around the earth at breakneck speed while communities stay rooted to the spot. As I write, the site is still desolate and empty.

This is why globalisation has become so unpopular. Before I left office I happened to see a Foreign Office briefing on attitudes to globalisation. The conclusion was candid: 'attitudes around the world towards globalisation remain frosty'. In America, the home of free trade, the same briefing pointed out, market researchers Pew found that 70% of Americans generally supported 'free markets'. But just 59% agreed that trade was good for their country, the lowest level of support in the 47-country study. We see the same thing here in the UK at election time. The British National Party stand on a platform that says: 'Britain and the British people believe we would be better off if we were free from and independent of the EU'. The UK Independence Party has a similar view.

Theory tells us that globalisation is good for us. Yet before the crash, the gap between theory and reality was taxing economists around the world.[342] Globalisation obviously brought access to a wider variety of goods and services, lower prices, more and better-paying jobs, improved health and higher overall living standards. Globalisation has been the key to what the Governor of the Bank of England Mervyn King once called the 'NICE decade', when economies enjoyed 'non-inflationary continuously expanding' growth. But data was beginning to show something going wrong: between 2000 and 2008, for example, only the top 2% in the US enjoyed increases in mean real income.

So what happened? Well, rapid global economic integration has radically narrowed inequality *between* nations. But income inequality *within* nations has exploded. When I worked at the Treasury I became obsessed with this problem. One day, I asked my civil servants to summarise just why we thought globalisation was fuelling inequality. This is what they said:[343]

1   Advanced countries have relatively more skilled workers than developing countries; conversely, developing countries have relatively more unskilled workers than advanced countries.

2   In all countries, workers (skilled and unskilled) tend to be less mobile than capital.

3   With open trade and financial flows, firms take advantage of the relative abundance of skilled workers in advanced countries and unskilled workers in developing countries, and move around their production units to maximise profits (for example, building big assembly plants in China).

4   In developing countries, wages of unskilled workers are bid up.

5   In advanced countries, skilled production increases and wages of skilled-workers are bid-upwards, but unskilled wages are depressed – leading to a growth in income inequality.

The consensus is that the adverse effect of *trade* on wages is not substantial. But *technology* and trade together have a massive impact. As more work is mechanised and as fewer people are needed for any task, demand for labour falls. Prevailing wages for that labour take a hit. Technological progress is therefore driving up inequality in both advanced and developing countries.

On balance, most economists will argue that the gains from globalisation and technological progress will outweigh losses. The problem is that winners and losers are too often different people. Globalisation does not, on its own, share the gains broadly. Indeed what we see in the real world is that when capital moves, communities stand still: worse, they are left to pick up the pieces. The 'big picture' is cold comfort to workers losing their jobs in communities forged in the Industrial Revolution, where the prospects of new, 'real' jobs are hard to see.

Gene Sperling, the brilliant former economic advisor to Bill Clinton, posed the dilemma well.[344] An open economy benefits an economy in ways that are 'invisible and diffuse'. Yet when a factory goes out of business it is not hard to point the finger at free trade. A thousand jobs created in a hundred companies across the UK do not create much news. A thousand jobs lost at a plant that closes certainly does. That's what I felt when I watched the tragic closure of LDV.

Building new links to China isn't going to solve Britain's problems on its own because it's not enough to create new wealth. We have to find new ways of making sure the price and the prize of globalisation are fairly shared. In the UK, that means we need a new approach to innovation policy – or industrial policy, as some would call it – that explicitly aims to generate 'good jobs' and rebalance away from dependence on low-wage industries. We need to improve access to education and training – to help develop worker skills necessary for keeping up with rapid technological change and innovation. We need better social protection for workers during what economists prosaically call the 'adjustment period' when old firms die, and new firms are yet to be born.

We have to find ways of helping workers boost their bargaining power at work; that means placing a responsibility on employers to create a role for workers on remuneration committees of public companies. We have to look at minimum wages, perhaps equipping the Low Pay Commission with the power to investigate the causes of low pay and make recommendations on how to tackle them. Government needs to use its procurement power to ensure that, across the economy, firms are not simply profiteering at the expense of decent pay for their staff. We are almost certainly going to need to reform corporate governance in some way, to include staff representation on remuneration committees to help tackle the crazy growth in pay at the very top. And we have to think about the way we negotiate free-trade agreements globally to make sure that, as an international community, we're not all charging forward in a race to the bottom.

Dani Rodrik is someone who has thought about this a lot is. Originally a citizen of Turkey, Rodrik is today Professor of International Political Economy at Harvard. On a trip back to Harvard to meet him, Rodrik made a point that stuck with me:

> The debate can't simply be about compensation for the losers created by globalisation. The response needs to address legitimacy, fairness, and who makes the decisions that affect whole communities through trade.
>
> It's not unreasonable for people to complain when their jobs are displaced to foreign countries who allow firms to employ workers in dangerous conditions, for example. Instead, we have to recognise that values can and should be applied internationally, without those complaining merely being dismissed as 'protectionist'.

Lower pay abroad in countries like China is not illegitimate. But we have a mutual interest in discussing what represents unfair or exploitative competition.

I am convinced that if we do not get the answers to some of these questions right, then people and policy-makers will quite simply turn their backs on a more open world. And if they do not vote to 'shut the door', they will drag their feet, safe in the knowledge that no one really has the political capital to go any faster or propose a different course.

Soft landing?

But, say the sceptics, is this entire argument not misplaced? Is there not a bigger risk, looming larger? That the Chinese economy is in fact not set for growth but for a mighty smash?

In the course of writing this book, I've met plenty of people in Britain and abroad who are profoundly worried about the pressures building up across China, not least in the banking system.

The argument put forward by the 'China bears' is straightforward. Deep flaws in China's political and economic model are stopping China adapt in the way it must to escape the 'middle income' trap. Exporting cheap goods, investing the revenues in infrastructure and allowing the cream of society to benefit from luxury consumption might work when the world is benign and full of limitless credit. But those days are numbered and, runs the argument, China's elite is too conflicted to change.

Economists and academics that I've met in China won't speak on the record about it. But in private they are deeply worried that the Communist Party's monopoly on power and the state's monopoly on the key factors of production – land, labour, capital – have created such a rich opportunity to cream off the super-profits that local and national elites have succumbed to temptation and greedily built a system hard-wired to profit the few and not the many. Floating on a sea of cheap Chinese credit, state-owned enterprises and local governments have spent a fortune building small empires over which they preside unchallenged and unchallengeable. Will Hutton, one of the leading 'China bears', puts it like this:

> A murky corporatist economic model has been created in which insiders, especially so-called princelings – sons and daughters of former revolutionary leaders such as Bo Xilai and his wife (both are children of revolutionary generals) – feather their nests with impunity. There is no impartial law; no checks and balances; nothing can be trusted. Party officials can make no claim to being revolutionary heroes as a reason for holding office; they are corrupt administrators just

about delivering the quid pro quo of rising living standards. But if they fail, it is clear the whole edifice will implode.[345]

One leading Chinese economist swore to me that there would be a banking crash within five years, triggered by a Chinese 'sub-prime crisis' as interest rates slowly rise and bad debts go wrong.

Over the course of 2012, warning signs began to flash to tell us that China's growth was indeed decelerating.

In July 2012, the International Monetary Fund concluded: 'The economy seems to be undergoing a soft landing, though global headwinds are increasing', and noted sustained property price falls in nearly two-thirds of China's 70 major cities.[346] The New York Times reported bankers saying that 'across China, developers have slowed construction to the most cash-conserving pace possible without activating default clauses on their loans ... and sending away the cranes'. Round the clock shifts in great cities like Chengdu were cut back to one a day.[347]

Politicians all over China began to see the slowdown in their budgets. Central government investment spending fell in late 2011. Local government investment (which is 18 times the size of central government's) grew at the slowest pace since December 2001. Wealthier places like Beijing, Shanghai, Zhejiang and Guangdong saw revenue growth slow to 10% a year – down from 20 to 30% the year before. Land sales, which are the main source of income for local governments, have fallen off a cliff. The excellent online news source Caixin reported that in the first half of 2012 land transfer fees collected in 300 cities fell 38% from the previous year. Some cities, it reported, were suspending construction projects. Others, like Shenzhen and Dongguan, were struggling to balance their books.[348]

The point I think we need to remember here is that a slowdown shouldn't be a surprise. It is part of the plan. When I spoke to economist Jim O'Neill, in the summer of 2012, I was keen to get his take on just what was happening. This is how he explained it:

> Chinese equities are really struggling and the cyclical indicators that we follow are weak. But when I really look at all the evidence I think the slowdown is because they want to slow down and they've deliberately slowed because of inflation. Two years ago they decided that it's not simply the quantity of growth that's important, it's the quality of growth.
>
> What global investors are struggling to get their heads round is that China is simply moving from a state when it was growing at 10% to a world when it's growing at 7.5% – the target set out in the five-year plan.

I think he's right. The Chinese government has very deliberately acted to cool what was beginning to look like an asset bubble.

By 2011, property investment had come to make up fully one quarter of total fixed-asset investment in China – in an economy where investment powered nearly half of all economic growth. As house-prices started to soar, the government reacted in 2010 with a battery of measures to deflate the property bubble before it got out of hand. In places like Hong Kong, where the property market was especially hot, 15% transaction taxes were introduced on anyone buying from outside the province. Cities like Beijing introduced new laws requiring residents to live in the city for at least five years before they could buy. Bigger and bigger deposits were demanded to get a mortgage. And the government vowed to build an astonishing seven million low-income housing units in 2012 alone as part of a push to build 36 million affordable units by 2015.[349] By the summer of 2012, Premier Wen could declare that 'controls over the real estate market are still in a critical period',[350] but it was clear the strategy was working.

Rarely is economics ever easy, however. And the complication for China is how to slow its property bubble when the Eurozone is going bang and China's exports are diving. This has hit China hard. The IMF forecast that a 1% slowdown in the world economy could knock as much as 4% of Chinese growth. Throughout the summer of 2012, policy analysts from various parts of the Chinese government were scouring European chancelleries with one question on their lips: 'What on earth was going to happen to the Eurozone?'

The dilemma for China's leaders is acute: the easiest way to restore big growth is to step back up investment. But that does nothing to deliver the longer-term aim of putting Chinese consumers into the economy's driving seat. Aggregate wages are still growing only marginally faster than productivity, which means that household income as a share of GDP is not yet on a firm upward trend. The reality is that China is going to suffer these setbacks along the way, as economist Gerard Lyons reminded me: 'The trend is up but there'll be setbacks. The key to long-term success is how they deal with the setbacks. Why do I say that? Because the business cycle exists in China too.' The sort of numbers the Chinese are talking about are huge. If consumption has to rise to 48% of the economy from where it is today, in order to give household income a fairer share of GDP, that's a massive change whichever way you cut it.

China's leaders can't abolish the business cycle. Its leaders are deliberately seeking a slower rate of growth. And we have to be careful we don't lose sight of how fundamentally the world economy is going to change, *even when* China's growth slows down.

Jim O'Neill had a few facts and figures for me to illustrate the point.[351]

China's growth in 2011 of more than $1.3 trillion was close to creating the equivalent of another Australia, Spain, Mexico,

South Korea or about two new Turkish economies … or another Greece every 11½ weeks.

Now think about a reasonable scenario for the future. A 'middle path' of around 10% average growth (in nominal US$ terms), out to 2020, means an impressive $7.7 trillion increase in consumption if China's economy rebalances so that consumption rises to 45% of GDP. If consumption stays stuck at around 35% of the economy, then that's still $3.5 trillion more consumer spending. That is simply gigantic.

Let's look now at Jim's 'hard landing' scenario: an average of 7% US$ nominal GDP growth rate until 2020. In this pessimistic scenario, China's GDP would still be some $13.5 trillion in 2020, and if consumer spending stayed stuck at 35% of GDP, it will have increased by another $2.1 trillion. 'To put this in perspective', comments Jim, 'the total size of India is yet to breach $2 trillion'.

China spring?

The well-spring of worry for the 'China bears' is a political system that is very different to ours, without democracy, strong human rights, free speech or consistent rule of law. Confucius plus communism gives you a very different politics to Christ and Kant. The 'China bears' worry that this has fostered a political class that is institutionally incapable of leading change.

They have a point. Every year, the Foreign and Commonwealth Office (FCO) publishes its excellent human rights report, summarising the state of play in China and elsewhere. In China, say the FCO report-writers, 'personal freedoms, such as the freedom of individuals to choose where they work and live, have grown, and, despite pervasive censorship, technology has rapidly expanded the space for public debate'.[352] The spread of technology has now created unprecedented public discussion of political issues. It is transforming the scale and scope of public expression of grievances.[353] New 'Regulations on Consultation and Mediation for Labour Disputes in Enterprises', which came into force on 1 January 2012, should improve resolutions surrounding labour disputes. That's the good news.

The bad news is that the advance of political and civil rights has stalled, as calls for a 'Jasmine Revolution' provoked a predictable response. In the first six months of 2011, protestors could find themselves locked away far from a police station or home. Mistreatment in detention and harassment of family members were reported.[354] The artist Ai Weiwei, for instance, was arrested and held at an unknown location for 81 days. Access to justice and a consistent rule of law remain very problematic. Recently, good steps have been taken to reduce the use of illegal evidence and to improve access to defence lawyers in China's recent reforms to the Criminal Procedure Law, the first substantive revision for 15 years. But lawyers still need permission to speak to their clients if their client is accused of 'endangering state security',[355] and forms of arbitrary detention known as 're-education through labour'[356] remain widespread. Human Rights Watch has highlighted the treatment meted out to citizens filing some of the 10 million petitions lodged since 2003. Thugs hired by local authorities were sent to Beijing to round up petitioners and deposit them in 'black jails' outside the judicial system where abuse can take place unchecked.[357] Capital punishment remains extremely common; indeed China executes more prisoners than the rest of the world put together. For all the multiplication of online space, censorship still limits freedom of expression in practice.[358]

My impression is that Britain's consistent, systematic approach, backed up as it is by EU investment in practical projects, like training judges, is bearing fruit. It is quiet, patient and consistent. It advances in small steps. Our foreign policy has long sustained a combination of high-level lobbying and engagement, bilateral human rights dialogue and financial support to projects in the country. The UK–China Human Rights Dialogues are now in their nineteenth round.

I think our lobbying work for improvements in human rights, democracy and the rule of law is important, but it is even more effective when we recognise the progress made and remember that the Communist Party of China is like every political party the world over. It has wings, divisions, factions. Hawks and doves. Hard-liners and reformers. And right now, they are debating the direction and speed of China's seminal next stage of reform.

Normally, these debates are private. But the Bo Xilai affair has projected the state of tension into the global media. Patricia (Tia) Thornton is a brilliant academic of Chinese studies at Oxford and, in July 2012, I listened enthralled to her lecture on the Bo affair.[359]

Tia reminded us that Cheng Li,[360] one of the most trusted commentators on Chinese elite politics in the US, branded the removal of Bo as 'the most serious political crisis since the 1989 Tiananmen incident – and perhaps since the 1971 flight and death of Lin Biao (Mao's erstwhile successor)'. Bo is the son of Bo Yibo, one of the so-called 'Eight Immortals' of the Mao-era Party elite, and his leadership of Chongqing created a flamboyant neo-Maoist model that had become revered by the left.

Quoting as his guide Deng Xiaoping's slogan that 'development is the ironclad principle' (*fazhan fangshi ying daoli*), Bo set out to reverse the vast growth in Chongqing's inequality,[361] ruthlessly targeted organised crime ('strike the black') and religiously toasted the Party's revolutionary heritage with public performances of 'red songs', mass mailings of 'red SMS text messages' (known as *hong duanzi*, or 'red blurbs'), fervent pro-Party broadcasting on Chongqing's satellite TV and routine attacks on Western firms like Wal-Mart (closed for two weeks in October 2011 and fined $420,000 for mislabelling pork).

Famously, Bo and his wife were arrested after his police chief Wang Lijun sought protection in the American consulate, and in his final press conference in mid-March 2012, Premier Wen Jiabao did not miss the chance to reinforce his oft-repeated calls for political reform, underlining his point with a warning:

> The evil legacy of the error of the Cultural Revolution and the influence of feudalism still haven't been eradicated completely. The development of economic reform produced problems, like the unequal distribution of wealth, the decline of honesty and sincerity, and corruption ... Reform has arrived at a stage that is under attack. Without successful political reform, it won't be possible to complete economic reform, and the gains we have made are in danger of being reversed. If we are unable to fundamentally resolve the new social problems that have arisen, a historical tragedy like the Cultural Revolution could occur anew. Each leading Party cadre and responsible Party member should feel the urgency here.[362]

As I write, Bo's wife is serving life imprisonment, and Bo is facing trial. The affair is so important because it is about much, much more than the 'right' style of leadership and the 'right' view of the past. It's about the future direction of China.

Many in China have simply not bought in to the modernisers' approach. Indeed, Tia Thornton noted that days after Wen's attack on Bo Xilai, the well-known left-leaning intellectual Wang Hui attacked the leadership for a 'piece of deliberate, deadly political theatre [designed] ... to distract attention from what has actually happened ... which is a palace coup within a party keen to stifle debate about its top-down, neoliberal model of economic growth'.[363] Wang observed that, soon after Bo's dismissal, the State Council's Development and Research Centre held a 'market fundamentalist' forum with prominent economists discussing full-scale 'privatisation of state enterprises, privatisation of land and liberalisation of the financial sector'. Days later, said Wang, the National Development and Reform Commission published plans for the privatisation of large sections of the railways, education, healthcare, communications and energy resources. 'What the Chongqing incident now offers the authorities', Wang charged, 'is an opportunity to resume its neoliberal programme'.[364]

But the Communist Party is now arguing about more than economics. It's arguing about politics and the roadmap to a democracy that we might recognise in the West.

Kerry Brown's excellent book about the myriad views in China on democracy, Ballot Box China: Grassroots Democracy in the Final Major One Party State, captures views of key players on the one million elections in 600,000 villages held since the introduction of direct ballots in 1988, the twin evils of nationalism and corruption, and the future of Chinese democracy.

Clear among the noise is an appreciation that unless democracy and the rule of law advance then the economy will stall. In 2010, Prof. He Chuanqi, Director of Modernisation Research at the Chinese Academy of Sciences, put it like this: 'Unless China embarks on reform in its basic political system, its chance of achieving full scale modernisation by the end of the century is next to zero.'[365]

The year before saw populist writers opine in China Is Not Happy[366] that official complicity in scandals like the poisoned milk-powder tragedy of 2008 required 'democracy and freedom to limit the powers of some officials'.[367] President Hu has talked much about the infrastructure required to deliver justice. Clearing up the chaos of the Cultural Revolution and managing the accession to the WTO has demanded China basically invent a judicial system from scratch, passing 450 pieces of legislation, train a million lawyers and construct five levels of courts from the village to Beijing.[368] The problem obviously is that the courts still ultimately report to the Party. But as China grows richer and richer, so the prizes of corruption multiply and the Party's challenge is to keep itself clean, which is why since the mid-2000s Hu Jintao authorised more talk of democracy, not in villages or towns but in the Party itself.

In 2007, a group of academics developed the argument in Storming the Fortress, a manifesto of sorts that argued for measures to 'push forward intra-party democracy through reform of the peoples' congresses, the government system and the legal system'.[369] Given the Party's monopoly on power and leadership, democracy and progress hinge not on a Western-style contest between parties, but on democracy within the Party. Here was a narrative, a practical blueprint and a timetable, 60 years long and stretching from the early 1980s, when village elections began, to 2040.[370] It is an argument that has gathered momentum; in 2009, leaders finally agreed 'careful management of the Party has never been so arduous and urgent ... intra-Party democracy is the lifeblood of the Party'.[371]

One of the clearest thinkers I've heard discuss this roadmap is Wang Changjiang, a professor at the CPC Central Party School. A month before the 2012 leadership change, Wang wrote a fascinating article warning that 'China's reform has entered a critical period and if reform does not accelerate it will be pushed back.' The call for political reform from both within society and the CPC was growing louder.[372]

Wang highlighted a series of protests in Wukan, where villagers demanded and won the right to elections as part of a deal to end unrest over land seizures by rural officials; Qidong, where thousands of protesters mobilised to stop a pipeline that allegedly increased pollution from a Japanese-owned paper mill; and Shifang, where again thousands mobilised in violent protest to halt the construction of a copper alloy plant. These incidents, argued Wang, shared a common cause: 'the current political system did not provide an effective platform for public participation'. And that is why change is afoot.

'The entire CPC', concludes Wang, 'has reached a consensus to follow the trend of the times and speed up reform', with 'a holistic plan to guide ongoing reform'. At the core of said plan, says Wang, needs to be a step up in intra-Party democracy 'to enable more CPC members and the public to participate in the selection of those in power'.

The lesson for us is this. China has reformers. They're arguing for change. That change is good for us. It offers the hope of a stronger Chinese economy, which is good for us, and a stronger Chinese democracy, which is good for China and us. But wading in as foreigners with loud, insistent arguments about what China's doing wrong and how it must change doesn't make the reformers' job easier. It makes it harder because it provokes the same kind of reaction you'd see in Britain if the French started lecturing us on why we don't work hard enough. We should remember that, like all politicians, China's leaders now contend with an online jungle of opinion and argument that mobilises political pressure quickly, especially on questions that invoke feelings of national pride and chauvinism.

Charles Grant, the excellent Director of the Centre for European Reform, told me of his surprise on a recent visit to China listening to senior policy-makers talk about their worry – indeed their fear – of the nationalism suffusing the Chinese blogosphere, a mobilisation of popular opinion that goes into overdrive whenever an incidents flares with Japan, and which now really affects the climate of opinion within which Chinese politicians can act. Some, says Charles, now self-censor for fear of what the netizens will say. China's netizens aren't neutral. They're nationalist.

British politicians should continue to make the case for progress on human rights, the rule of law and the evolution of democracy. Not just because these ideas are right in themselves, but because they are good for China's long-term development.

But let's be clear about something. We make these arguments because we aim for change, not because we want some crowd-pleasers for a home audience. And if we're aiming for real change, we need to reflect on the way we put our points across. Megaphone diplomacy never has worked and will not work, not least because China's leaders are perfectly within their rights to retort, after St Matthew, 'Why do you see the speck in your brother's eye but fail to notice the beam in your own eye?'[373]

Unlike China, which has no real history of foreign empire building, Britain, like most of our Western cousins, has a highly imperial past that drew to a close more recently than we might care to remember. Unlike Vasco da Gama or James Lancaster, Admiral Zheng He's epic journeys of the 1400s did not spark an attempt by the Chinese to project power forward into empire-building either across the Indian Ocean or the South China Sea.

When I met Peter Nolan, he was very eloquent on this point.[374] By 1900, the key territories across the South China Sea were all Western colonies; the Philippines were taken by the US in 1898 with enormous loss of life; Indonesia was ruled violently by the Dutch – 200,000 were killed for instance in the Javanese rebellion of 1820–5. After the second world war, the British occupation in support of Dutch rule provoked the battle of Surabaya,

in which 15,000 Indonesians were killed. The British government apologised in 2001. In Malaya, which the British ran after
the terrible Japanese occupation, we re-colonised and conducted
a vicious 12-year campaign against the Malaysian Communist
Party. Indo-China was run from Paris until the outbreak of the
second world war; 250,000 French troops were then deployed
in a barbarous conflict before the escalation of American military
action which from 1965 saw 190,000 troops engaged in total war
which killed two million people. Today, following the American
'pivot'[375] towards Asia, the Pentagon has hurried to develop its
air–sea battle concept spanning nearly 6,000 miles of ocean from
Diego Garcia to Guam aimed at China's 'access denial weapons'.

When we frame arguments about human rights, the rule
of law and democracy, we at least need the good grace and
self-awareness to know our history – because the Chinese do –
and acknowledge that we preach or teach as reformers who have
erred in the past. And we need to appreciate too that, just like the
Chinese, we're seeking to develop not just political and human
rights – but economic and welfare rights too. The 'rights' business is not a one-dimensional, singular affair. It's an agenda. And
on much of that agenda – like lifting 400 million people out of
poverty – China has made extraordinary progress in developing
the economic and welfare rights of its citizens.

Is its task finished? No. Should we lobby for more progress?
Yes. This isn't a counsel to stop calling for reform. It is advice on
the approach that might work fastest.

So, what next?

Over the past few years, it's been a huge privilege to interview
wise people in Britain, Europe and China, from the fields of poli-

tics, the arts, universities, business and the civil service about how we strengthen UK–China links.

Most of the people I've met are, on balance, optimists about our ability to tie these links tighter. But very few of the people I've met think we're proceeding in the perfect way. There's real worry. There's frustration. There's a sense that others – such as Germany – are pulling way ahead. And that's why they want a new determination to turn east.

I haven't set out to write a detailed blueprint for how Britain draws closer to China. I want to highlight how important this issue has become; I want to underline that we've got our work cut out; that others are ahead of us. I want people to debate the right way forward and I want us to learn from others. I've tried to offer the reflections of people who know an awful lot more than I do. And in that spirit, I want to conclude with a list of the seven 'crunch points', the key approaches, arguments, ideas and initiative that people put to me.

1. Re-orientate. With self-confidence. We are not irrelevant. Yet.

The overwhelming message from Britain's most experienced China-watchers is that we have to re-orientate fast. As a signed-up member of Britain's political classes I can tell you honestly that Britain's political elite, whether in Westminster or our great cities, is well behind our rivals in the US and Germany in understanding the changes now unfolding in China and what they mean for us. Our media elite are no better.

The weekend before the American presidential election and the Eighteenth CPC Congress, at which China changed its leadership team, was dominated by coverage not of China but America. Some newspapers, like the Sunday Times, relegated coverage of China's Congress to page 33 and then focused their story on the geopolitical significance of Xi Jinping's singing wife. Now, it's true; America was the greater drama. The American result was fraught. The Beijing 'result' was a foregone conclusion. But my friend Matthew d'Ancona of the Daily Telegraph provided a wonderful illustration of why really Britain's attention was fixed across the Atlantic:

> The gravitational pull of America is best captured in the obsessive love shared by politicians of all parties for Robert Caro's multi-volume biography of Lyndon Johnson – perhaps the one thing about which George Osborne and Gordon Brown truly agree. It is visible in Michael Howard's unexpected passion for baseball and the Boston Red Sox. Daniel Finkelstein, once William Hague's chief political adviser ... has a game he plays with Andrew Cooper, David Cameron's director of strategy, the object of which is to name ... as many losing vice-presidential candidates as you can ... Cooper and Finkelstein storm on, or rather backwards, into the Fifties.[376]

How many British politicians, or indeed journalists, can name the last three Chinese leaders? Or more than three members of the Politburo? Believe me, it's not many. Gerard Lyons told me a story about just how challenging this re-orientation business will be:

> One of our challenges is that we just don't think long term – and they [the Chinese] do. A few years ago, I was invited to go and give a presentation at the Map Room at the Foreign Office before the last prime minister's visit. It was absolutely packed. Standing room only. It was all the officials across Whitehall who dealt with China. I asked an official later how often people got together like that. This was the first time, he replied.

Yet, change in China could be *very* good for us – if we play our cards right. And if we get our skates on. Right now, we have a window of opportunity. But it won't last forever. Perhaps another five, or possibly 10 years at best. Chinese leaders know what they need to do to secure China's future. They will be ruthless in its pursuit. Yet we should be self-confident about what can be done together. Stephen Perry, Chairman of the 48 Group, underlined for me just why:

> British policy has long been characterised by this ambition for a special relationship with America but ... could China have a special relationship with Britain? Can we ride on the coat-tails of China? At the very least we should be seeking a relationship with special features. I don't think the door is closed. China is very interested in Britain. We're a member of some very important clubs like the UN Security Council; London is a major global centre; we're one of the world's great financial centres. There is an opportunity there to have a very substantial relationship. They want to know how we manage several hundred years of stability. They want to know about the rule of law and strong civil society – and they want to know where we got things wrong. They want to learn from our mistakes.

Dame Jessica Rawson is one of Britain's most eminent Sinologists, former Warden of Merton College and holder of the Leverhulme grant that helped establish the Contemporary China Studies Programme at Oxford. I met her at Oxford one hot July afternoon to get some advice on how we draw Britain and China closer. She underlined the virtue of optimism: 'The Chinese hugely want to learn from us', she said, but 'we simply haven't defined what we want to get out of China'. Of course there are lots of good ambitions for improvements to human rights, democracy, the rule of law. But what do we actually want to get out of the relationship?

This point is crucial, and it was underlined by Martin Davidson, the head of the British Council. Despite our often barbarous history, there is Chinese interest in a country like ours that boasts of a civilisation stretching back over a thousand years and yet has found ways to constantly renew. There is an interesting cultural affinity between us. One UK business leader explained it like this: 'I'm a real optimist. Deep down I think the UK and Chinese business cultures should work very well together. We're both very sociable. "Face" is important in the right way.[377] There are lots of traditions like courtesy which we both share.'

If we fail to seize this opportunity, we will not only lose an opportunity to grow faster, we will start to fall behind in the world. Prof. Andrew Dilnot explained it thus: 'There are 25 times as many of them as us. We're very small. Any strategy other than the fullest engagement will leave us left behind.'

But piecing together the UK's strategy for China has to be a long-term and, therefore, a cross-party affair. We could do with a place where long-term cross-party thinking comes together. Where politics, business, universities and cultural leaders mix together. We don't have such a place today. But we need one. As someone put it to me:

> What we need is a quality blue-sky group to think very long term about our relationship with China. It needs to be cross-party. You'd have to get all three parties involved and you'd have to get people in it who could do it and wouldn't be prone to lobbying.

Too much punditry about China tends to return to a broad debate: Whither China? Is it going to implode? Is it going to master a capacity to innovate? Is its economy going to land soft or hard? Will it ever improve its human rights record?

These questions are important, but we would do well if we spent half of our time reflecting not just on China's future, but on our shared future. And on this question, we must be clear about two things: What is it that we want out of the relationship, and what are Britain's strengths, in contrast to say France or Germany or America? This point was made to me time and time again by business leaders, and what one of them said bears repeating:

> So we have to think: What is our competitive advantage? What does China really need, and then how are we going to sell it? ... What are our competitive advantages? I don't think that we have many. Education is one; healthcare is another. We're good at building a services economy. We're a post-colonial power. We're not the US and we're not a threat.

Another businessman said:

> There is a real urge among the Chinese to see us as their best friends. The question is, how do you make the UK the hub? We've lost a lot of self-confidence. But we should be a good base for them. We're also very badly organised in the way we service our relationships with their key players.

We tend to forget that what attracts people to us is great assets – language, education, our way of life.

Crucially we cannot seek quick returns; it has to be a longer and deeper commitment, a commitment to broaden our links well beyond the industrial to people.

2. Innovate. Or we're finished.

Sorry to put it quite as starkly as this. But even the most casual study of what is about to happen in China's technology revolution is, I think, enough to persuade anyone that there is simply no future for Britain as a low-wage, low-tech economy. We won't stay ahead of China in a race to the top, nor – and this is the crucial point – forge a successful partnership with China, unless we become an even more innovative country. For China is moving 'up the value chain' very, very fast.

The great city of Tianjin is a perfect example of just how. One of the three great cities of ancient China, Tianjin is built on the confluence of five rivers and the Bohai Sea, and is the traditional port for Beijing, to which it is now linked by high-speed trains travelling at 300km/h. It is today the world's fourth biggest port. The city boasts one of the highest levels of GDP/capita in China – some $13–15,000 – and has been growing at a blistering 16% a year. That makes it one of China's most important engines of growth.

The dead flat green–brown plains that stretch to the horizon all around the city are carved into great lots with huge manufacturing plants and piles of containers and forests of 24-storey apartment blocks. Over lunch in the Renaissance Ballroom at the Tianjin Teda Convention Centre, I asked some senior city officials whether they found the rising standard of living and the concomitant rising wage costs were encouraging businesses to leave town. 'That's definitely a trend', said one, 'where we have low-value manufacturing. But in high-value manufacturing we have engineers that are still relatively cheap by international standards.'

This matched what an official at the People's Bank of China had told me in Beijing: 'Low-skill industries are losing their competitiveness. Manufacturing shoes and clothes, that's all moving inland. But in the electronics industries we still have a competitive advantage because the wages of engineers are so competitive.'

Tianjin's planners are responding by building business strength in precisely the sectors where we like to think we're strong: financial services, pharmaceuticals and aerospace. Airbus has a factory here knocking out four units a months. Standard Chartered is building a big processing hub. In the heart of the city, a new World Financial Center is rising from the river-front, and the city has a host of special freedoms designed to encourage new financial-services firms. Tianjin is climbing up the value chain fast and new advanced businesses have a huge talent pool to draw on. The city-region's 40 educational institutes and 1,000 science research centres are educating 300,000 students; 123,000 graduated last year.

That's already providing big opportunities for UK-based business. Local officials estimate some $2 billion of investment from the UK is here. Standard Chartered and HSBC are building up joint ventures. So is GlaxoSmithKline. The City of London has a training programme for local specialists. The point is that we can't compete with a low-wage, low-employment, low-tech economy. But we can partner where we are the world's best innovators.

The greatest wake-up call should be the outstanding performance now delivered by Chinese schools. In the 2009 PISA survey, students in Shanghai performed on average 15% better than young people in Britain,[378] and OECD specialists are full of praise for the way China works hard across the country to get its best teachers and school leaders into its toughest schools. I don't get the sense that Shanghai is a great outlier in the Chinese system.

We are a home to world-beaters. But we are a small market. To stay as one of the world's favourite places to invest, we need to be the world's favourite place to innovate. I've heard lots and lots of ideas on my travels. Talking to old 'China-hands', big multinationals in the UK, business leaders in Germany, and entrepreneurs in places like Israel, I was very struck by the fact that the best of British business does have a rare combination that is much prized: a capacity to innovate plus a high comfort level with doing business globally. That is immensely attractive to potential partners who might have innovation to offer. It's also immensely attractive to Chinese businesses which are at the beginning of a global journey. One business leader described their strategy as the challenge to think through how they partner with China globally, with Chinese firms who are just in the early stages of 'going out', or 'going global', and used a very nice term: 'Our goal is to grow with and within China.' That summarises the value proposition well. But the whole game will be lost unless we step up the pace of innovation here at home. Here's the shortlist of ideas – a seven-point plan – that needs some serious thought:

- Focus on city regions as the power-houses of innovative growth
- Set up a big 'Innovation Bridges' fund to help universities in our core cities develop R&D partnerships with hubs in China and elsewhere. Demand good partnerships with city councils and teaching hospitals as part of the deal
- Evolve the Technology Strategy Board (TSB) to take on the lessons of Israel's Office of the Chief Scientist; specifically think hard about creating a 'Chief Scientist'-like role for the TSB in our city regions, someone with a specific role to foster private-sector innovation, backed by TSB funds
- Explore how to earmark some of these funds for binational research or business ideas. Remember Israel's Chief Scientist spends 20% of his budget on binational projects
- Explore how we create stronger venture funds with a regional locus, packaging together national and European funds to lever in private-sector funds
- Perhaps appoint full-time regional ministers to make sure city regions have champions in government who are able to

join things up and make decisions quickly, especially around science, skills, transport, trade and culture

- Reform the governance of pension funds so there's a much stronger supply of 'patient (long-term) capital'

3. Educate. Our business leaders for today. And our children for tomorrow.

Wherever I went to research this book, I heard how Chinese leaders think long term, and we think short term. Many, many people said to me: we need to do far more to educate today's crop of business leaders to think ambitiously about China. Lots of UK business leaders simply do not think our exports to China are where they should be. Paul Walsh of Diageo said: 'I think what we've got to do is to capture the imagination of business in the UK – show them the gain.' Mike Wright, Executive Director of Jaguar Land Rover, added:

> I think it's interesting that the amount we export to China is still very modest. There needs to be a strategy that gets the larger companies and the mid-caps [medium-sized companies] to understand that China is a key source for growing your business.

If it were properly organised, I think there are lots of major UK businesses leaders who would be happy to organise trade visits for the key businesses in their own supply chain. Here, we need to take a leaf out of the Germans' text-book: there the business community is highly organised, gives lots of senior time to developing the China–Germany relationship, and ruthlessly focuses the way it asks politicians to advance its interests. And it thinks very, very long term.

But if we want to be really long term, then we have to start teaching our children far more about the country that will shape so significantly the world which they will inherit. As Paul Walsh put it: 'If 10 years is your time frame, then you've got to get to the schools. You've got to turn the lights on of our young people.'

Martin Davidson of the British Council agreed: investment in education, he said to me, is the huge transformer; school-to-school links are therefore vital because they are the key to widening the mindset of our own people. We don't find ways of encouraging Chinese students in Britain to come and spend any time in our classrooms. The exam system doesn't exactly encourage study of Mandarin, which is not easy to learn. Starting at age 11 doesn't set up a student to do well at GCSE. For all the warm words a few years ago, Mandarin teachers are still pretty rare in our secondary schools; and they are about as common as hen's teeth in primary school, where arguably Mandarin teaching has to start. Only 945 students are studying a first degree in Chinese studies. Only 2,245 students are studying A Level Chinese – fewer than 1%. When Stephen Twigg, Shadow Education Secretary, recently asked the government how many teachers were qualified to teach Mandarin and Cantonese in primary and secondary schools, he was told: 'The Department [for Education] does not collect information on the individual language subjects taught by all serving teachers.'[379]

4. Invest in institutions around money, health and law.

Over the next decade, a generation of politicians unscarred by personal experience of the Cultural Revolution will rise in the CPC. Many were student activists at the time of the Tiananmen Square protests. They face a country where the traditional language of the Communist Party is as resonant, in Kerry Brown's phrases, as 'medieval Latin', and where the CPC must craft a 'new emotional appeal'. They aspire to rule a country which has become more unequal, where oligarchs are stronger, more transparent for the revolution in social media, where local officials still exploit their rent-seeking powers, and where the tension between the old rights of farmers and the new ambitions of urban developers is far more taut. In short, CPC politicians foresee a society where the 'clash of interests' becomes ever more pronounced. One economist I spoke to, pondering the future path of China's economy offered this:

> The key issue for me isn't the hard infrastructure like roads or railways, or the soft infrastructure like skills and training. The Chinese are very good at both. The key is the institutional infrastructure – like the rule of law – which in Britain has been built up over the centuries. The problem for the Communist Party is that they are still running the country like it's a country that's very small.

Institutional infrastructure is something that Britain is a world expert in building. Our legal system is world-renowned. For all its travails, the City of London remains one of the world's financial centres. The combination of our National Health Service, world-leading life-science firms and cutting-edge medical researchers has created one of the globe's leading health centres. We should become far more systematic in the way we share our expertise not only because it is great for exports but because it is one of the leading ways in which we can help China grow.

5. Invest in hard interconnections between our key sectors and key cities. And use universities as the cutting edge.

If we learn one thing from China's plans for economic development, it is that cities drive forward economic growth. In Britain, however, most of our Westminster elite see our national interest and London as synonymous. But just as there is more to China than Beijing and Shanghai, so there is more to Britain than London. Yet, often our embassy staff don't have a clear map of Britain's provincial strengths. And our provinces don't have a good map of China and where their best partners might lie.

We need to get over this. When I asked people about the opportunities for Britain in China, I was struck by two things: that most people agreed on which sectors had potential, and that the list of sectors was quite long. Not endless. But in 10 key sectors we have tremendous potential. Each of these sectors has concentrations of excellence in Britain. I think the time has now come to start thinking through how we strengthen our key sectors in China by strengthening connections between cities and provinces. In so doing we create a much more sophisticated and intricate web of connections than merely a London–Beijing–Shanghai triangle. Chinese provinces have their own plans. As one economist put it to me: 'We need to be twinning cities and provinces in the UK with cities and provinces in China. McKinsey and Co. have done a lot of work on mega-cities and China's push west. Provinces have their own specialisation and strategies.'

We should be plugging our cities into these new networks. Writer Mark Leonard made the point to me that, in his travels around China, the Germans seemed far more plugged in at the regional level than we were; they understood regional politics and regional politicians and were investing long term in relationship building: 'I don't think we're as good at reaching out at the regional level; we don't have a good way of doing that. In a way we have to have much more of a political strategy.'

Every major city has its business leader, its great city council, its teaching hospital, a science park – and crucially a university or two. In other words, cities are 'hubs'. We need a plan for connecting every major hub in the UK to priority places in China. The cutting edge of this relationship is not hard to find. It is our universities: 'Without question, this is where the Chinese respect us', underlined Martin Davidson. This means sustaining a level of investment in universities, it means university-to-university links, and it means joint research, especially post-doctoral, where we have come to the party slightly later than the Germans. The key is then to 'spin in' commerce and business to this relationship, creating a new host of connections between the educational and the industrial.

Jessica Rawson emphasised the point. We have to work much harder to a support the role of our elite institutions:

> The Chinese are very good at empirical innovation. They are very good at doing things at scale, and we are too dismissive of this. But we have a causal view of the universe which shapes our ability to ask questions.

That helps make us good scientists. And very good inventors. We have to work much harder to support and develop the quality of our educational institutions because the Chinese immensely value our elite universities. Education is *absolutely* fundamental to our brand.

If we're to strengthen our interconnections to China, however, then there's a place we have to think about very, very hard: our border, our airports and, crucially, our visa system.

I should lay my cards on the table here. When I was Minister for Borders and Immigration, I was very struck by a story told me by a senior Chinese diplomat. A leader of China's sovereign wealth fund came to London, extolled its virtues and then went to New York and spent a fortune (several billion dollars' worth of fortune) on a joint venture there. Why? asked the diplomat. Because all our people have their networks in the US, came the answer. As it happened, I had just finished an around-the-country tour hosting local business leaders in conversations about border controls, and the new points system which I was busy importing from Australia. One manager of a major UK business based in Newcastle said to me bluntly: 'Well, look. We don't try to hire Chinese students from the university because they have to go after a year. It's just not worth us investing in them.'

This is crazy. We have 67,000 Chinese students studying at British universities. Any British exporters with eyes on the Chinese market should be building relationships now, for the future. Unless we alter the visa system to allow the best and brightest Chinese students studying here to apply for jobs and stay and build networks of their own before perhaps one day going back to China, then we will damage the networks that need to grow like coral reefs over long, long periods of time but which in time will be critical to the UK and China drawing together. And we will throw in the bin one of the few aces that we happen to hold. The visa issue came up time and time again in the conversations I've had.

6. Use our culture.

I must say that when I started writing this book, I hadn't given much thought to the importance of culture. In fact at times, I thought it might be a bit of a sideshow. I was absolutely wrong. Promoting our culture is one of *the* key ways we can advance our relationship with China. In part this is because command of English is such a prized possession in China. An economist I interviewed told me about what they had seen on their travels around rural China: 'One of the most striking things I saw when I was travelling around was a small village where on a wall someone had written in great huge letters, "Success in English = success in life".'

Alex Wilson from Flamingo Research explained to me that when the Chinese think of Britain, they think of lots of entrenched old-fashioned views: top hats and high society. But when they think of London, they think of something else entirely: cool, cosmopolitan, music, fashion. It appeals because it breaks lots of rules. 'It fills', said Alex, 'a gap, another void [Chinese popular culture], a cultural abyss that you see in the lack of proper film or proper pop music'. If you're opening a theatre a week and a new cinema every day, then the creative industries are a very good market to be in.

But many told me that organisations like Visit Britain are simply under-resourced; our different agencies in China don't operate in a single, simple framework for the story we're trying to project.

The awareness of and appetite for British chic and excellence are very good for our creative industries. But they're also very good for our more traditional exporters. When I asked Mike Wright at Jaguar Land Rover what kind of thing we needed more of to help businesses like his, he didn't miss a beat:

> Anything that can be done to reinforce the UK brand is good for us. From a consumer point of view we're associated with design and engineering excellence; anything that reinforces that we're at the forefront of design and engineering is good. Anecdotally, the Olympic opening ceremony did a huge amount of good for us. It challenged the anachronisms, showed all the good things, and was inclusive.

The French have understood this for years. As one of my interviewees put it to me: 'They painted the Eiffel Tower red, for heaven's sake. That's commitment. But France is less relevant to the international community. We are. For a bit.'

Our culture is quite simply one of our greatest blessings; our language that is in such demand; our education system and tradition of university excellence, and our creativity. For a country like China that is anxious to become a nation of intellectual property creators, those are good cards to hold and trade. If you want to do good business, you have to invest in culture. The Heatherwick pavilion at the Shanghai Expo made a huge impact on Britain's image in China. The truth is Harry Potter and Norman Foster do more than a few business delegations led by the Prime Minister.

7. Use our club. Our membership of Europe is mission-critical to a closer relationship with China. So, for heaven's sake, let's start using it.

My final point is not about China, but Europe. I had a sneaking suspicion that this was important before I sat down to write this. But I hadn't realised quite *how* important. Now it's quite possible our civil servants in Brussels are making sure British interests are top of the European Commission's agenda. No doubt they are. But if so, they are working untroubled by any wider debate in Westminster. We never debate how Europe can be used to promote our interests in China. Yet the EU Investment Memorandum with China could be the most important step forward in our trading relationship for years and years.

We have crucial interests to advance, especially given that the barriers created by the Ministry of Commerce's Catalogue on Foreign Investment stop two of our strongest sectors, telecoms and banking, expanding fluently. Equally the EU Free Trade Agreements with China's close neighbours, Japan and South Korea, are absolutely critical assets for British business seeking to build supply chains close to the honey-pot of Chinese markets.

One business leader with huge experience of trading with China explained it to me like this:

> We actually have to learn from Mao's lesson to 'search for the main contradiction'. The main contradiction now in China is how to restrain the behaviour of the US. Restraining the

relationship of the US means that a strong Asia is important; a strong Africa is important; and a strong Europe is vital. Within Europe an informal group of the UK, Germany and France could provide leadership that others would follow.

Looking back on his time as the EU Trade Commissioner, Peter Mandelson posed the question as acutely as this:

> Absolutely key to unlocking that trade relationship is that Britain is part of a big free-trade club called Europe. So, first of all please understand our interest to China is largely because we are in the EU. A Britain which is independent of the EU is of no great interest or value. Indeed, I found in a whole succession of talks that Britain is valued because we're seen at the free trade end of the argument, always arguing against protectionism unlike, for instance, the French.

And the irony is that we could make a difference to the EU's agenda in China, frankly, with some ease. As one senior Commission official put it to me:

> The Commission [does] put the stress on speaking with one voice. We lose credibility when we speak apart. Too often we see China play to a strategy of divide and rule. So yes, there is a concern to coordinate what EU members are talking about. The UK is seen as seeing trade as one of the biggest reasons to be in the EU. The UK is potentially one of the most important advocates of this.

This is a really important point: at a time when many in the European Parliament are raising the ante about the lack of reciprocity in our trade relations, it is up to Britain to weigh in with arguments for an answer that hinges on knocking down trade barriers in China, rather than putting up protectionist fences in Europe. With the weight of Europe behind us, we'd make an awful lot more progress than having the argument on our own, not least because when we negotiate as the EU, we can talk far tougher. When Peter Mandelson arrived in Brussels as EU Trade Commissioner towards the end of 2004, he was handed a decision to unilaterally reimpose controls on the importation of Chinese textiles, flying in the face of the decade-long transition to free trade in textiles. He refused, and tried a different tack. Eventually the Chinese came to the table and agreed to start a negotiation which was widely acclaimed and became the template for Europe's subsequent approach to China: partnership, agreement, mutual benefit. But when China failed to reciprocate on market access, Peter halted normal relations and refused to relent until the Chinese established with Europe a high-level mechanism between China and the EU, on the model of the Americans' Strategic & Economic Dialogue. It was set up between Mandelson and Vice-Premier Wang Qishan, and it worked. It is simply not conceivable that the UK would have been able to secure the same kind of results acting alone. We need the EU club.

Final words

As I said in quoting Machiavelli above, nothing is as hard to do as to introduce a new order of things. Britain's alliance with America is based on what Churchill called 'a fraternal association of the English-speaking peoples', and he might have added a shared Protestant religion. Our Continental alliance, still controversial, is rooted in geography, democratic values and profound shared interests.

Our alliance with Asia will demand more creativity; we don't share a language. Democratic traditions are different. We are not neighbours. But our future interests are very much a shared concern. For centuries we were connected only by long and dangerous caravan routes along which we traded spices, silk – and myths. We don't trade so much spice and silk any more. But there are still plenty of myths. Myth-busting will demand we work very hard together on the business of mutual understanding. To succeed, more of our children must study in China, so must more of our teachers and academics. Chinese firms must do more business here – and more British firms must work in China. Managers and employees must pass back and forth. Brits should own great Chinese brands – and vice versa. Our politicians should know as much about Sun Yat-sen as they do about Abraham Lincoln. Chinese art and culture should not be alien. Globally, there should be causes – counter-poverty, climate change, tackling piracy – on which we work together. Our exchanges should become less ceremonial and more conversational.

Predictions, said Yogi Berra, are always difficult, especially when they are about the future. History is littered with forecasts of what never was. But the economic prize of globalisation and the huge new prize in Asia seems as certain as anything. A new global middle class is emerging, soon to be two billion citizens in size, on a planet where the majority of us live in cities, in a global economy of $150 trillion, three times greater than today. That great tripling could bring extraordinary new riches to Britain, greater even than the Empire 200 years ago. It would be almost impossible for Britain to shut itself off from change. But it is possible to imagine a country of merely grudging acceptance, where we limp along reluctantly at incalculable cost to ourselves.

If there's one lesson we should learn from Europe's truculent story and our economic success over three centuries of our history it is that we thrive on competition, the clashing of ideas and the curiosity that drove us to new horizons. Let's not lose that spirit now. Let's be self-confident enough to throw in our lot with the changing world around us, to become full-blooded globalisers. In this new world, let's resolve to build a more United Kingdom where we strike a better balance for working families between the prizes of globalisation and the price. Let's move beyond the comfort zone of our past and like the pioneers of centuries past let's look for new markets, new friends, new futures. But let's remember the lessons of our history. Times change. The world turns. The next few years may be very uncertain but it seems clearer now how this century is going unfold. So let's not hang around. Let's get on with the job of turning east.

ANNEX: STATISTICAL TABLES

Table 1.1: GDP growth forecasts

	2012	2013	2014	2015
OBR 2010	2.8	2.9	2.7	2.7
OBR 2012	0.8	2	2.7	3
Change	-2	-0.9	0	0.3

OBR = Office for Budget Responsibility

Table 1.2: UK economic statistics

		1997	2008	2009	2010	2011	Change since 2008
Business investment (£bn)		92.4	134.4	115	115	116	-£18.4
Exports (£bn)		278	440	404	429	449	£9
Cash balances (£bn)		191	698	626	676	733	-£35
Business start-ups	Births		267,000	236,000	235,000		-32,000
	Deaths		223,000	277,000	297,000		74,000
Net business creation			44,000	-41,000	-62,000		

Table 3.1: When China is expected to overtake the US

Institution	When	Date of forecast
Purchasing power parity terms		
Arvind Subramanian[1]	2010	January 2011
OECD[2]	2016	November 2012
IMF WEO[3]	2017	October 2012
PriceWaterhouseCoopers (PWC)[4]	Before 2020	January 2011
Market exchange rates terms		
Standard Chartered[5]	2020	2010
Economist Intelligence Unit[6]	2021	2011/2012
Goldman Sachs	2027	2009
PWC[7]	Before 2035	January 2011

1   Arvind Subramanian, 'Is China Already Number One? New GDP Estimates'. PIIE, 13 January 2011 (available at http://www.piie.com/blogs/realtime/?p=1935).

2   OECD, 'Looking to 2060: Long-term Global Growth Prospects: A Going for Growth Report'. OECD Publishing, November 2012 (available at http://www.oecd.org/eco/economicoutlookanalysisand forecasts/2060%20policy%20paper%20FINAL.pdf).

3   IMF, World Economic Outlook Database October 2012 (available at http://www.imf.org/external/pubs/ft/weo/2012/02/weodata/index.aspx).

4   PWC, 'The World in 2050: The Accelerating Shift of Global Economic Power: Challenges and Opportunities'. PWC, January 2011 (available at http://www.pwc.com/en_GX/gx/world-2050/pdf/world-in-2050-jan-2011.pdf).

5   Standard Chartered Global Research, 'The Super-Cycle Report, 2010'. Standard Chartered, 15 November 2010 (available at http://www.standardchartered.com/id/_documents/press-releases/en/The%20Super-cycle%20Report-12112010-final.pdf).

6   Free Exchange, 'You're On'. The Economist, 30 March 2012 (available at http://www.economist.com/blogs/freeexchange/2012/03/china-will-overtake-america-within-decade-want-bet).

7   PWC, 'The World in 2050'.

Table 3.2: Alternative profiles for exports to China and their GDP impact

Scenario	Required growth in exports (%)	Impact on GDP (£bn)	Impact on GDP (%)
Export growth doubles	31	5	0.3
Export growth trebles	47	7	0.5

A note on the model: The Pink Book (the British government's publication detailing the country's balance of payments) contains information on UK exports to individual countries (the latest data are for 2011). The model includes exports to both China and Hong Kong. In 2011, about 4% of our exports of goods and services went to China and Hong Kong, or about £19 billion (within this, £12.5 billion of exports goes to China alone). That amounted to 1.3% of GDP. This overstates the impact on GDP, since a proportion of exports will consist of imported inputs. The Office of National Statistics' 'supply and use' tables contain an estimate of the import content of exports – the most recent data are for 2005. As you would expect, that number is higher for goods, where the import content is 30%. The import content of services exports is 13%. Three-quarters of our exports to China are goods, while the rest are services; this suggests that 25% of overall exports consist of imported inputs. Accounting for the import content reduces the share of Chinese and Hong Kong exports in GDP from 1.3% to 1%.

Health warnings: This is a simple calculation that holds everything else constant.

• It doesn't take into account multiplier effects: increased exports would have knock-on effects on the rest of the economy through higher profits or wages in the export sector.

• It also doesn't take into account the potential impact on exchange rates: some offset is likely to come from the fact that as demand for UK exports goes up, sterling appreciates and some importers may decide either to switch to cheaper imports from a competitor country, or to consume domestically produced substitutes. The latter argument, however, would have a very small impact if movements in the renminbi continued to be tightly controlled.

Table 7.1: Britain's global R&D giants

Sector	Key UK firms	UK share of global spend	UK R&D spending (£m)	Global R&D spending (£m)
Mobile telecommunications	Vodafone	44%	£303	£696
Banks, insurance and financial services	RBS, Lloyds, Barclays	31%	£1,553	£5,029
Mining	RioTinto; BHP Billiton	23%	£216	£939
Food and drug retailers	Tesco; M&S	22%	£111	£494
Food producers	Unilever; Cadbury	19%	£864	£4,612
Tobacco	BAT	19%	£152	£784
Oil and gas producers	Shell; BP	17%	£1,060	£6,185
Media	BBC; BSkyB; Reed	15%	£292	£1,921
Fixed line telecommunications	BT	13%	£1,029	£7,633
Pharmaceuticals and biotechnology	GSK, AstraZeneca; Shire	10%	£6,824	£65,881
Aerospace and defence	Rolls-Royce; BAE Systems; Smiths Industries; Meggitt	7%	£859	£12,918

Source: Analysis based on Department for Business, Innovations and Skills, The 2010 R&D Scoreboard

Table 7.2: Tax receipts 2006/07 (£ billions)

Sector	Personal	Direct Business	Consumption	Property	Environment	Total
Business services	34,328	8,056	2,362	1,757	46	46,549
Education, health and social work	36,172	416	1,671	168	88	38,515
Financial intermediation	22,869	6,986	2,589	3,970	21	36,435
Insurance and pension funding	2,079	2,583	2,637	321	5	7,625
Manufacturing	27,528	4,172	1,906	2,052	369	36,026

Financial services pay more in Corporation Tax. But the picture changes once you take into account the personal taxes paid by people going to work in different sectors.

Table 13.1: UK overseas foreign direct investment stock

Rank	2010 (£bn)	Cumulative share of UK foreign investment	Share
United States	184	18%	18%
Netherlands	147	32%	14%
Luxembourg	138	45%	13%
France	54	50%	5%
Irish Republic	41	54%	4%
Belgium	41	58%	4%
China plus Hong Kong	36	61%	3%

Source: House of Commons library.

Table 13.2: UK overseas foreign direct investment: Fastest growing nations

	2010 (£m)	Change (2001–10)	Compound annual growth rate 2001–10
1 Arabian Gulf countries	16,344	1003%	31%
2 Russia	10,046	846%	28%
3 South Korea	3,984	628%	25%
4 India	10,830	628%	25%
5 Belgium	41,272	568%	24%
6 Cyprus	563	512%	22%
7 Spain	35,398	399%	20%
8 Hong Kong	29,850	350%	18%
9 China plus Hong Kong	35,854	310%	17%
10 Portugal	3,607	293%	16%

Source: House of Commons library.

Table 13.3: Inward direct investment positions in China (US$ millions)

	2009	2010
Japan	88,364	106,303
United States	55,265	63,454
South Korea	32,223	40,342
Germany	21,694	28,730
Netherlands	11,729	15,170
United Kingdom	13,446	13,483
France	10,344	13,226

Source: House of Commons library.

NOTES

1 Angus Maddison, *Monitoring the World Economy, 1820–1992*. OECD, 1995.

2 Exports were to be expanded by between 50 and 75%.

3 Alec Cairncross, *Years of Recovery: British Economic Policy 1945–1951*. Routledge, new edition, 2005.

4 Compared to 1946; ibid., pp. 24–6.

5 There was however still a deficit to the dollar area. By 1953, exports to the US covered only 85% the value of imports. But this was still up from merely a half in 1948–9. Restocking from America would not have been possible without a boom in our exports to the States. Ibid., p. 44.

6 Confucius, *The Analects*. Penguin Classics, 1979.

7 Scholars debate this point. The Florentine financiers had become over-extended in the Mediterranean and the English king perhaps spied his chance to renege on his debts. See Edwin Hunt, *The Medieval Super-Companies: A Study of the Peruzzi Company of Florence*. Cambridge UP, new edition, 2002.

8 Carmen Reinhart and Ken Rogoff, *This Time Is Different: Eight Centuries of Financial Folly*. Princeton UP, 2011, p. 150. Seven of these crashes unfolded after 1945.

9 Five of which were enormous: Spain 1977; Norway 1987; Finland 1991; Sweden 1991 and Japan 1992. Ibid., p. 216.

10 Thus by August 2005, Alan Greenspan was pondering a 'conundrum'. The Federal Reserve had raised interest rates from 1 to 3%. But the long-term rate on US Treasury bills was not rising; it was falling: from 4.9% to under 4%. As the Fed raised the headline interest rates between 2004 and 2006, from 1% to 5.25%, long-term rates and mortgage rates barely moved as a wall of demand from the East kept interest rates low.

11 16 June 2005.

12 Andrew Ross Sorkin, *Too Big To Fail*. Viking, 2009.

13 Reinhart and Rogoff, *This Time Is Different*.

14 John Irons, 'Economic Scarring: The Long-Term Impacts of the Recession'. Economic Policy Institute, September 2009 (available at http://www.epi.org/publication/bp243/).

15 Edmund Phelps, *Inflation Policy and Unemployment Theory: The Cost Benefit Approach to Monetary Planning*. Macmillan, 1972.

16 Work by Paul Gregg and Emma Tominey suggests that a man who has had a spell of unemployment of more than a year will have average pay at the age of 42 which is £7,143 less than someone who has not suffered unemployment: 'The Wage Scar from Youth Unemployment'. CMPO Working Paper Series No. 04/097, 2004 (available at http://www.bristol.ac.uk/cmpo/publications/papers/2004/wp97.pdf).

17 In autumn 2010 the Office for Budget Responsibility had forecast an increase in business investment of 1.3% in 2010 and 8.6% in 2011; it actually fell by 2.1% in 2010 and grew by just 1.2% in 2011.

18 Ray Barrell, Dawn Holland and Iana Liadze, 'Accounting for UK Economic Performance 1973–2009'. NIESR, August 2010, p. 27 (available at http://www.niesr.ac.uk/pdf/dp359.pdf).

19 http://www.bankofengland.co.uk/publications/Pages/other/monetary/TrendsinLending/2012/marchdataset.aspx

20 Exchange between David Willetts and Phil Willis, HC Deb, 27 October 2011, cc. 450–1.

21 'International Comparative Performance of the UK Research Base – 2011'. Department of Business, Innovation and Skills, 2011 (available at http://www.bis.gov.uk/assets/biscore/science/docs/i/11-p123-international-comparative-performance-uk-research-base-2011).

22 Adjusted for tax, inflation and household composition.

23 http://budgetresponsibility.independent.gov.uk/economic-and-fiscal-outlook-december-2012/

24 This is gross exports, not net exports.

25 Robert Cooper, 'The Post-Modern State and the New World Order'. Demos, 2000 (available at http://www.demos.co.uk/files/postmodernstate.pdf).

26 Ibid.

27 In *European Union: The Next 50 Years*, ed. Maurice Fraser. Financial Times Books, 2007, p. 5.

28 My old friend Mark Leonard put it like this. Europe was shaping a very post-modern kind of power: 'a network of power that binds states together with a market, common institutions, and international law –

rather than a hierarchical nation-state, it is increasingly writing the rules for the 21st century': *Why Europe Will Run the 21st Century*. Fourth Estate, 2011.

29 Tony Blair, 'Europe Moving Forward Again'. Policy Network, 2005 (available at http://www.policy-network.net/uploadedFiles/Publications/Publications/Blair.pdf).

30 Simon Tilford and Phillip Whyte, 'The Lisbon Scorecard X: The Road to 2020'. Centre for European Reform, 2010 (available at http://www.cer.org.uk/sites/default/files/publications/attachments/pdf/2011/rp_967-251.pdf).

31 This has been a standard get-out since at least the days of Thomas Gresham, who cleared Elizabeth I's debt in the 1560s by manipulating the English exchange rate to allow him to borrow more for his pound on the Amsterdam bond market.

32 Fareed Zakaria, 'The Future of American Power: How America Can Survive the Rise of the Rest'. *Foreign Affairs*, May / June 2008.

33 Robert Cooper, *The Breaking of Nations: Order and Chaos in the Twenty-First Century*. Atlantic Books, 2004.

34 Niall Ferguson, *Colossus: The Rise and Fall of the American Empire*. Penguin, 2005.

35 President Barack Obama, State of the Union Address, 24 January 2012 (available at http://www.whitehouse.gov/the-press-office/2012/01/24/remarks-president-state-union-address).

36 Joseph Nye, 'The Future of American Power: Dominance and Decline in Perspective'. *Foreign Affairs*, November / December 2010.

37 Paul Krugman, *The Conscience of a Liberal*. Penguin, 2009.

38 Robert Reich, *Supercapitalism*. Icon Books, 2009.

39 Jacob Hacker and Paul Pierson, *Winner-Take-All Politics*. Simon and Schuster, 2011.

40 Lane Kenworthy, 'Progress and Social Policy', in *After the Third Way*, ed. O. Cramme and P. Diamond. IB Taurus, 2012.

41 Krugman, *Conscience of a Liberal*.

42 'All rich countries', write Hacker and Pierson, 'have experienced the impact of technological change and globalisation and yet in many rich democracies increases in inequality and declines in economic security have been modest, and few have seen anything like the sharp upward shift of economic rewards, the implosion of unions or the breakdown of social benefits that have occurred in the United States.'

43 Barry Eichengreen, *Exorbitant Privilege*. Oxford UP, 2011, p. 118.

44 Ibid., p. 169.

45　Richard Nixon, 'Asia After Viet Nam'. *Foreign Affairs*, 1967.

46　Goldman Sachs, 'Dreaming with BRICs: The Path to 2050'. 2003 (available at http://www.goldmansachs.com/our-thinking/topics/brics/brics-dream.html).

47　Ibid.

48　Quoted in Xie Chuntao, *Why and How the CPC Works in China*. New World Press, 2011.

49　The phrase 'crossing the river' emerged in the 1980s, and has been popular ever since.

50　http://www.telegraph.co.uk/finance/financialcrisis/8900851/Jim-ONeill-Welcome-to-a-future-built-in-BRICs.html

51　OECD, 'Looking to 2060: Long-term Global Growth Prospects: A Going for Growth Report'. OECD Publishing, November 2012 (available at http://www.oecd.org/eco/economicoutlookanalysisand-forecasts/2060%20policy%20paper%20FINAL.pdf).

52　Jim O'Neill, *The Growth Map*. Penguin, 2011, p. 134.

53　And around 40 to 45% of global defence spending.

54　America accounts for around 40% of global R&D spending: $369 billion as against Asia's $338 billion.

55　Joseph Nye, *Soft Power: The Means to Success in World Politics*. Public Affairs, 2005.

56　Zakaria, 'The Future of American Power', p. 169.

57　Fareed Zakaria, *The Post-American World*. W.W. Norton & Co., 2008.

58　Maddison, *Monitoring the World Economy*.

59　Quoted in Daniel Walker Howe, *What Hath God Wrought: The Transformation of America 1815–1848*. Oxford UP, 2009.

60　Ibid.

61　Francis Parkman, *The Oregon Trail*. Oxford World Classics, 2008.

62　Alfred Chandler, *The Visible Hand: The Managerial Revolution in American Business*. Harvard UP, 1977, p. 90.

63　Ibid., p. 92.

64　Zakaria, *The Post-American World*, pp. 46–7.

65　Robert Kagan, 'Not Fade Away: The Myth of American Decline'. *The New Republic*, 11 January 2012 (available at http://www.tnr.com/article/politics/magazine/99521/america-world-power-declinism).

66　http://www.hks.harvard.edu/news-events/news/news-archive/american-power-21st-century

67　Martin Jacques, *When China Rules the World: The Rise of the Middle Kingdom and the End of the Western World*. Penguin, 2009, p. 281.

68　Neil MacGregor, *A History of the World in 100 Objects*. Allen Lane, 1st edition, 2010. The British Museum's Room 33 is in fact a catalogue of China's political, technological and cultural superiority over the West.

69   Jared Diamond, *Guns, Germs and Steel: A Short History of Everybody for the Last 13,000 Years.* Vintage: 1998.
70   Ibid., p. 252.
71   Sir Francis Bacon, in *The New Organon, or True Directions Concerning the Interpretation of Nature*, Book I, Chapter CXXIX (1620): 'Printing, gunpowder and the magnet ... whence have followed innumerable changes, insomuch that no empire, no sect, no star seems to have exerted greater power and influence in human affairs than these mechanical discoveries.' All four inventions were a central feature of China's Olympic opening ceremony; details can be found at http://www.chinadaily.com.cn/olympics/2008-08/12/content_6928189.htm
72   Diamond, *Guns, Germs and Steel*, p. 324.
73   Tacitus's *Germania*, written around AD98, described in detail the barbarian tribes to the north of the Roman empire.
74   Arrian, *Anabasis of Alexander*, Book V, Chapters 18–19. Hereabouts, Alexander founded the city of Bucephalus in memory of his horse who died there: 'not wounded by anyone', says Arrian, 'but worn out by heat and age'.
75   William Bernstein, *A Splendid Exchange: How Trade Shaped the World.* Atlantic Books, 2009.
76   Edward Gibbon, *The Decline and Fall of the Roman Empire.* Wandsworth Classics of World Literature, 1998.
77   John Julius Norwich, *Byzantium: The Early Centuries*, Vol. I. Penguin, new edition, 1990, p. 266.
78   Ibid., p. 204.
79   Geoffrey de Villehardouin (c.1160–c.1213), *Memoirs or Chronicle of The Fourth Crusade and The Conquest of Constantinople*, trans. Frank T. Marzials. J.M. Dent, 1908, p. 65. Much of the 'booty' can still be seen today adorning the Basilica of St Mark in St Mark's Square. Dandolo was buried in the Hagia Sophia, where a memorial to him still sits today. His bones were said to have later been fed to a dog.
80   Under the terms of the deal struck with the crusading princes, Venice secured three-eighths of the city and free trade in the Empire – from which Genoa and Pisa were to be excluded. John Julius Norwich, *Byzantium: The Early Centuries*, Vol. II. Penguin, new edition, 1990, pp. 180–1.
81   Fernand Braudel, *Civilization and Capitalism: 15th–18th Century*, Vol. III: *The Perspective of the World.* Weidenfeld and Nicolson, 2002.

82 Ruskin believed the church to be the first in Venice: 'the nucleus of future Venice and became afterwards the mart of her merchants'. John Ruskin, *The Stones of Venice*, Vol. III. Da Capo Press, 2003, p. 296. Ruskin was fascinated by the idea that Venice had created a new fusion between East and West.

83 Bernstein, *A Splendid Exchange*, p. 4.

84 Sir Henry Yule, Marco Polo's leading Victorian editor, aptly called it 'A book of great puzzles'. Sir Henry Yule, *The Book of Ser Marco Polo*, Vol. I. John Murray, 1903.

85 Bernstein, *A Splendid Exchange*.

86 In August 1492, a Spaniard, Alexander VI, was elected Pope and promptly began publishing a series of papal bulls awarding large parts of the planet to his royal patrons Ferdinand and Isabella of Spain. King João of Portugal was infuriated by Alexander's actions and demanded a better settlement of his neighbours who, keen to avoid a domestic fight, settled up on a June day in 1494, in the quiet market town of Tordesillas. The Iberians simply divided the world between them, along a line 1,270 miles west of Cape Verde. All land west of the line was Spanish, and all land east, Portuguese.

87 Herman Lopes de Castaneda, *The First Book of the Historie of the Discoveries and Conquests of the East India by the Portingals*, London, 1582, in *A General History and Collection of Voyages and Travels*, ed. Robert Kerr, Vol. II. London, 1824.

88 Jonathan Spence, *The Search for Modern China*. W.W. Norton & Co., 2001.

89 Julia Lovell, *The Great Wall: China Against the World*. Atlantic Books, 2007, pp. 256–7.

90 Niall Ferguson, *Civilization: The Six Killer Apps of Western Power*. Penguin, 2012, p. 32. (Published in the US as *Civilization: The West and the Rest*.)

91 See for example the wonderful David Landes, *The Wealth and Poverty of Nations*. Abacus, 1999.

92 Wall-building is a tradition that stretches back to at least the 9th century BC.

93 Lovell, *The Great Wall*, pp. 54–5.

94 Ibid., Chapter 8.

95 Ibid., p. 8.

96 He ruled 1572–1620.

97 Lovell, *The Great Wall*, pp. 256–7.

98 Henry Kissinger, *On China*. Penguin, 2012, p. 33.

99   Peter Perdue, *China Marches West*. Harvard UP, 2005.

100 Kissinger, *On China*, p. 33.

101 Ibid.

102 Of the 44 merchants interested in the Guinea voyage of 1558, twenty-two were named in the Muscovy Company charter of 1555. Nine of the Turkey Company's original investors were investors in the Muscovy Company, and 10 were Spanish Company members. Of all the active Levant Company traders, 40–50% had fathers or fathers-in-law or brothers already engaged in the trade. Robert Brenner, *Merchants and Revolution*, Verso Books, 2003, p. 72.

103 To Russia (1555), Guinea (1558), Spain (1573), Turkey, and then Venice (1583). Finally in 1592 the Venice and Turkey Companies joined forces to create the Levant Company, which was in turn to lay the foundations for the greatest English company of all: the Company of Merchants of London Trading into the East Indies, or the East India Company, which received its charter from Queen Elizabeth on New Year's Eve 1600.

104 In the late 1580s and 1590s the Levant Company's shareholders made small fortunes from stealing vast quantity of sugar from the Portuguese ships returning from Brazil. James Watts, Lord Mayor of London in 1607, who was described by the Spanish ambassador as the greatest 'pirate', was a member of the Spanish Company, the Levant Company, the Virginia Company and the East India Company.

105 Born in Basingstoke in the mid 1550s, Lancaster had made a fortune in Portugal as a merchant and a soldier, before having to leave in a hurry when the Portuguese crown passed to the Spanish in 1580. Lancaster probably served with Drake and was well trained for his venture east.

106 *The Diary of Samuel Pepys 1600*. Echo Library, 2006, p. 194.

107 The first request for a pot of tea had been recorded 45 years earlier by a Mr R. Wickham, an agent of the East India Company.

108 Niall Ferguson, *Empire: How Britain Made the Modern World*. Penguin, 2003, p. 12.

109 Until the 1820s, when it was overtaken by raw cotton.

110 Ferguson, *Empire*, p. 15.

111 *Lord Macartney's Embassy to Peking*, ed. J.L. Cranmer-Byng. Hong Kong UP, 1961, p. 12.

112 William J. Duiker and Jackson J. Spielvogel, *The Essential World History*, Vol. II: *Since 1500*. Wadsworth, 2010, p. 543.

113 Kissinger, *On China*, p. 37.

114 Historically designated for the transport of tribute-grain from the south and east to the imperial capital.

115 Wen later signed a deal with Volkswagen to build a new factory in Xinjiang province in western China.

116 Ralph Atkins, 'Germany: The Miraculous Machine'. *Financial Times*, 19 April 2012 (available at http://www.ft.com/cms/s/0/dff3976a-8a08-11e1-87f0-00144feab49a.html).

117 The euro slid around 15% against the Chinese *yuan* in the first half of 2010.

118 Hans Kundnani and Jonas Parello-Plesner, 'China and Germany: Why the Emerging Special Relationship Matters for Europe'. European Council on Foreign Relations, May 2012 (available at http://ecfr.eu/page/-/ECFR55_CHINA_GERMANY_BRIEF_AW.pdf).

119 Jeff Black, 'Germany's Future Rising in East as Exports to China Eclipse US'. Bloomberg News, 7 April 2012 (available at http://www.bloomberg.com/news/2011-04-06/germany-s-future-rising-in-east-as-exports-to-china-eclipse-u-s-.html).

120 Hans Kundnani, quoted in Didi Kirsten Tatlow, 'Germany and China: Too Close for Some'. *International Herald Tribune*, 16 May 2012 (available at http://rendezvous.blogs.nytimes.com/2012/05/16/germany-and-china-a-special-relationship/).

121 President Clinton, 'Letter to Speaker Hastert'. 23 May 2000 (available at http://clinton6.nara.gov/2000/05/2000-05-23-letter-from-the-president-to-speaker-hastert.html).

122 Hillary Clinton, 'Remarks at the Strategic and Economic Dialogue US Press Conference'. 4 May 2012 (available at http://m.state.gov/md189315.htm).

123 Robert Scott and Hilary Wething, 'Jobs in the US Auto-Parts Industry'. Economic Policy Institute Briefing Paper, 31 January 2012 (availableathttp://www.epi.org/publication/bp336-us-china-auto-parts-industry/).

124 Eichengreen, *Exorbitant Privilege*, p. 118.

125 Susan V. Lawrence and Thomas Lunn, 'US–China Relations: Policy Issues'. Congressional Research Service, 11 March 2011, p. 20 (available at http://assets.opencrs.com/rpts/R41108_20110311.pdf).

126 Daniel Rosen and Thilo Hanemann, 'An American Open Door?'. Asia Society, May 2011, p. 1 (available at asiasociety.org/policy/center-us-china-relations/american-open-door).

127 Lawrence and Lunn, 'US–China Relations: Policy Issues'.

128 The Defense Department on military developments; State Department on Tibet; and US Trade Representative on WTO compliance.

129 Lawrence and Lunn, 'US–China Relations: Policy Issues', pp. 42–3.

130 Galina Hale and Bart Hobijn, 'The US Content of "Made in China"'. Federal Reserve Bank of San Francisco, 8 August 2011 (available at http://www.frbsf.org/publications/economics/letter/2011/el2011-25.html).

131 Laura Tyson and Stephen Roach, 'Opportunities and Challenges in the US–China Economic Relationship'. Evidence to the US Senate Foreign Relations Committee Hearing on 'The New US–China Relationship: Living with Friction', 23 June 23 2010 (available at http://www.foreign.senate.gov/imo/media/doc/Tyson,%20Dr.%20Laura.pdf).

132 Ibid.

133 Martin Jacques provides a superb summary in *When China Rules the World*.

134 See Chapter 4.

135 Elizabeth Economy, 'The Game Changer'. *Foreign Affairs*, November / December 2010.

136 Quoted in ibid.

137 Thomas Christensen, 'The Advantages of an Assertive China'. *Foreign Affairs*, March / April 2011.

138 Robert Kaplan, 'The Geography of Chinese Power'. *Foreign Affairs*, May / June 2010, p. 23.

139 Ibid.

140 S. Pushpanathan, 'The ASEAN–China Relationship'. *China Brief Magazine*, 7 May 2010.

141 Theodore Roosevelt, *The Winning of the West*, Vol. IV: *Louisiana and the Northwest, 1791–1807*. G.P. Putnam's Sons, 1807, p. 342.

142 Barry Eichengreen, Donghyun Park and Kwanho Shin, 'When Fast Growing Economies Slow Down: International Evidence and Implications for China'. March 2011 (available at http://iis-db.stanford.edu/evnts/6930/session_3.3_kwan_stanford.pdf).

143 An excellent summary of Kerry's argument is 'China: Great Leap into the Unknown'. *The World Today*, April / May 2012.

144 Its motto is an echo of Deng Xiaoping's edict to 'seek truth from facts'.

145 Fubing Su and Tao Ran, 'Asian Tiger or Fragile Dragon? Understanding China's Development Model'. Unpublished.

146 Poverty Reduction and Economic Management (PREM) Network of the World Bank, *Economic Growth in the 1990s: Learning from a Decade of Reform*. World Bank Publications, 2005.

147 As Fubing Su and Tao Ran point out, Japan, South Korea and Taiwan all put tight restrictions on unions during the cold war, ostensibly as a safeguard against communism; workers' collective bargaining power was thus severely limited.

148 Nomura, 'China Economy'. Nomura Anchor Report on China, November 2011, p. 13 (available at http://www.scribd.com/doc/72251949/Nomura-China-Anchor-Nov-2011).

149 In 1984, more than 40% of government revenues went to the central coffers, but that ratio had diminished to only 22% in 1993.

150 However, ultimately only 25% of VAT receipts and 40% of enterprise income taxes will be retained locally.

151 On the supply side, the close ties between local governments and bank branches enabled officials to access loans and credits. They provided implicit guarantees for these loans or, in some cases, used their power to pressure banks to extend credits to their own enterprises.

152 Su and Ran, 'Asian Tiger or Fragile Dragon?'

153 World Bank/DRC, *China 2030*. World Bank, 2012, p. 15 (available at http://www.worldbank.org/content/dam/Worldbank/document/China-2030-complete.pdf).

154 Charles E. Morrison, Cheng Siwei, et al., 'The Asia–Pacific Role in the New Global Economic Order'. Remarks to 18th Pacific Economic Cooperation Council, Washington DC, 2009.

155 Stephen Roach, 'China's 12th Five-Year Plan'. Morgan Stanley, April 2011, p. 1 (available at http://www.morganstanley.com/im/emailers/inst/pdf/China_12th_Five_Year_Plan.pdf).

156 World Bank/DRC, *China 2030*, p. 12.

157 Ferrari's chief executive Amedeo Felisa delivered one of the firm's super-cars to Ferrari's 999th customer in 2011 with the prediction that the firm was about to spread dealerships from the coast to inland: 'China has the potential to be No. 1 for the luxury segment some day, with growth much faster than the US ever experienced', Felisa told the press (reported in *China Daily*, 15 January 2011).

158 Nomura, 'China Economy', p. 28.

159 Ming Zeng and Peter Williamson, 'How To Meet China's Cost Innovation Challenge'. *Ivey Business Journal*, November / December 2008, p. 1 (available at http://www.iveybusinessjournal.com/topics/innovation/how-to-meet-chinas-cost-innovation-challenge).

160 Ming Zeng and Peter Williamson, *Dragons at your Door*. Harvard Business School Press, 2007, p. 46.

161 Simon Rabinovitch, 'Shanghai Vows to Expand Capital Markets'. *Financial Times*, 30 January 2012 (available at http://www.ft.com/cms/s/0/8d30af66-4b1c-11e1-a325-00144feabdc0.html#axzz1zp5IXDrP).

162 Jonathan Watts, 'Inner Mongolia Protests Prompt Crackdown'. *The*

Guardian, 30 May 2011 (available at http://www.guardian.co.uk/ world/2011/may/30/mongolia-protests-communist-party-crackdown).

163 http://www.telegraph.co.uk/news/worldnews/asia/china/ 9734322/Openness-reform-and-peacefulness-is-transforming-modern-China.html

164 http://www.worldbank.org/content/dam/Worldbank/document/ China-2030-complete.pdf

165 US Senate Foreign Relations Committee, 'The New US–China Relationship: Living with Friction'. 23 June 2010.

166 Exports to Europe have grown by around £63 billion compared to £9 billion in export growth to China.

167 My thanks to Prof. Peter Nolan for these important details.

168 McKinsey and Co., 'Meet the 2020 Chinese Consumer'. McKinsey Insights China, March 2012 (available at http://www.mckinseychina. com/wp-content/uploads/2012/03/mckinsey-meet-the-2020-consumer.pdf).

169 Max Magni and Yuval Atsmon, 'Getting the Most from Your R&D in China'. *Harvard Business Review*, 30 September 2011 (available at http://blogs.hbr.org/cs/2011/09/getting_the_most_from_your. html).

170 Christina Savvas, 'Wen Jiabao Hails MG as Symbol of China's Friendship with UK'. *Birmingham Post*, 27 June 2011 (available at http://www.birminghampost.net/news/mgrover/2011/06/27/ wen-jiabao-hails-mg-as-symbol-of-china-s-friendship-with-uk-65233-28946600/#ixzz1zpsrYiHM).

171 Standard Chartered Global Research, 'The Super-Cycle Report, 2010'. Standard Chartered, 15 November 2010, p. 153 (available at http:// www.standardchartered.com/id/_documents/press-releases/en/ The%20Super-cycle%20Report-12112010-final.pdf).

172 http://www.hsbc.com/1/2/about/history/history

173 Stefan Wagstyl, 'Tesco: Asia overtakes Europe'. *Financial Times*, 19 April 2011 (available at http://blogs.ft.com/beyond-brics/2011/04/19/ tesco-asia-overtakes-europe/#axzz210aQWBJw).

174 See McKinsey and Co., 'Meet the 2020 Chinese Consumer', p. 14.

175 These take-off points vary between cities (the good citizens of Wuhan spend far more on yoghurt than their countrymen in Hefei, for instance).

176 McKinsey and Co., 'Meet the 2020 Chinese Consumer'.

177 Ibid.

178 Ibid.

179 David Sainsbury, *The Race to the Top: A Review of Government's Science and Innovation Policies.* HMSO, 2007, p. 19.

180 UKTI.

181 12% of output, 10% of employment.

182 The breakdown from Her Majesty's Revenue and Customs is presented in Table 7.2.

183 Department for Business, Enterprise and Regulatory Reform, 'Building Britain's Future: New Industry, New Jobs'. April 2009 (available at www.berr.gov.uk/files/file51023.pdf).

184 UKTI.

185 China already has twelve nuclear reactors; twenty-four are under construction, and forty more are in the pipeline, demanding $120 billion of investment by 2020. If China wants to meet its clean energy targets by 2020, then it needs the equivalent of 834 million tonnes of oil from alternative sources: the nuclear and wind energy sectors will grow exponentially; renewable energy investment is already twice the level of the US, at $34 billion (in 2009) – most of it into wind energy. Standard Chartered, 'The Super-Cycle Report, 2010'.

186 Coal accounts for over half of Asia's energy production. Ibid.

187 ONS.

188 Aaron Fischer, 'Dipped in Gold: Luxury lifestyles in China/HK'. CLSA Asia–Pacific Markets, January 2011 (available at http://www.iberglobal.com/Archivos/china_luxury_clsa.pdf).

189 Standard Chartered, 'The Super-Cycle Report, 2010', p. 68.

190 See McKinsey and Co., 'Meet the 2020 Chinese Consumer', p. 23.

191 HM Treasury.

192 Marcos Chamon, Kai Liu and Eswar Prasad, 'The Puzzle of China's Rising Household Saving Rate'. *Vox*, 18 January 2011 (available at http://www.voxeu.org/article/puzzle-china-s-rising-household-saving-rate).

193 Marcos Chamon, Kai Liu and Eswar Prasad, 'Income Uncertainty and Household Savings in China'. NBER Working Paper No. 16565, December 2010 (available at http://www.nber.org/papers/w16565).

194 And author of the excellent *Modern China: A Very Short Introduction.* Oxford UP, 2008.

195 For an excellent summary see Yanzhong Huang, 'The Sick Man of Asia: China's Health Crisis'. *Foreign Affairs*, November / December 2011.

196 Ibid., p. 119.

197 Ibid., p. 129.

198 Ibid., p. 130.

199 Available at http://www.fdi.gov.cn/pub/FDI_EN/Laws/GeneralLaws andRegulations/MinisterialRulings/P020071121358108121219.pdf

200 As Clay put it: 'We must speedily adopt a genuine American policy. Still cherishing the foreign market, let us create also a home market, to give further scope to the consumption of the produce of American industry.' Henry Clay, Speech on American Industry in the House of Representatives, 30 March 1824.

201 Third Meeting of the EU–China High Level Economic and Trade Dialogue (HED) in Beijing. MEMO/10/698, Brussels, 21 December 2010 (available at http://europa.eu/rapid/press-release_MEMO-10-698_en.htm).

202 USTR, '2011 Report to Congress on China's WTO Compliance'. 2011 (available at http://www.ustr.gov/webfm_send/3189).

203 See for example ibid.; Assistant USTR for China Affairs Claire Reade, 'Testimony before the Congressional–Executive Commission on China'. 13 December 2011 (available at http://www.ustr.gov/about-us/press-office/speeches/transcripts/2011/december/testimony-as-sistant-united-states-trade-rep); Angelos Pangratis, 'Statement of the EU Ambassador to the World Trade Organisation Fourth Trade Policy Review of China', 12 and 14 June 2012 (available at http://trade.ec.europa.eu/doclib/docs/2012/june/tradoc_149542.pdf); 'Motion for a European Parliament Resolution on EU and China: Unbalanced Trade?' European Parliament ref. 2010/2301(INI), 20 April 2012 (available at http://www.europarl.europa.eu/sides/getDoc.do?type=REPORT&reference=A7-2012-0141&language=EN#title1).

204 'Statement by EU Ambassador Angelos Pangratis on the Final Transitional Review of China's Protocol of Accession to the WTO Agreement', 30 November 2011 (available at http://trade.ec.europa.eu/doclib/docs/2011/december/tradoc_148450.pdf).

205 'Motion for a European Parliament resolution on EU and China: Unbalanced Trade?'

206 Thus, the European Parliament has called on China to comply with the OECD Arrangement on Guidelines for Officially Supported Export Credits; and on the Commission to support OECD efforts to involve China in this Arrangement.

207 The WTO Agreement on Subsidies and Countervailing Measures (ASCM) demands systematic notification of specific subsidies.

208 WTO, 'Report on China, 2011'. WTO ref. WT/TPR/S/264.

209 China recently committed to sever the link between China's innovation policies and government procurement preferences, including through

the elimination of all indigenous innovation government procurement catalogues and the issuance of a State Council measure mandating that, by 1 December 2011, provincial and local governments must eliminate any policies that are inconsistent with the de-linking commitment; and China confirmed that it will not require foreign automakers to transfer technology to Chinese enterprises nor to establish Chinese brands in order to invest and sell electric vehicles in China: USTR, 'US–China Economic Issues'. January 2011 (available at http://www.ustr.gov/about-us/press-office/fact-sheets/2011/january/us-china-economic-issues).

210 The subject of a WTO ruling against China of 5 July 2011, which was upheld on appeal.

211 WTO members agree to protect IPRs under the WTO Agreement on Trade-Related Aspects of IPRs (the TRIPS Agreement).

212 European Commission, 'Facts and Figures on EU–China Trade'. 2012 (available at http://trade.ec.europa.eu/doclib/docs/2009/september/tradoc_144591.pdf).

213 China established a new, permanent-vice-premier-led IP enforcement structure that will allow much better government coordination of IP enforcement efforts and stronger outcomes on the ground. China committed to increased resources and further efforts to improve the effectiveness of its government software legalisation programme, as well as further work to promote the use of licensed software in enterprises: STR, 'China's Compliance with WTO Accession Commitments Subject of Annual USTR Report'. Sandler, Travis and Rosenberg Report, 14 December 2011 (available at http://www.strtrade.com/publications-7199.html).

214 'Statement of the EU Ambassador to the World Trade Organisation Fourth Trade Policy Review of China'.

215 Originally the Chinese side fielded MofCom's predecessor, the Ministry of Foreign Economic Relations and Trade. The process was 'upgraded' in 2003, when President Bush and Premier Wen decided annual meetings should be chaired at Cabinet / Vice-Premier level.

216 USTR, '2011 Report to Congress on China's WTO Compliance'.

217 Kundnani and Parello-Plesner, 'China and Germany'.

218 $280 billion.

219 Kundnani and Parello-Plesner, 'China and Germany'.

220 *China Statistical Yearbook*. China Statistics Press, 2010.

221 Germany, incidentally, has done this with France, Israel and India.

222 Xin Dingding and Wang Qian, 'Day of Pride from Orbit to Ocean'.

China Daily, 25 June 2012 (available at http://www.chinadaily.com. cn/china/Shenzhou-IX/2012-06/25/content_15520107.htm).

223 Sunny Ye, 'Can Sina Weibo Become the Facebook of China?' Tech Rice, 24 May 2011 (available at http://techrice.com/2011/05/24/ can-sina-weibo-become-the-facebook-of-china-2/).

224 Leon Lazaroff, 'China to Capitalize on Nasdaq Jump with Tech IPOs, BNY Says'. Bloomberg, 7 May 2012 (available at http://www. bloomberg.com/news/2012-05-07/china-to-take-advantage-of-nasdaq-jump-with-tech-ipos-bny-says.html).

225 John Tozzi, 'China's Next Export: Venture Capital'. *Bloomberg Business Week*, 17 May 2012 (available at http://www.businessweek.com/ articles/2012-05-17/chinas-next-export-venture-capital).

226 KPMG, 'China Projected to be on Par with US as a Future Tech Innovation Leader; Cloud, Mobile to Drive Breakthroughs in Coming Years'. KPMG Survey, 27 June 2012 (available at http://www.kpmg.com/ us/en/issuesandinsights/articlespublications/press-releases/pages/ china-projected-to-be-on-par-with-us-as-tech-innovation-leader.aspx).

227 Gao Yuan, 'China to Further Encourage Software Exports'. *China Daily*, 15 June 2012 (available at http://www.chinadaily.com.cn/ business/2012-06/15/content_15505674.htm).

228 See for instance Michael Spence, *The Next Convergence: The Future of Economic Growth in a Multispeed World*. Farrar, Straus and Giroux, 2011, p. 265.

229 Will Hutton, *The Writing on the Wall: China and the World in the 21st Century*. Abacus, 2008.

230 Ibid., preface, p. 2.

231 Ibid., p. 187.

232 See for instance, E.J. Jones, *The European Miracle*. Cambridge UP, 1987; Diamond, *Guns, Germs and Steel*; Landes, *Wealth and Poverty of Nations*, and Ferguson, *Civilization*, for a more recent take.

233 Dani Rodrik and Arvind Subramanian, 'The Primacy of Institutions'. *Finance and Development*, June 2003, pp. 31–4.

234 'Geography' here is short-hand for climate, natural resource endowments, disease burdens, transport costs and the ease of technological diffusion.

235 As indeed several writers have argued including Diamond, *Guns, Germs and Steel*.

236 Joel Mokyr, *The Lever of Riches: Technological Creativity and Economic Progress*. Oxford UP, 1992, p. 155.

237 Jones, *European Miracle*, p. 202.

238 Ferguson, *Civilization*, p. 22.

239 Between 1580 and 1650, the Chinese population fell by some 35–40%. Ibid., p. 44.

240 See Peter Perdue's extraordinary account, *China Marches West*.

241 E.J. Jones puts it thus: 'There was expansion, not growth. But there was expansion, in the sense of the replication of millions of tiny farms and the growth of the elite on the backs of peasants. The prospects of colonisation were far beyond anything open to either the Ottoman or Mughal empires': *European Miracle*, p. 217.

242 'To put it bluntly', says Hutton, 'the banking system is the essential and indispensable tool of the Leninist party-state': *Writing on the Wall*, p. 155.

243 Ibid.

244 Ibid., p. 3.

245 Ibid., pp. 45–7.

246 Andrew Szamosszegi and Cole Kyle, 'An Analysis of State-owned Enterprises and State Capitalism in China'. US–China Economic and Security Review Commission, 26 October 2011, pp. 17, 25 (available at http://www.uscc.gov/researchpapers/2011/10_26_11_Capital TradeSOEStudy.pdf).

247 Ibid., p. 6.

248 *OECD Economic Survey of China, 2005*. OECD, 2005, p. 111.

249 Hutton, *Writing on the Wall*, p. 148.

250 Nomura, 'China Economy', p. 29.

251 Hutton *Writing on the Wall*, p. 162.

252 Wei Tian, 'China to tighten approval for SOE investments'. *China Daily*, 12 July 2012 (available at http://www.chinadaily.com.cn/china/2012-07/12/content_15571581.htm).

253 Nomura, 'China Economy', p. 32.

254 See the excellent *New York Times* series: http://www.nytimes.com/2012/01/22/business/apple-america-and-a-squeezed-middle-class.html?pagewanted=all&_moc.semityn.www

255 Zeng and Williamson, *Dragons at your Door*, p.158.

256 Prof. Richard Suttmeier, quoted in Testimony to US–China Economic and Security Review Commission, 112th Congress, 10 May 2012.

257 (Xinhua), 'Hu Pins Hope on Innovation'. *China Daily*, 11 June 2012 (available at http://www.chinadaily.com.cn/china/2012-06/11/content_15493919.htm).

258 See 'The iPhone challenge' in Chapter 6 above.

259 See Micah Springut, Stephen Schlaikjer and David Chen, 'China's

Program for Science and Technology Modernization'. Submission to US–China Economic and Security Review Commission, May 2012 (available at http://www.uscc.gov/researchpapers/2011/USCC_REPORT_China%27s_Program_forScience_and_Technology_Modernization.pdf). Others now talk of the *xietong chuangxin*, or collaborative innovation.

260 Robert D. Atkinson, quoted in Testimony to US–China Economic and Security Review Commission, 112th Congress, 10 May 2012.

261 The EU-15 are Austria, Belgium, Denmark, Finland, France, Germany, Greece, Ireland, Italy, Luxembourg, Netherlands, Portugal, Spain, Sweden and the United Kingdom.

262 First university degrees in natural science and engineering leapt from 280,000 in 2000 to over a million in 2008. National Science Board, *Science and Engineering Indicators, 2012*, p. 7 (overview) (available at http://www.nsf.gov/statistics/seind12/pdf/seind12.pdf).

263 Prof. Simon, quoted in Testimony to US–China Economic and Security Review Commission, 112th Congress, 10 May 2012.

264 Springut, Schlaikjer and Chen, 'China's Program for Science and Technology Modernization', p. 15.

265 Ibid., p. 37.

266 Ibid., p. 56.

267 Atkinson, quoted in Testimony to US–China Economic and Security Review Commission, 112th Congress, 10 May 2012.

268 Dan Breznitz, Testimony to US–China Economic and Security Review Commission, 10 May 2012.

269 Quoted in McKinsey and Co., 'Three Snapshots of Chinese Innovation'. McKinsey Quarterly, February 2012 (available at http://www.mckinsey quarterly.com/Three_snapshots_of_Chinese_innovation_2918).

270 Andy Grove, 'How America Can Create Jobs'. *Bloomberg Business Week*, 1 July 2010 (available at http://www.businessweek.com/magazine/content/10_28/b4186048358596.htm).

271 Jenny Wivell, 'World's Fastest Train Unveiled in China'. BBC, 10 December 2009 (available at http://news.bbc.co.uk/1/hi/8406910.stm).

272 Xin Dingding, 'China Rejects Japan's Rail Patents Claims. *China Daily*, 8 July 2011 (available at http://www.chinadaily.com.cn/china/2011-07/08/content_12858878.htm).

273 River Path, 'Shanghai Expo 2010. Briefing on Visitor Preferences'. 9 April 2009. Information provided by the FCO.

274 In other words, adding together those who 'strongly trust' and 'tend to trust' and subtracting those who 'strongly distrust' and 'tend to distrust'.

275 David Sainsbury, forthcoming.

276 'This House Believes that Industrial Policy Always Fails'. Economist Debates, July 2010 (available at www.economist.com/debate/days/view/541).

277 See the excellent summary Philippe Aghion, et al., 'Rethinking Industrial Policy'. Bruegel Policy Brief, June 2011.

278 See Pascal Lamy's excellent introduction to the World Trade Organisation's Annual Report 2011 (available at http://www.wto.org/english/res_e/booksp_e/anrep_e/anrep11_e.pdf).

279 *OECD Science, Technology and Industry Outlook 2008*. OECD, 2008.

280 Sainsbury, *Race to the Top*, p. 153.

281 Ibid., p. 55.

282 Ibid., p. 63.

283 Sainsbury, ibid., estimated the level stabilised at around £6–700 million a year.

284 GERD (Gross Expenditure on Research and Development) as a percentage of GDP in UK (1.78%) is below the OECD average (2.26%) and below the rates in the top performing OECD countries. These figures probably underestimate the UK's true innovation performance, because they don't capture innovation in services or the creative industries, where the UK is strong. Almost all of this gap with, say, the US or Germany can be accounted for by our different industrial structure: our big financial services and oil and gas industries are innovative but simply don't report R&D as significant proportion of their sales, and never have.

285 Dan Senor and Saul Singer, *Start-Up Nation*. Twelve Books, 2011, p. 262.

286 Ibid., p. 13.

287 Ibid., p. 183.

288 Ibid., p. 86.

289 In interview with Philip Salter in *City A.M.*, 20 February 2012 (available at http://www.cityam.com/business-features/israel-national-hub-intense-innovation).

290 Ed has written up his remarkable story in a wonderful memoir, which he was kind enough to send me: Ed Mlavsky, *Milk and Honey and Hi-Tech*. Weill Publishers, 2009.

291 Senor and Singer, *Start-Up Nation*, p. 200.

292 Sainsbury, *Race to the Top*, p. 24.

293 McKinsey Global Institute, 'Preparing for China's Urban Billion'. McKinsey and Co., March 2009, p. 26.

294 Provided in private briefing.

295 Stephen Cohen and Bradford DeLong, *The End of Influence: What Happens When Other Countries Have Money*. Basic Books, 2010.

296 Prof. Simon, quoted in Testimony to US–China Economic and Security Review Commission, 112th Congress, 10 May.

297 Unpublished note.

298 The World Bank, *Doing Business 2010: Reforming through Difficult Times*. The World Bank, IFC and Palgrave Macmillan, 2009, p. 16 (available at http://www.doingbusiness.org/~/media/GIAWB/Doing%20Business/Documents/Annual-Reports/English/DB10-Full Report.pdf).

299 OECD, *Product Market Regulation Database*. OECD, 2011 (available at www.oecd.org/economy/pmr).

300 UKTI.

301 International Telecommunications Union, *Measuring the Information Society*. ITU, 2011, p.110 (available at http://www.itu.int/net/pressoffice/backgrounders/general/pdf/5.pdf).

302 Average of 25 OECD countries: OECD, *Economic Policy Reforms: Going for Growth*. OECD, 2009.

303 Quoted in House of Commons, *Infrastructure (Financial Assistance) Bill*. Commons Library Research Paper, 2012 (available at http://www.parliament.uk/briefing-papers/RP12-54).

304 Ibid.

305 Sir Rod Eddington, *The Eddington Transport Report*. Department of Transport, 2006 (available at http://webarchive.nationalarchives.gov.uk/+/http:/www.dft.gov.uk/about/strategy/transportstrategy/eddingtonstudy/).

306 Ibid.

307 Quoted in House of Commons, *Infrastructure (Financial Assistance) Bill*.

308 British Chambers of Commerce, *The Case for a British Investment Bank*. Policy Paper, September 2012 (available at http://www.britishchambers.org.uk/assets/downloads/policy_reports_2012/12-09-03%20State%20Backed%20Business%20Bank%20Report.pdf).

309 Montfort Mlachila and Misa Takebe, 'FDI from BRICs to LICs: Emerging Growth Driver?' IMF Working Paper WP/11/178, July 2011, p. 4 (available at www.imf.org/external/pubs/ft/wp/2011/wp11178.pdf).

310 Mlachila and Takebe, 'FDI from BRICs to LICs', p. 11.

311 Title of policy brief: François Godement and Jonas Parello-Plesner with Alice Richard, 'The Scramble for Europe'. European Council on Foreign Relations, July 2011 (available at http://www.ecfr.eu/page/-/ECFR37_Scramble_For_Europe_AW_v4.pdf).

312 Daniel Rosen and Thilo Hanemann, 'China Invests in Europe'. Rhodium Group, 7 June 2012, p.13 (available at http://rhgroup.net/reports/china-invests-in-europe-patterns-impacts-and-policy-issues).

313 Zeng and Williamson, *Dragons at your Door*, p. 163.

314 Ibid., p. 116.

315 Ibid., p. 147.

316 Peter Nolan, *Is China Buying the World?* Polity, 2012, p. 9.

317 http://unctad.org/en/pages/PublicationArchive.aspx?publicationid=753, quoted in ibid.

318 Department for Business, Innovation and Skills, *2008 R&D Scoreboard*.

319 Ibid., p. 48.

320 Ibid., pp. 59–60.

321 Ibid., p.112.

322 Ibid., p. 86.

323 Pascal Lamy, '"Made in China" Tells us Little about Global Trade'. *Financial Times*, 24 January 2011 (available at http://www.ft.com/cms/s/0/4d37374c-27fd-11e0-8abc-00144feab49a.html#axzz2DiwJTVxY); Nolan, *Is China Buying the World?*, p. 12.

324 Graham Ruddick, 'Jaguar Land Rover Rewards Tata's faith and investment'. *The Telegraph*, 26 May 2011 (available at http://www.telegraph.co.uk/finance/newsbysector/transport/8539245/Jaguar-Land-Rover-rewards-Tatas-faith-and-investment.html).

325 BBC News, 'Tata Buys Jaguar in £1.5bn Deal'. BBC News Online, 26 March 2008 (available at http://news.bbc.co.uk/1/hi/7313380.stm).

326 The Economist, 'North–South FDI: Role Reversal: Emerging Market Firms are Increasingly Buying up Rich World Ones'. *The Economist* Special Report, 24 September 2011 (available at http://www.economist.com/node/21528982).

327 Rosen and Hanemann, 'China Invests in Europe', p. 5.

328 UKTI, Great Britain and Northern Ireland Inward Investment Report 2011/12. UKTI, July 2012, p. 5 (available at www.ukti.gov.uk/uktihome/aboutukti/item/344820.html).

329 Zeng and Williamson, 'How To Meet China's Cost Innovation Challenge'.

330 Godement, et al., 'The Scramble for Europe'.

331 I thank Charles Grant for this point.

332 Quoted in Rosen and Hanemann, 'China Invests in Europe', p. 69.

333 Ibid., p. 65.

334 Nick Butler, 'Energy Beyond Nationality'. FT.com, 17 July 2012 (available at http://blogs.ft.com/nick-butler/2012/07/17/energy-beyond-nationality/).

335 Xiao Xiangyi, 'A British Man Keen on the *baijiu*'. *China Daily*, 3 October 2012 (available at http://www.chinadaily.com.cn/business/2012-10/03/content_15795913.htm).

336 Kissinger, *On China*, p. 37.

337 *An Embassy to China: Being the Journal Kept by Lord Macartney during his Embassy to the Emperor Chien-Lung*, ed. J.L. Cranmer-Byng. Longmans, 1962, p. 7.

338 Ibid., p. 150.

339 Stephen Perry, 'Written Evidence'. BIS Committee, 4 April 2011 (available at http://www.publications.parliament.uk/pa/cm201012/cmselect/cmbis/735/735vw21.htm).

340 EU Chamber of Commerce in China with Roland Berger Strategy Consultants, 'European Business in China: Business Confidence Survey'. EU Chamber of Commerce in China, 2012 (available at https://www.rolandberger.com/media/pdf/Roland_Berger_China_Business_Confidence_Survey_20120531.pdf).

341 Reported in 'EU Trade Chief Calls for New Chinese Investment Deal'. *The Star* online, 8 June 2012 (available at http://biz.thestar.com.my/news/story.asp?file=/2012/6/8/business/11439385&sec=business).

342 The IMF, for example, devoted a chapter to it in its October 2007 edition of the *World Economic Outlook Database*.

343 Thanks to my former colleagues in the Treasury for summarising this so simply.

344 Gene Sperling, *The Pro- Growth Progressive*. Simon and Schuster, 2005.

345 Will Hutton, 'Beyond the Scandal Lies a Crisis at the Heart of China's Legitimacy'. *The Observer*, 15 April 2012 (available at http://www.guardian.co.uk/commentisfree/2012/apr/15/will-hutton-chinese-spring-inevitable).

346 IMF, 'People's Republic of China: Staff Report for the 2012 Article IV Consultation'. IMF Country Report No. 12/195, July 2012 (available at http://www.imf.org/external/pubs/cat/longres.aspx?sk=26097.0).

347 Keith Bradsher, 'Construction and Real Estate Hinder China's Growth'. *The New York Times*, 9 September 2012 (available at http://

www.nytimes.com/2012/09/10/business/global/10iht-yuan10. html?pagewanted=all&_r=0).

348 'Learning to Cope with Lean Times'. CaixinOnline, 12 September 2012 (available at http://english.caixin.com/2012-09-12/100436728_all. html).

349 Xinhua, 'Wen: Property Controls still in "Critical Period"'. *China Daily*, 3 September 2012 (available at http://europe.chinadaily.com. cn/business/2012-09/03/content_15727961.htm).

350 Ibid.

351 Jim O'Neill, 'Pondering Ahead of the Autumn, Especially on China'. Viewpoints, Goldman Sachs Asset Management, 30 August 2012 (available at http://www.goldmansachs.com/gsam/advisors/education/ viewpoints_from_chairman/viewpoints-pdfs/q3_2012/2012-08-30. pdf).

352 FCO, *Human Rights and Democracy: The 2011 Foreign and Commonwealth Office Report*. HMSO, April 2012, p. 192.

353 Ibid., p. 194.

354 Ibid., p. 195.

355 Ibid., p. 196.

356 Ibid., p. 197.

357 Kerry Brown, *Ballot Box China: Grassroots Democracy in the Final Major One-Party State*. Zed Books, 2010, p. 134.

358 FCO, *Human Rights and Democracy*, p. 194.

359 Patricia Thornton, 'The Rise and Fall of Bo Xilai: Or What the Future Can Tell Us About the Past'. Unpublished.

360 Director of Research and a Senior Fellow at the Brookings Institution.

361 In 2011, Bo Xilai announced that one of the municipality's chief goals was to reduce the Gini coefficient measure of inequality from 0.42 back down to 0.35, a mere 0.02 points above what it had been in 1978 at the beginning of market reform.

362 Quoted in Thornton, 'The Rise and Fall of Bo Xilai'.

363 Quoted in Didi Kirsten Tatlow, 'Questioning Workings of a Rumor Mill'. *The New York Times*, 2 May 2012 (available at http://www. nytimes.com/2012/05/03/world/asia/03iht-letter03.html?_r=0).

364 A report on 'Important Points and Perspectives on the Deepening of Economic Structural Reform Priorities'. See Wang Hui, 'The Rumour Machine'. *London Review of Books*, 10 May 2012 (available at http:// www.lrb.co.uk/v34/n09/-wanghui/the-rumour-machine).

365 Brown, *Ballot Box China*, p. 118.

366 By Song Qiang, et al., March 2009.

367 Brown, *Ballot Box China*, p. 119.

368 Ibid., p. 125.

369 Ibid., p. 152.

370 Ibid., p. 158.

371 Ibid., p. 147.

372 Wang Changjiang, 'Reform of China's Political System Imperative'. China.org.cn, 21 October 2012 (available at http://www.china.org. cn/opinion/2012-10/21/content_26834176.htm).

373 Matthew 7:3.

374 See Peter's excellent paper: Peter Nolan, 'A New Peloponnesian War? China, the West and the South China Seas'. Centre for Development Studies, University of Cambridge. Unpublished.

375 'The future of politics', said Hillary Clinton in 2011, 'will be decided in Asia, not Afghanistan or Iraq and the United States will be right at the centre of the action'. Quoted Nolan, 'A New Peloponnesian War?', p. 7.

376 Matthew d'Ancona, 'David Cameron Fears a Chill Wind Blowing across the Atlantic'. *The Telegraph*, 3 November 2012 (available at http:// www.telegraph.co.uk/news/worldnews/us-election/9652766/ David-Cameron-fears-a-chill-wind-blowing-across-the-Atlantic.html).

377 'The term *face* may be defined as the positive social value a person effectively claims for himself by the line others assume he has taken during a particular contact. Face is an image of self delineated in terms of approved social attributes.' Erving Goffman and Joel Best, *Interaction Ritual: Essays in Face to Face Behavior*, Aldine Transaction, 2005.

378 See http://www.oecd.org/pisa/pisaproducts/46619703.pdf. PISA, the Programme for International Student Assessment, is run by the OECD and provides annual comparative assessments of the performance of 15-year-old school pupils across the world. Students in Shanghai ranked 556. UK students were batting at around the OECD mean of 494.

379 Parliamentary Answer to Stephen Twigg MP, from David Laws MP, 5 November 2012 (available from: http://www.publications.parliament. uk/pa/cm201213/cmhansrd/cm121105/text/121105w0002. htm#12110545000617).

INDEX